MW01709638

BASIC PHRASAL VERBS

NTC's Super-Mini BASIC PHRASAL VERBS

Richard A. Spears, Ph.D.

NTC

NTC Publishing Group
NTC/Contemporary Publishing Company

Library of Congress Cataloging-in-Publication Data
is on file at the United States Library of Congress

Originally published as *Basic Phrasal Verbs*

Published by NTC Publishing Group
An imprint of NTC/Contemporary Publishing Company
4255 West Touhy Avenue, Lincolnwood (Chicago),
Illinois 60646-1975 U.S.A.

Printed in the United States of America
International Standard Book Number: 0-8442-0457-9
13 12 11 10 9 8 7 6 5 4 3 2

TO THE USER

Basic Phrasal Verbs is designed to be an easy-to-use tool for learners of English. The dictionary contains over 6,000 examples illustrating the correct usage of over 2,200 commonly used phrasal verbs. Phrasal verbs are combinations of a verb and an adverb or preposition that function together as a single unit of meaning. Many of the phrases that contain these sequences are idiomatic. That is, even if one knows all the words in a phrase and understands all the grammar of the phrase, the meaning may still not be clear. Many readily understandable phrases are also included since this book is intended for people who are new-to-English as well as for the fluent speaker.

An important feature for the learner is the indication of human and nonhuman direct objects. Typical standard dictionary entries for phrasal verbs omit all references to direct objects, as in **put on hold, bail out,** or **see through**. This dictionary uses the pronouns *someone* and *something* to indicate whether the verb in the phrase calls for an object, where the object should go in the sentence, whether the object can be human, nonhuman, or either one, and if there are different meanings depending on whether the object is human, nonhuman, or either one. All that information is vital to learners of English, although it seems to come perfectly naturally to lifelong English speakers. For example, there is a big difference between **put someone on hold** and **put something on hold**, and between **bail someone out** and **bail something out**. There is also an important difference between **see something through** and **see through something**. These differences would never be evident if the entry heads were listed as **put on hold, bail out,** and **see through** with no object indicated.

Many phrases containing verb + particle collocations have optional parts. In fact, a phrase may seem hard to understand simply because it is really just a shortened form of a longer, less difficult phrase. This dictionary shows the extended forms of the verb phrases with the frequently omitted parts in parentheses. For example: **bark something (out) (at someone), battle (with someone) (over someone or something), bend over backwards (to do something) (for someone).**

How to Use This Dictionary

1. An entry head may have one or more alternate forms. The entry head and its alternates are printed in boldface type, and the alternate forms are preceded by AND. Additional alternate forms are set off by semicolons.

2. Many of the entry phrases have more than one major sense or meaning. These senses or meanings are numbered with boldface numerals.

3. Individual numbered senses may have additional forms that appear in boldface type, in which case the AND and the additional form(s) follow the numeral.

4. The boldface entry head (together with any alternates) is usually followed by a definition. Alternate definitions are separated by semicolons.

5. A definition may be followed by comments in parentheses that give some variations of the phrase, explain what the definition alludes to, or indicate cross-referencing.

6. Some definitions contain additional information in square brackets. This notation supplies information about the typical grammatical context in which the phrase is found.

7. Simple examples of the entry head are introduced by a □ and are in italic type.

8. Examples where the particle and a direct object are transposed are introduced by a [T] and are in italic type.

9. Entry heads appear in slanted type whenever they are referred to in a definition or cross-reference.

10. Some entry heads stand for two or more expressions. Parentheses are used to show which parts of the phrase may or may not be there. For example: **back out (of something)** stands for **back out** and **back out of something.**

NTC's Super-Mini
BASIC PHRASAL VERBS

A

act something out **1.** to perform in real life a role that one has imagined in a fantasy. ☐ *When I was onstage, I was really acting an old fantasy out.* 🆃 *Todd acted out his dreams.* **2.** to convert one's bad feelings into action rather than words. ☐ *Don't act your aggressions out on me!* 🆃 *Don't act out your aggressions on me!* **3.** to demonstrate or communicate something through action rather than words. 🆃 *Act out your request, if you can't say it.* ☐ *Fred, who had lost his voice, had to act his requests out.*

act up [for a thing or a person] to behave badly. ☐ *This car is acting up again.* ☐ *Andy, stop acting up!*

act (up)on something **1.** to take action on a particular problem. (*Upon* is formal and less commonly used than *on.*) ☐ *You should act upon this problem at once.* ☐ *I will act on this immediately.* **2.** to take action because of some special information. ☐ *The police refused to act upon the information they were given.* ☐ *They will act on your suggestion today.*

admit something into something to allow something to be introduced into something else. ☐ *You cannot admit this document into the body of evidence.* ☐ *The attorney admitted questionable evidence into the record.*

advance (up)on someone or something to move toward someone or something. (Typically in military maneuvers or in team sports, such as American football. *Upon* is formal and less commonly used than *on.*) ☐ *The troops advanced on the opposing army.* ☐ *They advanced upon the town.*

advise someone against someone or something to give someone advice about something or about choosing someone for some purpose. ☐ *I must advise you against trying that again.* ☐ *I advised them against Wally.*

agree to something to consent to something; to allow something to be done; to approve something. ☐ *I wish you would agree to my request.* ☐ *I will not agree to it.*

agree (up)on someone or something to agree to the choice of someone or something. ☐ *Couldn't we just agree on John rather than going over the whole list of candidates?* ☐ *Let's try to agree upon a date.*

agree with someone [for something] to be acceptable to someone as food. (Idiomatic. Usually negative.) ☐ *Onions do not agree with me.* ☐ *Some foods do not agree with people.*

agree with someone (about someone or something) AND **agree with someone (on someone or something)** to hold the same opinion as someone else about someone or something; to be of the same mind as someone else about someone or something. ☐ *I agree with you on that point.* ☐ *We do not agree with you about Tom.*

agree with someone (on someone or something) See the previous entry.

agree with something **1.** [for something] to look good or go well with something else. ☐ *This dress does not agree with these shoes, does it?* ☐ *Your dress agrees with your bag.* **2.** [for something] to be in accord with something else. ☐ *The texture of the flooring agrees with the straight lines of the wall covering.* ☐ *Your analysis agrees with mine.*

aim something at someone or something to point or direct something at someone or something. ☐ *Wally aimed the hose at Sarah.* ☐ *He aimed the hose at the base of the bush.*

air something out to allow fresh air to freshen something, such as clothing, a stale-smelling room, etc. ☐ *Should I air my jacket out?* 🅃 *Please air out your woolen jacket.*

allow for someone or something to provide for someone or something. ☐ *Be sure to allow for a large number of sick people.* ☐ *Please allow for Liz also.*

allow someone or something in (something) to permit someone or something to enter something or some place. ☐ *Will they allow you in the restaurant without a tie?* ☐ *They won't allow me in.*

amount to something **1.** [for someone or something] to become worthwhile or valuable. ☐ *I hope Charles amounts to something some day.* ☐ *I doubt that this whole business will ever amount to a hill of beans.* **2.** [for something] to be the equivalent of something. ☐ *Why, this amounts to cheating!* ☐ *Your comments amount to treason.*

amount to the same thing (as something) to be the same (as something); to be the equivalent of something. ☐ *Whether it's red or blue, it amounts to the same thing.* ☐ *It all amounts to the same thing.*

answer for someone [for someone] to speak for someone else. ☐ *I can't answer for Chuck, but I do have my own opinion.* ☐ *I will answer for him.*

appear before someone **1.** to show up in the presence of someone, suddenly. ☐ *The butler appeared before us with no sound or other warning.* ☐ *A frightful specter appeared before me.* **2.** to stand up in front of a particular judge in court. (Legal.) ☐ *You have to appear before Judge Cahill tomorrow.* ☐ *Have you ever appeared before him?*

apply something to something **1.** to put something onto something. ☐ *Apply the decal to the surface of the glass.* ☐ *A decal has been applied to the glass.* **2.** to use something, such as force, effort, etc., on something or in the performance of some task. ☐ *Apply more effort to the job.* ☐ *An even greater effort has been applied to the task.*

appoint someone to something to select or assign someone to serve in a particular role. (Usually focusing on the role of the person or on a group of persons with similar roles. *Someone* includes *oneself.*) ☐ *I am going to appoint you to the position of treasurer.* ☐ *Fred appointed himself to the board of directors, but was sued for doing it.*

arch over someone or something to bend or curve over someone or something; to stand or remain bent or curved over someone or something. ☐ *The trees arched gracefully over the walkway.* ☐ *A lovely bower of roses arched over the bride.*

argue against someone or something **1.** [for someone] to make a case against someone or something; to oppose the choice of someone or something in an argument. □ *I am preparing myself to argue against the case.* □ *Liz argued against Tom, but we chose him anyway.* **2.** [for something, such as facts] to support a case against someone or something in an argument; [for something, such as facts] to support a case against the choice of someone or something in an argument. □ *I have uncovered something that argues against continuing this discussion.* □ *His own remarks argue against the candidate, but he probably will be elected anyway.*

argue one's way out (of something) to talk and argue oneself free of a problem. □ *You can't argue your way out of this!* □ *It's a problem, and there is no way that you can argue your way out.*

argue someone down to defeat someone in a debate. □ *Sally could always argue him down if she had to.* 🅃 *She tries to argue down everyone she meets.*

argue something down **1.** to defeat a proposal or a motion in a meeting through discussion. □ *I am prepared to argue the proposal down in court.* 🅃 *She will argue down the proposal in the council meeting.* **2.** to reduce something, such as a bill or a price, by arguing. □ *I tried to argue the price down, but it did no good.* 🅃 *Tom could not argue down the bill.*

arise from something AND **arise out of something** **1.** to get up from something. □ *What time did you arise from bed?* □ *I arose out of bed at dawn.* **2.** to be due to something; to be caused by something. □ *This whole problem arose from your stubbornness.* □ *The problem arose out of mismanagement.*

arise out of something See the previous entry.

arouse someone from something to activate a person out of a state of rest, sleep, or inaction. (*Someone* includes *oneself.*) □ *I could not arouse her from her sleep.* □ *She aroused herself from a deep sleep.*

arrange something with someone or something to prepare or plan something that will include someone or something. □ *I will arrange a fancy dinner with wine and cloth napkins.* □ *Paul arranged a meeting with the opposition.*

arrive at something **1.** to reach a place. □ *When will we arrive at the resort?* □ *We will arrive at home soon.* **2.** to reach a conclusion; to make a decision. □ *Have you arrived at a decision yet?* □ *We will arrive at an answer tomorrow.*

arrive (up)on the scene (of something) to reach the location of an event in progress. (*Upon* is formal and less commonly used than *on.*) □ *The police arrived on the scene of the crime.* □ *What did they do when they arrived upon the scene?*

ask after someone to inquire about the health and well-being of someone. □ *Molly asked after you.* □ *I asked after Molly and her family.*

ask someone in((to) some place) to invite someone inside some place. □ *We asked them into the house.* □ *We asked them in.*

ask someone out (for something) See the following entry.

ask someone out (to something) AND **ask someone out (for something)** to invite someone to go out to something or some place [on a date]. □ *He asked her out to dinner, but she had other plans.* 🅃 *She couldn't go, so he asked out someone else.* □ *Liz asked Carl out for dinner.*

ask someone over to invite someone who lives close by to come to one's home [for a visit]. (Maybe to a house or apartment.) □ *Can we ask Tom over?* □ *He has been asked over a number of times.*

ask someone up to ask someone to come to one's home for a visit. (Usually said when someone must travel north, up a hill, or to an upper-level apartment for the visit.) □ *Let's ask Judy up for the weekend.* □ *She has been asked up before.*

assign someone or something to someone or something to designate someone or something as belonging to someone or something. (*Someone* includes *oneself.*) □ *They assigned the new car to Roger.* □ *They assigned the new worker to the mail room.* □ *Fred assigned himself to the busiest committee.* □ *I assigned the three new clerks to Mrs. Brown.*

assign something to someone to attribute something to someone; to blame something on someone. □ *We were forced to assign the blame to Robert.* □ *Is the blame assigned to Robert now?*

attach oneself to someone **1.** to become emotionally attached to someone. ☐ *Fred seems to have attached himself to a much older woman, who has captured his attention.* ☐ *Somehow, Fred has attached himself emotionally to Susan, and neither of them has any idea of what to do about it.* **2.** to follow after someone; to become a constant companion to someone. ☐ *Andy's little brother attached himself to Andy and his friends—much to Andy's distress.* ☐ *John attached himself to his older brother and drove him crazy.*

attach oneself to something **1.** to choose to associate with a particular thing, group, or organization. ☐ *Todd attached himself to a volleyball team that practices at the school.* ☐ *The manager attached himself to the luncheon club and became a regular fixture there.* **2.** to connect or secure oneself to something. ☐ *Tony attached himself to the helm and proceeded to steer the boat.* ☐ *Susan attached herself to the seat with the belt provided for that purpose.*

auction something off to sell something [to the highest bidder] at an auction. ☐ *He auctioned his home off.* T *He auctioned off his home.* T *The duke was required to auction off his ancestral home.*

audition for something to try out for a part in something. (One's singing, speaking, or playing is heard and judged.) ☐ *I plan to audition for the play.* ☐ *Liz auditioned for* The Mikado.

audition someone for something to allow someone to try out for a part in a performance; to judge someone's singing, speaking, or playing potentiality for a part in a performance. ☐ *Will you audition anyone else for the part?* ☐ *Have you been auditioned for the part?*

average out to even out ultimately; to be fair over the long term. ☐ *Everything will average out in the end.* ☐ *Yes, it will all average out.*

B

back away (from someone or something) AND **back off (from someone or something)** **1.** to move backwards from a person or thing; to withdraw physically from someone or something. □ *You should back away from the fire.* □ *Please back off from the man who is threatening you.* □ *You should back off.* □ *Jane backed away.* **2.** to begin to appear uninterested in someone or something; to withdraw one's interest from someone or something. □ *The board of directors began to back away from the idea of taking over the other company.* □ *They backed off from the whole idea.*

back off (from someone or something) See the previous entry.

back out (of something) **1.** [for someone or something] to move out of something backwards. □ *The rabbit tried to back out of its burrow.* □ *The rabbit backed out.* **2.** [for someone] to withdraw from something. □ *Are you going to try to back out of our agreement?* □ *You won't back out, will you?*

back someone up to provide someone with help in reserve; to support someone. □ *Don't worry. I will back you up when you need me.* [T] *Will you please back up Nancy over the weekend?*

bail out (of something) **1.** to parachute out of an airplane. □ *The pilot bailed out of the plane at the last moment.* □ *At the last moment, he bailed out.* **2.** to escape from or abandon something. □ *I had to bail out of the company because I decided it was failing.* □ *I bailed out before it was too late.*

bail someone or something out (of something) to get someone or something out of trouble or difficulty. □ *I'm really late on this deadline and I need help. Can you bail me out?* [T] *The government will not bail out the failing banks.* □ *No one will bail us out of our difficulties.*

bail someone out (of something) to pay bail or bond money to get a person out of jail. (*Someone* includes *oneself.*) □ *Try to get someone to bail me out of jail.* T *Can you bail out your friend?* □ *I don't want to bail him out.* □ *She bailed herself out of jail with her last fifty dollars.*

band together (against someone or something) to unite in opposition to someone or something; to unite against someone or something. □ *We must band together against the enemy.* □ *Everyone banded together.*

bang into someone or something to knock or bump into someone or something. □ *Why did you bang into me with your car?* □ *I banged into the door by accident.*

bargain for something to expect or anticipate something; to foresee something. □ *I didn't bargain for this.*

barge in on someone or something to enter or come rudely into a place and interrupt people or their activities. □ *Albert barged in on Ted without knocking.* □ *I didn't mean to barge in on your meeting.*

barge into someone or something to bump or crash into someone or something, possibly on purpose. □ *She just barged into me and nearly knocked me over.* □ *Tom barged into the watercooler and hurt his knee.*

bawl someone out to scold someone. □ *Then Maggie proceeded to bawl Tony out.* T *You can't bawl out everyone who was involved. There are too many.*

be at someone to be argumentative or contentious with someone. □ *She is always at him about something.* □ *I wish you weren't at me all the time.*

be behind (in something) to have failed to do one's work on time; to have failed to keep up with one's work. □ *I can't go out tonight. I'm behind in my work.* □ *I don't like to be behind.*

be down **1.** to be depressed or melancholy. □ *Ann's down a little. I think it's just the weather.* □ *I'm always down after a performance.* **2.** to be inoperable; to be not working. (Typically and originally said of a computer.) □ *The computer is down again.* □ *My television set was down, and I couldn't watch the football game.*

be down (from some place) to have come down from some higher place. □ *Billy's down from his tree house.* □ *Is Billy down yet?*

be down with something to be sick with some disease. □ *She's down with the flu.* □ *Lily is down with a sore throat.*

be in to be in attendance; to be available; to be in one's office. □ *Is the doctor in?* □ *Mr. Franklin is not in.*

be in on something to share in something; to be involved in something. □ *I want to be in on the planning of the party.* □ *I wasn't in on it.*

be into something **1.** to interfere or meddle with something. □ *She is always into other people's business.* □ *I'm sorry I'm into your affairs so much.* **2.** to be interested or involved in something. (Slang.) □ *I'm into model planes right now.* □ *Are you into Chinese food?*

be off **1.** [for one's plans or predictions] to be incorrect or inexact. □ *My estimate was off a little bit.* □ *Your idea of the plane's arrival time was off, but it did land safely two hours later.* **2.** to be not turned on. (As with electric switches or the things they control.) □ *These switches are now off.* □ *Is the fan off?* **3.** to have started. (As with runners in a race or any similar contest.) □ *They're off!* □ *Are the horses off yet?*

be off on someone or something to be in a rage about someone or something; to be on a tirade about someone or something. □ *Are you off on Sally again? Why can't you leave her alone?* □ *I'm off on my boyfriend again.*

be off (on something) **1.** to be incorrect in one's planning or prediction. □ *I was off on my estimates a little bit.* □ *I guess I was off too much.* **2.** to have started on something, such as a task or a journey. □ *What time should we be off on our trip?* □ *We should be off by dawn.*

be on **1.** to be turned on. (As with electric switches or the things they control.) □ *Is the motor on?* □ *It's not on now.* **2.** [for some agreement or plan] to be confirmed and in effect. (Often used with a *for* phrase.) □ *Is everything still on for Friday night?* □ *Yes, the party is on.*

be on something **1.** to be resting on something. □ *Karen is on that rock over there.* □ *People were on anything that would hold them, resting after the long climb.* **2.** to be taking medication. □ *I am on an antibiotic for my chest cold.* □ *I want you to be on this drug for another week.* **3.** to be taking an illegal drug or controlled substance and acting strangely. □ *What is the matter with that kid? Is he on something?* □ *She acted as if she were on barbiturates or something.*

be onto someone to have figured out what someone is doing; to have figured out that someone is being dishonest. □ *No more cheating. I think they are onto us.* □ *I'm onto you!*

be onto something to have found something useful or promising; to be on the verge of discovering something. □ *I think we are really onto something this time.* □ *I am onto a new discovery.*

be out from under someone or something **1.** to be clear of and no longer beneath someone or something. □ *I was glad to be out from under the bed where I had been hiding.* □ *The football player wanted to be out from under the stack of other players.* **2.** to be free from the control of someone or something. □ *It's good to be out from under the dictator.* □ *I was very glad to be out from under my daily work pressure.*

be (out) in the open **1.** to be visible in an open space; to be exposed in an open area. □ *The trucks are out in the open where we can see them.* □ *They're in the open.* **2.** [for something] to be public knowledge. □ *Is this matter out in the open, or is it still secret?* □ *Her pregnancy is in the open now.*

be out (of something) **1.** to be gone; to have left some place; to be absent from a place. □ *The monkey is out of its cage.* □ *Sam is out of the building at present.* □ *Sam's out right now.* **2.** to have no more of something. □ *Sorry, we are fresh out of cucumbers.* □ *Sorry, we're out.*

be out (on strike) to be away from one's job in a strike or protest. □ *The workers are out on strike.* □ *We can't do anything while the workers are out.*

be out something to lack something; to have lost or wasted something. □ *I'm out ten bucks because of your miscalculation.* □ *I'm out the price of a meal.*

be through with someone or something to be finished with someone or something. ☐ *I'm all through with course requirements. Now I can learn something.* ☐ *Lily is through with Max.*

be up for something **1.** [for someone] to be mentally ready for something. ☐ *The team is up for the game tonight.* ☐ *We are all up for the contest.* **2.** [for something] to be available for something, such as auction, grabs, sale, etc. ☐ *The outcome of the game is up for grabs.* ☐ *The car is up for sale.*

be (up)on someone to be someone's obligation, responsibility. ☐ *The obligation is upon you to settle this.* ☐ *The major part of the responsibility is on you.*

be with it to be up-to-date; to be knowledgeable about contemporary matters. ☐ *You're just not with it.* ☐ *I will never be with it!*

bear down (on someone or something) to press down on someone or something. ☐ *Bear down on the pen. You have to make a lot of copies.* ☐ *Don't bear down too hard.*

bear someone or something up to hold someone or something up; to support someone or something. (*Someone* includes *oneself.*) ☐ *Will this bench bear me up?* 🆃 *This bench would bear up an elephant.* 🆃 *The bridge could not bear up the heavy truck.* ☐ *She bore herself up with the aid of a cane.*

bear someone up to sustain or encourage someone. (*Someone* includes *oneself.*) ☐ *Your encouragement bore me up through a very hard time.* 🆃 *I will bear up the widow through the funeral service as well as I can.* ☐ *He bore himself up with thoughts of a brighter future.*

bear up (under something) **1.** to hold up under something; to sustain the weight of something. ☐ *How is the new beam bearing up under the weight of the floor?* ☐ *It isn't bearing up. It broke.* **2.** to remain brave under a mental or emotional burden. ☐ *Jill did not bear up well under problems in her home.* ☐ *Jill bore up quite well.*

bear (up)on something [for information or facts] to concern something or be relevant to something. (*Upon* is formal and less commonly used than *on.*) ☐ *How do those facts bear on this matter?* ☐ *They do not bear upon this matter at all.*

bear with someone or something to be patient with someone or something; to wait upon someone or something. (Especially through difficulties.) □ *Please bear with me for a moment while I try to get this straightened out.* □ *Can you bear with the committee until it reaches a decision?*

beat down on someone or something to fall on someone or something. □ *The rain beat down on us for an hour.* □ *The rock slide beat down on the car and totally ruined the body.*

beat someone down to defeat or demoralize someone. (*Someone* includes *oneself.*) □ *The constant bombing finally beat them down.* 🅃 *The attackers beat down the defenders.* □ *She beat herself down with self-doubt and guilt.*

beat something down **1.** to break something in; to break through something. □ *Don't beat the door down! I'm coming!* 🅃 *Please don't beat down the door!* **2.** to flatten something. □ *Sam beat the veal down to the thickness of a piece of paper.* 🅃 *First you have to beat down the meat to a very thin layer.*

beat something into something to beat or whip something with a utensil, until it changes into something else. □ *Beat the white of the egg into stiff peaks.* □ *Beat the batter into a satiny paste.*

beat something up **1.** to whip up something, such as an egg. □ *Beat the egg up and pour it in the skillet.* 🅃 *Beat up another egg and do the same.* **2.** to ruin something; to damage something. □ *The banging of the door has really beat this wall up.* 🅃 *The door handle beat up the wall.*

bed down (for something) to lie down to sleep for a period of time. □ *After she had bedded down for the night, the telephone rang.* □ *All the chickens bedded down hours ago.*

beef something up to strengthen or fortify something. □ *Can we beef the last act up a little bit? It's really weak.* 🅃 *Try to beef up the defensive plays of the team.*

beg off ((on) something) to make excuses for not doing something. □ *I'm going to have to beg off on our date.* □ *I'm sorry, I have to beg off.*

beg something off to decline an invitation politely. □ *She begged the trip to the zoo off.* 🅃 *We all begged off the dinner invitation.*

belch out to burst, billow, or gush out. □ *Smoke belched out of the chimney.*

belt up to secure oneself with a belt, usually a seat belt. (Also a slogan encouraging people to use their seat belts.) □ *Please belt up. Safety first!*

bend down to curve downward; [for someone] to lean down. □ *Please bend down and pick up the little bits of paper you just dropped.* □ *The snow-laden bushes bent down.*

bend over [for someone] to bend down at the waist. □ *I bent over and picked up the coin.* □ *When he bent over, something ripped.*

bind someone or something up (with something) to tie someone or something with string or rope. □ *We bound her up with the drapery cords.* 🅃 *Please bind up both of them with twine.* 🅃 *Could you bind up the newspapers with twine?*

bind someone over (to someone or something) to deliver someone to some legal authority. (Legal.) □ *They bound the suspect over to the sheriff.* 🅃 *The sheriff will bind over the suspect to the police chief.* □ *When will you bind the prisoner over?*

bite on something **1.** to chew on something; to grasp something with the teeth. □ *The injured cowboy bit on his wallet while they probed for the bullet.* □ *Don't bite on your collar.* **2.** to respond to a lure. □ *Do you think the fish will bite on this?* □ *No one would bite on that bait. Try another approach.*

black out **1.** to pass out; to become unconscious. □ *After I fell, I must have blacked out.* □ *I think I am going to black out.* **2.** [for lights] to go out. □ *Suddenly the lights blacked out.*

black something out **1.** to cut or turn out the lights or electric power. □ *The lightning strike blacked the entire town out.* 🅃 *The manager blacked out the whole building during the emergency to prevent an explosion.* **2.** to prevent the broadcast of a specific television or radio program in a specific area. (Usually refers to a sports event.) □ *Will they black the game out around here?* 🅃 *They blacked out the basketball game in this area.*

blame someone for something to hold someone responsible for something; to name someone as the cause of something. (*Someone* includes *oneself.*) □ *Please don't blame Jill for it.* □ *She blamed herself for everything that went wrong.*

blame something on someone to say that something is someone's fault; to place the guilt for something on someone. □ *Don't blame it on me.* □ *I blamed it all on someone else.*

blank something out **1.** to forget something, perhaps on purpose; to blot something out of memory. □ *I'm sorry, I just blanked your question out.* Ⓣ *I blanked out your question. What did you say?* **2.** to erase something, as on a computer screen. Ⓣ *Who blanked out the information that was on my screen?* □ *Please blank your password out as soon as you type it.*

blast off (for some place) **1.** [for a rocket ship] to take off and head toward a destination. □ *The rocket blasted off for the moon.* □ *Will it blast off on time?* **2.** [for someone] to leave for a destination. (Jocular.) □ *Ann blasted off for the library, so she could study.* □ *I've got to blast off. It's late.*

blaze down (on someone or something) [for the sun or other hot light] to burn down on someone or something. □ *The sun blazed down on the people on the beach.* □ *The stage lights blazed down on the set while the actors rehearsed.*

blaze up **1.** [for flames] to expand upward suddenly. □ *The fire blazed up and warmed all of us.* □ *As the fire blazed up, we moved away from the fireplace.* **2.** [for trouble, especially violent trouble] to erupt suddenly. □ *The battle blazed up again, and the fighting started to become fierce.* □ *As the battle blazed up, the cowards fled into the hills.*

blend in (with someone or something) to mix well with someone or something; to combine with someone or something. □ *Everyone there blended in with our group.* □ *This color doesn't blend in with the upholstery fabric I have chosen.*

blend in(to something) to combine nicely with something; to mix well with something. □ *The oil won't blend into the water very well.* □ *It simply won't blend in.*

blend something in(to something) to mix something evenly into something else. □ *We should blend the strawberry jam into the peanut butter slowly.* [T] *You should blend in some more jam.*

blend something together (with something) to mix something evenly with something else. □ *Blend the egg together with the cream.* □ *Blend the ingredients together and pour them into a baking pan.*

blink back one's tears to fight back tears; to try to keep from crying. □ *She blinked back her tears and went on.* [T] *He blinked his tears back.*

block something off to prevent movement through something by putting up a barrier; to close a passageway. □ *Sam blocked the corridor off with a row of chairs.* [T] *He used some chairs to block off the hallway.*

block something out **1.** to lay something out carefully; to map out the details of something. □ *She blocked it out for us, so we could understand.* [T] *Let me block out this project for you right now.* **2.** to obscure a clear view of something. □ *The trees blocked the sun out.* [T] *The bushes blocked out my view of the car that was approaching.*

block something up to obstruct something; to stop the flow within a channel. (Also without *up*, but not eligible as an entry.) □ *The heaps of debris blocked the channel up.* [T] *It blocked up the channel.*

blot someone or something out to forget someone or something by covering up memories or by trying to forget. □ *I try to blot those bad thoughts out.* [T] *I tried to blot out those unhappy thoughts.* □ *I blotted David out and tried to keep him out of my mind.*

blot something out to make something invisible by covering it with a spot or smudge. □ *Don't blot the name out on the application form.* [T] *Who blotted out the name on this form?*

blow away [for something light] to be carried away by the wind. □ *The leaves blew away on the autumn winds.* □ *My papers blew away!*

blow in [for something] to cave in to the pressure of moving air. □ *The door blew in during the storm.* □ *The window blew in.*

blow itself out [for a storm or a tantrum] to lose strength and stop; to subside. □ *The storm blew itself out.*

blow off 1. [for something] to be carried off of something by moving air. □ *The leaves of the trees blew off in the strong wind.* □ *My papers blew off the table.* 2. [for a valve or pressure-maintaining device] to be forced off or away by high pressure. □ *The safety valve blew off and all the pressure escaped.* □ *The valve blew off, making a loud pop.*

blow over [for something] to diminish; to subside. (As with a storm or a temper tantrum.) □ *Her display of temper finally blew over.* □ *The storm will blow over soon, I hope.*

blow someone or something away [for the wind] to carry someone or something away. □ *The wind almost blew her away.* 🅃 *The high wind blew away the entire barn.* 🅃 *It nearly blew away all of us.*

blow someone or something down [for a rush of air] to knock someone or something over. □ *The wind blew Chuck down.* 🅃 *It blew down many people.* □ *It almost blew the barn down.*

blow someone or something over [for the wind] to move strongly and upset someone or something. □ *The wind almost blew us over.* 🅃 *The wind blew over the shed.*

blow someone or something up 1. to destroy someone or something by explosion. (*Someone* includes *oneself.*) □ *The terrorists blew the family up as they slept.* 🅃 *The villains blew up the whole family!* 🅃 *They blew up the bridge.* □ *He blew himself up with the bomb he was making.* 2. to exaggerate something [good or bad] about someone or something. (*Someone* includes *oneself.*) □ *I hope no one blows the story up.* 🅃 *The press always blows up reports of bad behavior.* □ *The press blew the story up unnecessarily.* □ *She blows herself up whenever she gives an interview.*

blow something out to extinguish a flame by blowing air on it. □ *I blew the candle out.* 🅃 *I blew out the candle.*

blow something up 1. to inflate something. □ *He didn't have enough breath to blow the balloon up.* 🅃 *They all blew up their own balloons.* 2. to enlarge a photograph. □ *How big can you blow this picture up?* 🅃 *I will blow up this snapshot and frame it.*

blow up **1.** [for something] to explode. ☐ *The bomb might have blown up if the children had tried to move it.* ☐ *The firecracker blew up.* **2.** [for someone] to have an outburst of anger. ☐ *She got mad and blew up.*

bog down to become encumbered and slow down; to slow down. (As if one were walking through a bog and getting stuck in the mud.) ☐ *The process bogged down and almost stopped.* ☐ *The whole thing bogged down soon after it started.*

boil down to something **1.** [for a liquid] to be condensed to something by boiling. ☐ *Boil this mixture down to about half of what it was.* **2.** [for a complex situation] to be reduced to its essentials. ☐ *It boils down to the question of who is going to win.* ☐ *It boils down to a very minor matter.*

boil over [for a liquid] to overflow while being boiled. ☐ *The pudding boiled over and stuck to the stove.* ☐ *Don't let the stew boil over!*

boil something out (of something) to remove something from something by boiling. ☐ *I boiled the cleaning fluid out of the cloths.* 🅃 *I boiled out the cleaning fluid.* ☐ *We boiled the oily stuff out.*

book someone through (to some place) to make transportation arrangements for someone that involve a number of changes and transfers. (*Someone* includes *oneself.*) ☐ *The travel agent booked me through to Basra.* ☐ *I would be happy to book you through if you would like.* ☐ *She booked herself through to Budapest.*

boom out [for a loud sound] to sound out like thunder. ☐ *His voice boomed out so everyone could hear.* ☐ *An explosion boomed out and frightened us all.*

boot someone out (of something) to force someone to leave something or some place. ☐ *The board booted Greg out of the job.* 🅃 *After a unanimous vote, they booted out all the old guard.*

boot (something) up to start up a computer. ☐ *She booted her computer up and went to work.* 🅃 *Please go boot up your computer so we can get started.* ☐ *He turned on the computer and booted up.* ☐ *Try to boot up again and see what happens.*

border (up)on something **1.** [for something] to touch upon a boundary. (*Upon* is formal and less commonly used than *on.*) ☐ *Our* *property borders on the lakeshore.* □ *The farm borders upon the railroad right-of-way.* **2.** [for some activity or idea] to be very similar to something else. (Not usually physical objects. *Upon* is formal and less commonly used than *on.*) □ *This notion of yours borders upon mutiny!* □ *It borders on insanity.*

boss someone around to order someone around. □ *Please don't boss me around so much.* 🆃 *You boss around everybody!*

botch something up to mess something up; to do a bad job of something. □ *You really botched this up.* 🆃 *I did not botch up your project.*

bottle something up (inside (someone)) [for someone] to keep serious emotions within and not express them. □ *Don't bottle it up inside you.* 🆃 *Don't bottle up all your feelings.* □ *You can't just bottle it up.*

bottom out finally to reach the lowest or worst point. □ *The prices on the stock market finally bottomed out.* □ *When the market bottoms out, I'll buy some stock.*

bounce off ((of) something) to rebound from something. (The *of* is colloquial.) □ *The ball bounced off the wall and struck a lamp.* □ *It hit the wall and bounced off.*

bounce out (of something) to rebound out of or away from something. □ *The ball bounced out of the corner into my hands.* □ *The window was open and the ball bounced out.*

bounce something off (of) someone or something **1.** to make something rebound off someone or something. (The *of* is colloquial.) □ *She bounced the ball off the wall, turned, and tossed it to Wally.* □ *She bounced the ball off of Harry, into the wastebasket.* **2.** to try an idea or concept out on someone or a group. (Figurative. The *of* is colloquial.) □ *Let me bounce this off of the committee, if I may.* □ *Can I bounce something off you people, while you're here?*

bow out (of something) to withdraw from something. □ *I decided to bow out of the organization.* □ *The time had come for me to bow out.*

bowl someone over **1.** to knock someone over. □ *The huge dog ran by and bowled me over.* 🆃 *The wind bowled over all the pedes-*

trians. **2.** to astound someone. (Figurative.) □ *His statement just bowled me over.* [T] *The announcement bowled over everyone.*

box someone or something in to trap or confine someone or something. (Literal and figurative uses. *Someone* includes *oneself.*) □ *He boxed her in so she could not get away from him.* [T] *They tried to box in the animals, but they needed more space.* □ *Don't try to box me in.*

brace someone or something up to prop up or add support to someone or something. (*Someone* includes *oneself.*) □ *They braced the tree up for the expected windstorm.* [T] *They braced up the tree again after the storm.* □ *Help me brace him up until we get his bed made.* □ *He had to brace himself up with a splint before he could walk.*

branch off (from something) to separate off from something; to divide away from something. □ *A small stream branched off from the main channel.* □ *An irrigation ditch branched off here and there.*

branch out to develop many branches, tributaries, or interests. □ *I got tired of sales and branched out.* □ *The river branches out near its mouth.*

branch out (from something) **1.** [for a branch] to grow out of a branch or trunk. (Having to do with plants and trees.) □ *A twig branched out of the main limb and grew straight up.* □ *The bush branched out from the base.* **2.** to expand away from something; to diversify away from narrower interests. □ *The speaker branched out from her prepared remarks.* □ *The topic was very broad, and she was free to branch out.*

branch out (into something) to diversify and go into new areas. □ *I have decided to branch out into some new projects.* □ *Business was very good, so I decided to branch out.*

break away (from someone) AND **break free (from someone); break loose (from someone)** **1.** to get free of the physical hold of someone. □ *I tried to break away from him, but he was holding me too tight.* □ *She broke free from him, at last.* □ *I broke free from the intruder.* □ *I could not break loose from my captors.* □ *At* *last, I broke free.* **2.** to sever a relationship with another person, especially the parent-child relationship. □ *He found it hard to break away from his mother.* □ *She was almost thirty before she finally broke free.* □ *I found it hard to break loose from my parents.*

break down **1.** [for a mechanical device] to cease working. □ *The car broke down in the middle of the expressway.* **2.** [for someone] to have an emotional or mental collapse. □ *Finally, after many sleepless nights, he broke down totally.*

break down (and do something) to surrender to demands or emotions and do something. □ *Max finally broke down and confessed.* □ *I knew he would break down.* □ *I had to stop and break down and cry. I was so depressed.* □ *I was afraid I would break down and cry.*

break free (from someone) See *break away (from someone).*

break in (on someone) **1.** to burst into a place and violate someone's privacy. □ *The police broke in on him at his home and arrested him.* □ *They needed a warrant to break in.* **2.** to interrupt someone's conversation. □ *If you need to talk to me, just break in on me.* □ *Feel free to break in if it's an emergency.*

break in on something to interrupt something; to intrude upon something. □ *I didn't mean to break in on your discussion.* □ *Please don't break in on us just now. This is important.*

break into something See *break up (into something).*

break in(to something or some place) to force entry into something or a place criminally; to enter some place forcibly for the purpose of robbery or other illegal acts. □ *The thugs broke into the liquor store.* □ *They broke in and took all the money.*

break loose (from someone) See *break away (from someone).*

break off (from something) [for a piece of something] to become separated from the whole. □ *This broke off from the lamp. What shall I do with it?* □ *This piece broke off.*

break out **1.** [for widespread fighting] to emerge, erupt, or begin. □ *Fighting broke out again in the streets.* **2.** [for a disease] to erupt and become epidemic. □ *Chicken pox broke out in Tony's school.*

break (out) into tears to begin to cry. □ *Every single child broke out into tears in the movie.* □ *The child broke into tears and started howling.*

break out of something to get out of a confining place or situation; to escape from something or some place. □ *He couldn't break out of a paper bag!*

break out (with something) [for the skin] to erupt with a specific disease such as measles, chicken pox, rubella, etc. □ *Nick and Dan broke out with chicken pox.* □ *They both broke out at the same time.*

break someone down to cause a person to submit; to pressure a person to submit to something. □ *The police broke her down, and she confessed.* [T] *They found it easy to break down the suspect.*

break someone in to train someone to do a new job; to supervise someone who is learning to do a new job. (*Someone* includes *oneself.*) □ *Who will break the new employee in?* [T] *I have to break in a new typist* □ *She broke herself in on the new job by practicing at home.*

break someone up to cause someone to begin laughing very hard. (*Someone* includes *oneself.*) □ *Everything she says just breaks me up.* [T] *The joke broke up the audience.* □ *He broke himself up with the realization of what a silly mistake he had made.*

break something down to destroy a barrier. □ *The court broke a number of legal barriers down this week.* [T] *I did not break down your door!*

break something in **1.** to crush or batter something to pieces. □ *Why are you breaking the door in? Here's the key!* [T] *Who broke in the door?* **2.** to use a new device until it runs well and smoothly; to wear shoes, perhaps a little at a time, until they feel comfortable. □ *I can't travel on the highway until I break this car in.* [T] *I want to go out this weekend and break in the car.* [T] *I hate to break in new shoes.*

break something off ((of) something) to fracture or dislodge a piece off something. (The *of* is colloquial.) □ *He broke a piece of the decorative stone off the side of the church.* [T] *He didn't mean to break off anything.* □ *He didn't mean to break it off.*

break something up to put an end to some kind of fighting or arguing. ☐ *Okay, you guys, break it up!* ☐ *Break it up and leave the area!* 🅃 *The teacher broke up the fight in the school yard.*

break something up (into something) to break something into smaller pieces. ☐ *We broke the crackers up into much smaller pieces.* 🅃 *Please break up the crackers into smaller pieces if you want to feed the ducks.* ☐ *They broke the crackers up.*

break through (something) to force [one's way] through an obstruction. ☐ *The fire fighters broke through the wall easily.* ☐ *They broke through with no difficulty.*

break up 1. [for something] to fall apart; to be broken to pieces. (Typically said of a ship breaking up on rocks.) ☐ *In the greatest storm of the century, the ship broke up on the reef.* ☐ *It broke up and sank.* **2.** [for two people] to end a romance; [for lovers] to separate permanently. ☐ *Terry and Albert broke up. Did you hear?* **3.** [for married persons] to divorce. ☐ *After many years of bickering, they finally broke up.* **4.** [for a marriage] to dissolve in divorce. ☐ *The marriage finally broke up.* ☐ *It broke up almost immediately.* **5.** to begin laughing very hard. ☐ *The comedian told a particularly good joke, and the audience broke up.* ☐ *I always break up when I hear her sing. She is so bad!*

break up (into something) AND **break into something** to divide into smaller parts. ☐ *The glass broke up into a thousand pieces.* ☐ *It hit the floor and broke up, flinging bits everywhere.*

break up (with someone) to end a romantic relationship with someone. ☐ *Jill broke up with Albert.* ☐ *I just knew they would break up.*

breathe something in to take something into the lungs, such as air, medicinal vapors, gas, etc. ☐ *Breathe the vapor in slowly. It will help your cold.* 🅃 *Breathe in that fresh air!*

breathe something out to exhale something. ☐ *At last, he breathed his last breath out, and that was the end.* 🅃 *Breathe out your breath slowly.*

breeze along to travel along casually, rapidly, and happily; to go through life in a casual and carefree manner. ☐ *Kristine was just* *breezing along the road when she ran off onto the shoulder.* □ *We just breezed along the highway, barely paying attention to what we were doing.* □ *Don't just breeze along through life!*

breeze in(to some place) to enter a place quickly, in a happy and carefree manner. □ *She breezed into the conference room and sat down at the head of the table.* □ *Jerry breezed in and said hello.*

breeze through (something) **1.** to complete some task rapidly and easily. □ *I breezed through my calculus assignment in no time at all.* □ *It was not hard. I just breezed through.* **2.** to travel through a place rapidly. □ *They breezed through every little town without stopping.* □ *We didn't stop. We just breezed through.*

brew something up **1.** to brew something, as in making coffee or tea. □ *Can somebody brew some coffee up?* 🅃 *Let me brew up a pot of coffee, and then we'll talk.* **2.** to cause something to happen; to foment something. (Figurative.) □ *I could see that they were brewing some kind of trouble up.* 🅃 *Don't brew up any trouble!*

brew up to build up; [for something] to begin to build and grow. (Typically said of a storm.) □ *A bad storm is brewing up in the west.* □ *Something serious is brewing up in the western sky.*

bring a verdict in [for a jury] to deliver its decision to the court. □ *Do you think they will bring a verdict in today?* 🅃 *The jury brought in their verdict around midnight.* □ *A verdict was finally brought in by the jury.*

bring someone down **1.** to assist or accompany someone from a higher place to a lower place. □ *Please bring your friends down so I can meet them.* 🅃 *She brought down her cousin, who had been taking a nap upstairs.* □ *Aunt Mattie was brought down for supper.* **2.** to bring someone to a place for a visit. □ *Let's bring Tom and Terri down for a visit this weekend.* 🅃 *We brought down Tom just last month.* □ *They were brought down at our expense for a weekend visit.* **3.** to restore someone to a normal mood or attitude. (After a period of elation or, perhaps, drug use.) □ *The bad news brought me down quickly.* 🅃 *I was afraid that the change of plans would bring down the entire group.*

bring someone in (on something) to include someone in some deed or activity. □ *I'm going to have to bring a specialist in on* *this.* [T] *Please bring in several specialists on this.* □ *Let's bring Dave in before we go any further.* □ *Dave was brought in at the last minute.*

bring someone or something up **1.** to cause someone or something to go up with one from a lower place to a higher place. □ *We brought them up and let them view the city from the balcony.* [T] *Why did you bring up Tom? Wasn't he comfortable down there?* [T] *I brought up some binoculars so you can enjoy the view from up here.* □ *They were brought up from below.* **2.** to mention someone or something. (*Someone* includes *oneself.*) □ *Why did you have to bring that up?* [T] *Must you bring up bad memories?* [T] *Why did you bring up Walter?* □ *Walter was brought up for discussion.* □ *He brought himself up again and again. What a self-centered person!* **3.** to raise someone or something; to care for someone or something up to adulthood. □ *We brought the dog up from a pup.* [T] *We brought up the dog carefully and sold it for a good profit.* □ *I brought Sammy up the best I could.* □ *Sammy was brought up with the best child-raising methods.*

bring someone to to help someone return to consciousness. □ *We worked to bring him to before he went into shock.* □ *He was finally brought to with the smelling salts.*

bring someone up for something **1.** to suggest someone's name for something. (*Someone* includes *oneself.*) □ *I would like to bring Beth up for vice president.* [T] *I will bring up Beth for this office if you don't.* □ *Beth has been brought up for another office already.* □ *Tom always brings himself up for head of the department.* **2.** to put someone's name up for promotion, review, discipline, etc. (*Someone* includes *oneself.*) □ *We brought Tom up for promotion.* [T] *The boss brought up Tom too.* □ *Tom was brought up for something also.* □ *I had to bring myself up for promotion.*

bring someone up on something to provide something while raising a child to adulthood. □ *She brought her children up on fast food.* □ *We were all brought up on television cartoons.* [T] *You shouldn't bring up your children on that kind of entertainment!*

bring something about to make something happen. □ *I am unable to bring the desired result about.* [T] *He claimed he could bring about a miracle.*

bring something back to restore an earlier style or practice. ☐ *Please bring the good old days back.* 🅃 *Bring back good times for all of us.* ☐ *Those days cannot be brought back.*

bring something back (to someone) to remind someone of something. ☐ *The funeral brought memories back.* 🅃 *The warm winds brought back the old feeling of loneliness that I had experienced so many times in the tropics.*

bring something down **1.** to move something from a higher place to a lower place. ☐ *Bring that box down, please.* 🅃 *And while you're up there, please bring down the box marked winter clothing.* ☐ *The box was brought down as requested.* **2.** to lower something, such as prices, profit, taxes, etc. ☐ *The governor pledged to bring taxes down.* 🅃 *I hope they bring down taxes.* ☐ *Taxes were never brought down. In fact, they went up.* **3.** to defeat or overcome something, such as an enemy, a government, etc. ☐ *The events of the last week will probably bring the government down.* 🅃 *The scandal will bring down the government, I hope.* ☐ *The government was brought down by the scandal.*

bring something in to earn something—an amount of money; to draw or attract an amount of money. ☐ *My part-time job brings thirty dollars in every month.* 🅃 *She brings in a lot of money.* ☐ *A lot of money was brought in by Lily's parents.* 🅃 *Their appeal for donations brought in a lot of contributions.*

bring something on **1.** to cause something to happen; to cause a situation to occur. ☐ *What brought this event on?* 🅃 *What brought on the event?* ☐ *My comments were brought on by something I read last night.* **2.** to cause a case of, or an attack of, a disease. ☐ *What brought your coughing fit on?* ☐ *Something brought it on.* ☐ *The attack was brought on by allergy.*

bring something on someone to cause something to go wrong for someone. (*Someone* includes *oneself.*) ☐ *You brought it on yourself. Don't complain.* ☐ *Max brought this problem on all of us.*

bring something out to issue something; to publish something; to present something [to the public]. ☐ *I am bringing a new book out.* 🅃 *I hear you have brought out a new edition of your book.* ☐ *A new edition has been brought out.*

bring something out (in someone) to cause a particular quality to be displayed by a person, such as virtue, courage, a mean streak, selfishness, etc. ☐ *You bring the best out in me.* 🅃 *This kind of thing brings out the worst in me.* ☐ *This brings the worst out.*

brown out [for the electricity] to decrease in power. (Causing electric lights to dim. Not quite a blackout.) ☐ *The lights browned out and almost went out altogether.* ☐ *After the lights browned out, they stayed on for an hour.*

brush by someone or something AND **brush past someone or something** to push quickly past someone or something. ☐ *She brushed by the little group of people standing there talking.* ☐ *I brushed by the plant, knocking it over.* ☐ *You just brushed past me!*

brush past someone or something See the previous entry.

brush someone off **1.** to remove something, such as dust or lint, from someone by brushing. ☐ *The porter brushed Mr. Harris off and was rewarded with a very small tip.* 🅃 *The porter had never brushed off such a miserly man before.* **2.** to reject someone; to dismiss someone. ☐ *He brushed her off, telling her she had no appointment.* 🅃 *He brushed off Mrs. Franklin, who was only trying to be nice to him.* ☐ *Mr. Franklin should not be brushed off.*

brush something away (from something) to remove something from something by brushing; to get dirt or crumbs off something by brushing. ☐ *He brushed a bit of lint away from Tom's collar.* 🅃 *She brushed away the crumbs from the table.* ☐ *Liz brushed the crumbs away.* ☐ *The dust was brushed away from his shoes.*

brush something down to clean and neaten fur or fabric by brushing. ☐ *Why don't you brush your coat down? It's very linty.* 🅃 *I brushed down my trousers, and they looked much better.* ☐ *My coat was brushed down before I left home.*

brush something off ((of) someone or something) to remove something from someone or something by brushing. ☐ *I brushed a little lint off her collar.* 🅃 *I brushed off the lint that was on her collar.* ☐ *Liz brushed it off.*

brush (up) against someone or something to move past and touch someone or something. ☐ *I brushed up against the freshly* *painted wall as I passed.* □ *I guess I brushed against Walter as I walked by.* □ *The houseplant was brushed up against so much that it finally lost all its leaves.*

brush up (on something) to improve one's knowledge of something or one's ability to do something. □ *I need to brush up on my German.* □ *My German is weak. I had better brush up.*

bubble over **1.** [for boiling or effervescent liquid] to spill or splatter over the edge of its container. □ *The pot bubbled over and put out the cooking fire.* □ *The stew bubbled over.* **2.** [for someone] to be so happy and merry that it spills over onto other people. □ *She was just bubbling over, she was so happy.* □ *Lily bubbled over with joy.*

buckle someone in to attach someone securely with a vehicle's seat belts. (This includes airplane seat belts. *Someone* includes *oneself.*) □ *Don't forget to buckle the children in.* 🅃 *Did you buckle in the children?* □ *The children are all buckled in.* □ *Please buckle yourself in.*

buckle someone or something up to attach someone or something securely with straps that buckle together. (This emphasizes the completeness and secureness of the act. *Someone* includes *oneself.*) □ *Buckle the children up before we leave.* 🅃 *Buckle up your shoes.* 🅃 *I will buckle up Jimmy.* □ *Buckle yourself up, if you please.*

buckle up to buckle one's seat belt, as in a car or plane. □ *Please buckle up!* □ *I wish you would obey the law and buckle up.*

buddy up (to someone) to become overly familiar or friendly with someone. □ *Don't try to buddy up to me now. It won't do any good.* □ *He always tries to buddy up, no matter how badly you treat him.*

buddy up (with someone) to join with another person to form a pair that will do something together or share something. □ *I buddied up with Carl, and we shared the canoe.* □ *Carl and I buddied up, and we shared the canoe.* □ *Let's buddy up, okay?* □ *They buddied up with each other.*

build on((to) something) to add to something by constructing an extension. □ *Do you plan to build onto this house?* □ *Yes, we are going to build on.*

build someone in(to something) to make a person an integral part of an organization or a plan. ☐ *We built the mayor's nephew into the organizational structure of the town.* 🅃 *He built in his relatives from the very beginning.* ☐ *He built them in while he was president.*

build someone up **1.** to strengthen someone; to make someone healthier or stronger. (*Someone* includes *oneself.*) ☐ *You need more exercise and better food to build you up again.* 🅃 *The coach wanted to build up Roger into a stronger player.* ☐ *I need to do some exercises to build myself up.* **2.** to praise or exalt someone. (*Someone* includes *oneself.*) ☐ *Claire liked to build Tom up, because she was in love with him.* 🅃 *Mary also liked to build up Tom.* ☐ *Don't build yourself up so much.*

build someone up (for something) to prepare someone for something; to lead a person into a proper state of mind to receive some information. (*Someone* includes *oneself.*) ☐ *We built them up for what was about to happen.* 🅃 *We had to build up the woman for what we were going to tell her.* ☐ *They built John up carefully and then told him the bad news.* ☐ *She built herself up for a wonderful evening.*

build something in(to something) **1.** to make a piece of furniture or an appliance a part of a building's construction. ☐ *We will build this chest into the wall about here.* 🅃 *We are going to build in a second chest.* ☐ *Then we will build another one in.* **2.** to make a particular quality a basic part of something. ☐ *We build quality into our cars before we put our name on them.* 🅃 *We build in quality.* ☐ *We build quality in.* **3.** to make a special restriction or specification a part of the plan of something. ☐ *I built the restriction into our agreement.* 🅃 *I built in the rule.* ☐ *We built the rule in.*

build something out of something to construct something from parts or materials. ☐ *She built a tower out of the blocks.* ☐ *They will build the tower out of cast concrete.*

build something up **1.** to add buildings to an area of land or a neighborhood. ☐ *They are really building this area up. There is no more open space.* 🅃 *They built up the area over the years.* **2.** to develop, accumulate, or increase something, such as wealth, business, goodwill, etc. ☐ *I built this business up through hard work and hope.* 🅃 *She built up a good business over the years.* **3.** to praise or exalt something; to exaggerate the virtues of something. ☐ *The master of ceremonies built the act up so much that everyone was disappointed when they saw it.* 🅃 *He built up the act too much.*

build up to increase; to develop. ☐ *The storm clouds are building up. Better close the windows.* ☐ *The bad weather has been building up for days.*

bump (up) against someone or something to strike someone or something accidentally, usually relatively gently. ☐ *The car bumped up against the curb.* ☐ *This wall has been bumped against a lot. It needs painting.*

bunch someone or something up to pack or cluster things or people together. ☐ *Bunch them up so you can squeeze them into the sack.* 🅃 *Kelly bunched up the roses and put them in a vase.* ☐ *Bunch the people up so more will fit in.*

bunch up to pack together or cluster. ☐ *Spread out. Don't bunch up!*

bundle off to leave in a hurry; to take all one's parcels and leave in a hurry. ☐ *She got ready and bundled off after her bus.* ☐ *Lily bundled off just in time.*

bundle (oneself) up (against something) to wrap oneself up in protective clothing or bedding as protection against the cold. ☐ *Please bundle yourself up against the frigid wind.* ☐ *Bundle yourself up.* ☐ *Better bundle up.* ☐ *Be sure and bundle yourself up against the cold. It's freezing out there.*

bundle someone in(to something) **1.** to put someone, usually a child, into heavy outdoor clothing. (*Someone* includes *oneself.*) ☐ *Bill bundled Billy into his parka.* ☐ *He was hard to bundle in because he wouldn't stand still.* ☐ *Tom bundled himself into his parka and opened the door to go out.* **2.** to put someone, usually a child, into bed. ☐ *She bundled Sarah into bed just in time.* ☐ *June pulled back the sheets and bundled Sarah in.*

bundle someone up (in something) to wrap someone up in protective clothing or bedding. (*Someone* includes *oneself.*) ☐ *Bill bundled Billy up in his parka.* 🅃 *Bill bundled up Mary in her parka.*

☐ *He bundled her up.* ☐ *The child bundled himself up into the covers and went to sleep.*

bundle something off (to someone or some place) to send something off in a bundle to someone. ☐ *He bundled his laundry off to his mother, who would wash it for him.* 🅃 *Mary bundled off the package to her brother.* ☐ *She put stamps on the package and bundled it off.*

buoy someone or something up to keep someone or something afloat. (*Someone* includes *oneself.*) ☐ *Use this cushion to buoy yourself up.* 🅃 *The log buoyed up the swimmer until help came.* ☐ *The air trapped in the hull buoyed the boat up.*

buoy someone up to support, encourage, or sustain someone. (*Someone* includes *oneself.*) ☐ *The good news buoyed her up considerably.* 🅃 *Her good humor buoyed up the entire party.* ☐ *She buoyed herself up by keeping in touch with friends.*

burn away **1.** [for something] to burn until there is no more of it. ☐ *All the oil burned away.* ☐ *The fuel burned away and things are cooling down.* **2.** for something to keep on burning rapidly. ☐ *The little fire burned away brightly, warming the tiny room.* ☐ *The candle burned away, giving a tiny bit of light to the huge room.*

burn down **1.** [for a building] to be destroyed by fire. ☐ *The barn burned down.* ☐ *There was a fire, and the barn was burned down.* **2.** [for a fire] to burn and dwindle away. ☐ *The flame burned down and then went out.* ☐ *As the fire burned down, it began to get cold.*

burn (itself) out **1.** [for a flame or fire] to run out of fuel and go out. ☐ *Finally, the fires burned themselves out.* ☐ *The fire finally burned out.* ☐ *The flame burned itself out.* **2.** [for an electrical part] to fail and cease working or make a larger unit cease working. ☐ *The motor finally burned itself out.* ☐ *The motor burned out.*

burn off [for some excess volatile or flammable substance] to burn away or burn up. ☐ *A film of oil on the surface of the water was burning off, making dense black smoke.* ☐ *The alcohol burned off and left a delicious flavor in the cherries jubilee.*

burn (oneself) out to stay at a task so long that one's limit is reached and one is no longer effective. ☐ *I didn't want to burn* *myself out on the job, so I quit on my own.* ☐ *Finally, I just burned out.*

burn someone out to wear someone out; to make someone ineffective through overuse. (*Someone* includes *oneself.*) ☐ *Facing all these problems at once will burn Tom out.* 🅃 *The continuous problems burned out the office staff in a few months.* ☐ *She burned herself out as a volunteer in the state prison.*

burn someone up **1.** to destroy someone by fire. ☐ *The barn fire burned Walter up.* 🅃 *The fire burned up both of them.* **2.** to make someone very angry. (Figurative.) ☐ *You really burn me up! I'm very angry at you!* 🅃 *The whole mess burned up everyone.*

burn something away to remove or destroy something by burning. ☐ *The doctor burned the wart away.* 🅃 *The doctor burned away the wart.*

burn something down [for a fire] to destroy a building completely. ☐ *The fire burned the barn down.* 🅃 *It burned down the barn.*

burn something off ((of) something) to cause excess volatile or flammable substance to burn until there is no more of it. (The *of* is colloquial.) ☐ *We burnt the gasoline off the water's surface.* 🅃 *Why did you burn off the gasoline?* ☐ *I burned the vapors off.*

burn something out **1.** to burn away the inside of something, getting rid of excess deposits. ☐ *The mechanic burned the carbon out of the manifold.* 🅃 *He burned out the carbon.* **2.** to wear out an electrical or electronic device through overuse. ☐ *Turn it off. You're going to burn it out!* 🅃 *He burned out the motor.*

burn something up to destroy something by fire. ☐ *Take this and burn it up.* 🅃 *The fire burned up the papers and left no trace.*

burn up to become destroyed or consumed by fire. ☐ *The wood burned up and left only ashes.* ☐ *The deed burned up in the fire.*

burst in ((up)on someone or something) to intrude or come in thoughtlessly and suddenly, interrupting someone or something. (*Upon* is formal and less commonly used than *on.*) ☐ *I didn't mean to burst in on you.* ☐ *She feared that someone would burst in upon her.* ☐ *He just burst in!*

burst in (with something) to interrupt with some comment. □ *Ted burst in with the good news.* □ *He burst in to tell us the news.*

burst in(to some place) to intrude or come into a place thoughtlessly and suddenly. □ *Ted burst into the room and sat down right in the middle of the meeting.* □ *Why did you just burst in?*

burst out to explode outward; to break open under force. □ *The door burst out and released the trapped people.* □ *When the glass burst out, Gerald was injured.*

burst out doing something to begin to do something suddenly, such as cry, laugh, shout, etc. □ *Suddenly, she burst out singing.* □ *Ted burst out smiling.*

burst (out) into something **1.** [for plants or trees] to open their flowers seemingly suddenly and simultaneously. □ *The flowers burst out into blossom very early.* □ *They burst into blossom during the first warm day.* **2.** [for someone] to begin suddenly doing a particular activity, such as crying, laughing, chattering; or to begin producing the evidence of such activities as laughter, chatter, tears, etc. □ *Suddenly, she burst out into laughter.* □ *The child burst into tears.*

burst out (of some place) [for people] to come out of a place rapidly. □ *Everyone burst out of the burning building.* □ *Suddenly, they all burst out.*

burst out of something to explode out of something; to become [suddenly] too big for something, such as clothes, a house, etc. □ *She is bursting out of her dress.* □ *The butterfly burst out of the chrysalis.*

burst out with something to utter something loudly and suddenly. □ *The child burst out with a scream.* □ *Lily burst out with song.*

burst through something to break through or penetrate something with force. □ *The tank burst through the barrier easily.* □ *The workers burst through the wall after a lot of hard work.*

burst (up)on someone [for an idea] to strike someone suddenly. (*Upon* is formal and less commonly used than *on*.) □ *Then, this really tremendous idea burst upon me.* □ *It burst on me like a bolt of lightning.*

burst (up)on the scene to appear suddenly somewhere; to enter or arrive suddenly some place. (*Upon* is formal and less commonly used than *on*.) □ *The police suddenly burst upon the scene.* □ *They burst on the scene and took over.*

bury someone or something away (some place) to bury or hide someone or something some place. (*Someone* includes *oneself*.) □ *The dog buried the bone away under a bush.* □ *They buried her uncle away in the cemetery.* □ *They buried him away.* □ *Don't bury yourself away. Get out and have some fun.*

bush out [for something] to develop many small branches or hairs. (Said of a plant, bush, beard, head of hair, etc.) □ *His beard bushed out and really needed trimming.* □ *I hope the hedge bushes out nicely this year.*

butt in (on someone or something) to interrupt or intrude on someone or something. □ *I didn't mean to butt in on your conversation.* □ *Please don't butt in.* □ *How can we talk when you keep butting in on us?*

butt into something to intrude upon something; to break into a conversation. □ *Please don't butt into my conversation.* □ *I don't like my conversations being butted into by perfect strangers!*

butt (up) against someone or something to press against someone or something firmly. □ *This board is supposed to butt up against the one over there.* □ *The goat butted against Fred, but didn't hurt him.*

butter someone up AND **butter up to someone** to flatter someone; to treat someone especially nicely in hopes of special favors. □ *A student tried to butter the teacher up.* 🅃 *She buttered up the teacher again.* □ *She is always buttering up to the teacher.*

butter up to someone See the previous entry.

button something up to fasten the edges of something with buttons. □ *Button your shirt up, please.* 🅃 *I will button up my shirt.*

button up to fasten one's buttons. □ *Your jacket's open. You'd better button up. It's cold.* □ *I'll button up in the car.*

buttress something up **1.** to brace something; to provide architectural support for something. ☐ *We have to buttress this part of the wall up while we work on it.* 🅃 *The workers buttressed up the wall.* **2.** to provide extra support, often financial support, for something. (Figurative.) ☐ *We rounded up some money to buttress the company up through the crisis.* 🅃 *The loan buttressed up the company for a few minutes.*

buy in(to something) to purchase shares of something; to buy a part of something, sharing the ownership with other owners. ☐ *I bought into a company that makes dog food.* ☐ *Sounds like a good company. I would like to buy in.*

buy one's way out (of something) to get out of trouble by bribing someone to ignore what one has done wrong. ☐ *You can't buy your way out of this mess, buster!* ☐ *You made this mess and you can't buy your way out!*

buy someone off to bribe someone to ignore what one is doing wrong. ☐ *Do you think you can buy her off?* 🅃 *Max tried to buy off the cops.*

buy someone or something out to purchase full ownership of something from someone or a group. ☐ *We liked the company, so we borrowed a lot of money and bought it out.* 🅃 *Carl bought out the owners of the company.* ☐ *He bought the company out.*

buy something back (from someone) to repurchase something that one has previously sold from the person who bought it. ☐ *Can I buy it back from you? I have decided I need it.* 🅃 *He bought back his book from George.* ☐ *I sold it too cheap. I want to buy it back.*

buy something out to buy all of a particular item. ☐ *The kids came in and bought all our bubble gum out.* 🅃 *They bought out the bubble gum.*

buy something up to buy all of something; to buy the entire supply of something. ☐ *He bought the oranges up.* 🅃 *He bought up all the oranges and drove up the price.*

buzz in(to some place) to come into a place rapidly or unexpectedly. ☐ *The child buzzed into the shop and bought a nickel's worth of candy.* ☐ *I just buzzed in to say hello.*

C

call back **1.** to call [someone] again on the telephone at a later time. ☐ *Call back later, please.* ☐ *I will call back when you are not so busy.* **2.** to return a telephone call received earlier. ☐ *The note says I am to call back. What did you want?* ☐ *This is Bill Wilson calling back.*

call in (to some place) to telephone to some central place, such as one's place of work. ☐ *I have to call in to the office at noon.* ☐ *I will call in whenever I have a chance.*

call out to shout; to call. ☐ *Someone called out. Was it you?* ☐ *Yes, I called out.*

call out to someone to call or shout to someone. ☐ *She called out to Mike, but he didn't hear her.* ☐ *Sue called out to her friends.*

call someone back **1.** to call someone again on the telephone. ☐ *Since she is not there, I will call her back in half an hour.* 🅃 *Carl called back the person who called earlier.* **2.** to return a telephone call to a person who had called earlier. ☐ *I have to call Judy back now.* ☐ *I will call him back tomorrow.*

call someone down to criticize or scold someone; to ask someone to behave better; to challenge someone's bad behavior. ☐ *The teacher called Todd down for being late.* 🅃 *The teacher called down all the students who were late.*

call someone in (for something) **1.** to request that someone come to have a talk. ☐ *The manager called Karen in for a talk.* 🅃 *The manager called in Gary for questioning.* ☐ *She called Gary in.* **2.** to request a consultation with a specialist in some field. ☐ *We will have to call a specialist in for a consultation.* 🅃 *We called in another specialist for an opinion.* ☐ *We called someone else in.*

call someone or something back to call out that someone or something should come back. □ *As she left, the clerk called her back.* 🅃 *The clerk called back the customer.* □ *They had to call the order back because it was incomplete.*

call someone or something out to request the services of someone or a group. □ *Things got bad enough that the governor called the militia out.* 🅃 *The governor called out the militia.* 🅃 *The governor called out his hatchet man for the job.*

call someone or something up **1.** to request that someone or a group report for active military service. □ *The government called the fourth battalion up for active service.* 🅃 *They called up another battalion.* **2.** to call someone, a group, or a company on the telephone. □ *I will call them up and see what they have to say.* 🅃 *Please call up the supplier.*

call someone over (to some place) to request that someone come to where one is. □ *I will call her over to us, and you can ask her what you want to know.* 🅃 *Call over the waitress so we can order.* □ *I called Ted over.*

call something (back) in to order that something be returned. □ *The car company called many cars back in for repairs.* □ *They called a lot of cars in.* 🅃 *They called in a lot of defective cars.*

call something off to cancel something. □ *We had to call the picnic off because of rain.* 🅃 *Who called off the picnic?*

call something out **1.** to draw on something, such as a particular quality or talent. □ *It's times like these that call the best out in us.* 🅃 *These times call out our best.* **2.** to shout out something. □ *Who called the warning out?* 🅃 *You should call out a warning to those behind you on the trail.*

call (up)on someone **1.** to visit someone. (*Upon* is formal and less commonly used than *on*.) □ *My mother's friends call upon her every Wednesday.* □ *Let's call on Mrs. Franklin this afternoon.* **2.** to choose someone to respond, as in a classroom. □ *The teacher called upon me, but I was not ready to recite.* □ *Please don't call on me. I can't remember a thing.*

call (up)on someone (for something) to choose someone to do or to help with some particular task. (*Upon* is formal and less commonly used than *on*.) ☐ *Can I call upon you for help?* ☐ *You can call on me at any time.*

calm down to relax; to become less busy or active. ☐ *Now, now, calm down. Take it easy.* ☐ *Please calm down. Nothing bad is going to happen.*

calm someone or something down to cause someone or some creature to be less active, upset, or unsettled. (*Someone* includes *oneself*.) ☐ *Please try to calm yourself down!* 🅃 *Can you calm down your dog?* ☐ *Please calm your horse down.* ☐ *Can you calm yourself down?*

camp out to live out of doors temporarily in a tent or camping vehicle, as on a vacation or special camping trip. ☐ *I love to camp out in the winter.* ☐ *We plan to camp out again next month.*

cancel out (of something) to withdraw from something. ☐ *I hate to cancel out of the event at the last minute, but this is an emergency.* ☐ *It's too late to cancel out.*

carry on (about someone or something) **1.** to talk excitedly or at length about someone or something. ☐ *She was carrying on about the new governor.* ☐ *Jane was carrying on about her job.* ☐ *Stop carrying on, Jane.* **2.** to have an emotional display of distress about someone or something; to behave badly or wildly about someone or something. ☐ *Must you carry on so about virtually nothing?* ☐ *Jane carried on about her husband.* ☐ *Jane is carrying on again.*

carry on (with someone) to flirt with someone; to have a love affair with someone. ☐ *It looks like Heather is carrying on with James.* ☐ *Heather, stop carrying on!*

carry on (with something) to continue doing something. ☐ *Please carry on with your singing.* ☐ *Oh, do carry on!*

carry over (to something) **1.** [for a sum or other figure] to be taken to another column of figures. ☐ *This amount carries over into the next column.* ☐ *Yes, this number carries over.* **2.** to last or continue until another time. ☐ *Will this enthusiasm carry over to the following week?* ☐ *Of course, it will carry over.*

carry someone or something about to carry someone or something with one; to carry someone or something from place to place.

☐ *Do I have to carry these books about all over campus?* ☐ *You are too heavy, sweetie. I don't want to carry you about all day.*

carry someone or something away to take or steal someone or something. ☐ *Someone carried our lawn furniture away.* 🅃 *The kidnappers carried away the child.* ☐ *They carried the child away.*

carry someone or something off to take or steal someone or something. ☐ *The kidnappers carried the child off.* 🅃 *They carried off the child.* ☐ *Someone carried the patio chairs off.*

carry something off **1.** to make something happen; to accomplish something. ☐ *Do you think you can carry the deal off?* 🅃 *Sure, I can carry off the deal.* **2.** to make some sort of deception believable and successful. ☐ *It sounds like a great trick. Can you carry it off?* 🅃 *I can carry off the entire scheme perfectly.*

carry something on **1.** to do something over a period of time. ☐ *Do you think you can carry this on for a year?* 🅃 *I will carry on this activity for three years if you want.* **2.** to continue to do something as a tradition. ☐ *We intend to carry this celebration on as long as the family can gather for the holidays.* 🅃 *We will carry on this tradition for decades, in fact.*

carry something on(to something) to take something onto a vehicle. ☐ *Do you plan to carry this bag onto the plane?* 🅃 *I'd like to carry on two bags.* ☐ *Can I carry them on?*

carry through (on something) to carry something out satisfactorily; to complete some act as promised. ☐ *I hope you will carry through on this project.* ☐ *Yes, I'll carry through.*

cart someone or something off to take or haul someone or something away. (When used with *someone*, the person is treated like an object.) ☐ *The police came and carted her off.* 🅃 *Let's cart off these boxes.* ☐ *They carted the trash off.*

carve something in(to something) to cut letters or symbols into something. ☐ *He carved his initials into a tree.* 🅃 *He carved in the letters.* ☐ *He carved them in.*

carve something into something to create a carved object by sculpturing raw material. ☐ *She carved the soap into a little elephant.* ☐ *Ken carved the apple into a tiny snowman.*

carve something out to hollow something out by carving; to make something hollow by carving. □ *Can he carve a bowl out?* [T] *He carved out the bowl of the pipe and then began to sand it.*

carve something out (of something) to remove something from the inside of something else by carving or cutting. □ *She carved the insides out of the pumpkin.* [T] *She carved out the insides of the pumpkin.* □ *John carved the insides out.*

carve something up to divide something up, perhaps carelessly. □ *You can't carve the country up!* [T] *You can't just carve up one country and give the pieces away.*

cash in on something to take advantage of something; to earn a profit by exploiting something. □ *Everyone was trying to cash in on the current interest in the military.* □ *I want to cash in on the idea.*

cash (one's chips) in **1.** to turn in one's gaming tokens or poker chips when one quits playing. □ *When you leave the game, you should cash your chips in.* [T] *Cash in your chips before you go.* □ *I'm going to cash in.* **2.** to quit [anything], as if one were cashing in gaming tokens. (Figurative.) □ *I guess I'll cash my chips in and go home.* [T] *Well, it's time to cash in my chips and go home.* □ *I've eaten enough. I'm going to cash in.* **3.** to die. (Slang. Using the same metaphor as sense 2.) □ *There's a funeral procession. Who cashed his chips in?* [T] *Poor Fred cashed in his chips last week.* □ *He took a slug in the gut and cashed in.*

cast off (from something) [for the crew of a boat or ship] to push away from the dock or pier; to begin the process of undocking a boat or ship. □ *The crew cast off from the dock.* □ *It's time to cast off.*

cast someone or something off to dispose of someone or something; to throw someone or something aside or away. □ *You can't just cast me off like an old coat!* [T] *She cast off her husband of three months.* [T] *Lee cast off his coat.*

cast someone or something out to throw someone or something out. (Stilted.) □ *You are not going to cast me out on a night like this!* [T] *Jane cast out the cat and slammed the door.* □ *I cast the offensive child out.*

cast someone or something up [for the waves] to bring up and deposit someone or something on the shore. ☐ *The waves cast the body of the sailor up, and it was found on the shore.* 🅃 *The waves cast up the body of a sailor.* ☐ *The action of the waves cast a lot of driftwood up.*

catch on (to someone or something) to figure out someone or something. ☐ *I finally caught on to what she was talking about.* ☐ *It takes a while for me to catch on.*

catch on (with someone) [for something] to become popular with someone. ☐ *I hope our new product catches on with children.* ☐ *I'm sure it will catch on.*

catch someone up in something [for excitement or interest] to extend to and engross someone. ☐ *The happenings caught everyone up in the excitement.* ☐ *The accident caught us all up in the resultant confusion.*

catch someone up (on someone or something) to tell someone the news of someone or something. (*Someone* includes *oneself*.) ☐ *Oh, please catch me up on what your family is doing.* ☐ *Yes, do catch us up!* ☐ *I have to take some time to catch myself up on the news.*

catch up (on someone or something) to learn the news of someone or something. ☐ *I need a little time to catch up on the news.* ☐ *We all need to catch up on Tony.* ☐ *I need some time to catch up.*

catch up (on something) to bring one's efforts with something up to date; to do the work that one should have done. ☐ *I need a quiet time so I can catch up on my work.* ☐ *I have to catch up and become more productive.*

catch up (to someone or something) to get even with, or equal to, someone or something. ☐ *I finally caught up to Fred, who was way ahead of me in the race.* ☐ *Jane caught up to the bus that had almost left her behind.* ☐ *Don't worry, I'll catch up.*

catch up (with someone or something) to increase the rate of movement or growth to become even with or equal to someone or something. ☐ *Martin is finally catching up with his taller brother.* ☐ *This puppy will never catch up with the others.* ☐ *The compet-*

ing companies will never catch up with this one. □ *I'm smaller than the others. Will I ever catch up?*

cave in (on someone or something) [for a roof or ceiling] to collapse on someone or something. □ *The roof caved in on the miners.* □ *The roof caved in.*

cave in (to someone or something) to give in to someone or something. □ *Finally, the manager caved in to the customer's demands.* □ *I refuse to cave in.*

center something on someone or something to base something on someone or something. □ *Let us center the discussion on Walter.* □ *We centered our whole meeting on the conservation question.*

chalk something out 1. to draw a picture of something in chalk, especially to illustrate a plan of some type. □ *The coach chalked the play out so the players could understand what they were to do.* [T] *She chalked out the play.* **2.** to explain something carefully to someone, as if one were talking about a chalk drawing. (Often figurative.) □ *Here, let me chalk it out for you. Listen carefully.* [T] *She chalked out the details of the plan.*

chalk something up 1. to write something on a chalkboard. □ *Let me chalk this formula up so you all can see it.* [T] *I'll chalk up the formula.* **2.** to add a mark or point to one's score. □ *Chalk another goal up.* [T] *Chalk up another basket for the other side.*

chalk something up to something to account for something with something else; to blame something on something else. □ *You can chalk her mistake up to ignorance.* □ *Chalk Ted's success up to preparedness.* [T] *I will chalk up this defeat to his youth.*

chance (up)on someone or something to find someone or something by accident; to happen on someone or something. (*Upon* is formal and less commonly used than *on*.) □ *I chanced upon a nice little restaurant on my walk today. The prices looked good too.* □ *I chanced on an old friend of yours in town today.*

change out of something to take off a set of clothing and put on another. □ *I have to change out of these wet clothes.* □ *You should change out of your casual clothes and put on something more formal for dinner.*

charge in(to some place) to bolt or run wildly into a place. □ *The people charged into the store on the day of the sale.* □ *They all charged in like thirsty camels.*

charge off to bolt or run away. □ *He got angry and charged off.* □ *Juan charged off to talk to the boss.*

charge out of some place to bolt or stomp out of some place. □ *Carol charged out of the house, trying to catch Sally before she got on the bus.* □ *Juan got mad and charged out of the office.*

charge someone up to excite someone; to make a person enthusiastic about something. (*Someone* includes *oneself.*) □ *The excitement of the day charged them up so they could not sleep.* 🅃 *The speaker charged up the crowd.* □ *He reread the report, hoping to charge himself up enough to make some sensible comments.*

charge something up **1.** to apply an electrical charge to a battery. □ *How long will it take to charge this battery up?* 🅃 *It takes an hour to charge up your battery.* **2.** to load or fill something, such as a fire extinguisher. □ *We had to send the extinguishers back to the factory, where they charged them up.* 🅃 *How much does it cost to charge up an extinguisher?* **3.** to reinvigorate something. □ *What can we do to charge this play up?* 🅃 *A murder in the first act would charge up the play.*

charge something (up) to someone or something to place the cost of something on the account of someone or a group. □ *I will have to charge this up to your account.* □ *Do you have to charge this to my account?* □ *Is this order charged to anyone yet?*

chart something out (for someone or something) to lay out a plan or course for someone or something. □ *The first mate charted the course out for the skipper.* 🅃 *The first mate charted out the course for us.* □ *Shall I chart it out?* 🅃 *I will chart out the course for our journey.*

chase someone or something down to track down and seize someone or something. □ *Larry set out to chase Betsy down.* 🅃 *The police chased down the suspect.* □ *They chased her down.*

cheat someone out of something to get something from someone by deception. (*Someone* includes *oneself.*) □ *Are you trying to* *cheat me out of what is rightfully mine?* □ *She cheated herself out of an invitation because she lied about her affiliation.*

check back (on someone or something) to look into the state of someone or something again at a later time. □ *I'll have to check back on you later.* □ *I'll check back later.*

check back (with someone) to inquire of someone again at a later time. □ *Please check back with me later.* □ *Okay. I'll check back.*

check in (at something) to go to a place and record one's arrival. □ *When you get there, check in at the front office.* □ *All right. I'll check in when I arrive.*

check in on someone or something to go into a place and look in on someone or something there. □ *I think I will go check in on Timmy.* □ *Let me check in on how things are going in the kitchen.*

check into something **1.** to investigate a matter. □ *I asked the manager to check into it.* □ *Something is wrong, and I will check into it.* **2.** to sign oneself into a place to stay, such as a hotel, hospital, motel, etc. □ *She checked into a private hospital for some kind of treatment.* □ *They checked into the first motel they came to on the highway.*

check on someone or something to look into the legitimacy or condition of someone or something. □ *Sarah will check on the matter and report to us.* □ *I will check on Jeff.* □ *While you're upstairs, would you check on the baby?*

check out [for someone or something] to prove to be correctly represented. □ *Everything you told me checks out.* □ *Your story checks out, Max.*

check out (from something) to do the paperwork necessary to leave a place and then leave. □ *I will check out from the office and come right to where you are.* □ *I'll be there as soon as I check out.*

check out (of something) to do the paperwork necessary to leave a place, such as a hotel. □ *I will check out of the hotel at about noon.* □ *I check out at noon.*

check someone in to record the arrival of someone. (*Someone* includes *oneself.*) □ *Ask the guard to check you in when you get* *there.* 🆃 *Tell the guard to check in the visitors as they arrive.* □ *She checked herself in and went on to the dressing room.*

check someone or something off to mark or cross out the name of a person or thing on a list. (*Someone* includes *oneself.*) □ *I am glad to see that you were able to come. I will check you off.* 🆃 *I checked off the recent arrivals.* □ *I checked the items off.* □ *Mary checked herself off and proceeded to start the day's work.*

check someone or something out to evaluate someone or something. (*Someone* includes *oneself.*) □ *It sounds good. I'll check it out.* 🆃 *I'll check out everyone else.* □ *The doctor will check you out.* □ *She checked herself out, but found no broken bones.*

check someone or something over to examine someone or something closely. (*Someone* includes *oneself.*) □ *You should have the doctor check you over before you go back to work.* 🆃 *The doctor checked over the children who had shown the worst symptoms.* □ *The mechanic checked the car over.* □ *After checking herself over, Sally picked up her parcels, got up, and continued to walk down the street.*

check something in **1.** to record that someone has returned something. □ *I asked the librarian to check the book in for me.* 🆃 *Did the librarian check in the book?* **2.** to take something to a place, return it, and make sure that its return has been recorded. □ *I checked the book in on time.* 🆃 *Did you really check in the book on time?* **3.** to examine a shipment or an order received and make certain that everything ordered was received. □ *I checked the order in and sent a report to the manager.* 🆃 *Tim checked in the order from the supplier to make sure that everything was there.*

check up (on someone or something) to determine the state of someone or something. □ *Please don't check up on me. I can be trusted.* □ *I see no need to check up.*

cheer someone up to make a sad person happy. (*Someone* includes *oneself.*) □ *Let's try to cheer Karen up.* 🆃 *Yes, let's cheer up Karen.* □ *Usually I can cheer myself up on days like this, but not today.*

cheer up [for a sad person] to become happy. □ *After a while, she began to cheer up.* □ *Cheer up! Things could be worse.*

chew something off ((of) something) to bite or gnaw something off something. (The *of* is colloquial.) □ *The puppy chewed the heel off of my shoe.* □ *The puppy chewed the heel off.*

chew something up to grind food with the teeth until it can be swallowed. □ *You had better chew that stuff up well.* 🅃 *Please chew up your food well.*

chime in (with something) to add a comment to the discussion. □ *Little Billy chimed in with a suggestion.* □ *He chimed in too late.*

chip away [for something] to break off or break away in small chips. □ *The edges of the marble step chipped away over the years.* □ *Some of the stone figures had chipped away so badly that we couldn't see what they were.*

chip in (on something) (for someone) to contribute money toward something for someone. □ *Would you please chip in on the present for Richard?* □ *Will you chip in for Randy?* □ *I would like to chip in on the gift.* □ *I won't chip in.*

choke on something to begin to gag and cough because of something stuck in the throat. □ *The dog choked on the meat.* □ *The restaurant patron began to choke on a fish bone.*

choke someone up to cause someone to feel like sobbing. □ *Sad stories like that always choke me up.* □ *Your complaints choke me up considerably.*

choke something back to fight hard to keep something from coming out of one's mouth, such as sobs, tears, angry words, vomit, etc. □ *I tried to choke the unpleasant words back, but I could not.* 🅃 *She choked back her grief, but it came forth nonetheless.* □ *I could hardly choke my tears back.*

choke something down to work hard to swallow something, usually because it tastes bad. □ *The medicine was terrible, but I managed to choke it down.* 🅃 *She choked down the horrible medicine.*

choke something up **1.** to clog something up; to fill up and block something. □ *Branches and leaves choked the sewer up.* 🅃 *Rust choked up the pipes.* **2.** to cough or choke until something that has blocked one's windpipe is brought up. □ *The old man was unable* *to choke the candy up that was stuck in his windpipe.* 🅃 *He choked up the chunk of meat and could breathe again.*

choke up **1.** to feel like sobbing. □ *I choked up when I heard the news.* □ *He was beginning to choke up as he talked.* **2.** to become frightened or saddened so that one cannot speak. □ *I choked up when he came in.* □ *I was choking up, and I knew I would not be able to go on.* □ *Henry was so choked up he couldn't speak.*

choke up (about someone or something) to become very emotional about someone or something. □ *I choke up about Tom every time I think about his illness.* □ *I choked up at the thought.*

choose up sides to select opposing sides for a debate, fight, or game. □ *Let's choose up sides and play basketball.* □ *The children chose up sides and began the game.*

chop someone off to stop someone in the middle of a sentence or speech. □ *I'm not finished. Don't chop me off!* 🅃 *The moderator chopped off the speaker.*

chop something down to fell a tree or a pole; to fell a person by cutting with a sword or something similar. □ *George chopped the tree down for some unknown reason.* 🅃 *He chopped down the cherry tree.* 🅃 *The knight chopped down the peasant.*

chop something off to cut something off, perhaps with an axe. □ *Chop this branch off, please.* 🅃 *I'll chop off the branch.*

circulate something through something to route something through something; to make something travel through something. □ *Walter circulated the memo from the boss through the department.* □ *I would like for you to circulate this through the members of the club.* □ *This pump circulates the hot water through the heating pipes.*

circulate through something **1.** [for a fluid in a closed system of pipes or tubes] to flow through the various pathways of pipes and tubes. □ *Cold water circulates through the entire building and keeps it cool.* □ *Blood circulates through the veins and arteries, carrying food to, and wastes away from, all parts of the body.* **2.** to travel through something; to make the rounds through something. □

Rumors circulated through the department about Tom's retirement. ☐ *Please circulate through the room and hand out these papers to each person over thirty.*

clamp down (on someone or something) to restrain or limit someone or someone's or something's actions. ☐ *The police clamped down on the gang.* ☐ *They had to clamp down to keep the streets safe.*

claw something off ((of) someone or something) to rip or tear something off from someone or something. ☐ *We saw a guy clawing his burning clothes off himself.* 🅃 *He clawed off his burning clothes.* ☐ *He clawed them off.*

clean one's act up to start behaving better. ☐ *You had better clean your act up and be a better citizen.* 🅃 *Clean up your act!*

clean someone or something down to clean someone or something by brushing or with flowing water. (*Someone* includes *oneself.*) ☐ *He was covered with mud, and we used the garden hose to clean him down.* 🅃 *Please clean down the sidewalk.* ☐ *He was so dirty I just wanted to clean him down!* ☐ *He cleaned himself down with water from the hose.*

clean someone or something out (of something) to remove people or things from something or some place. ☐ *Someone should clean those bums out of political office.* 🅃 *Yes! Clean out those bums.* ☐ *Clean the dust out of the cupboards.* ☐ *Clean them out!*

clean someone or something up to get someone or something clean. (*Someone* includes *oneself.*) ☐ *Please go into the bathroom and clean yourself up.* 🅃 *I'll clean up the kids a little bit before we leave for dinner.* ☐ *Can you clean this place up a little?* ☐ *Oh, go clean yourself up. You're a mess.*

clean something off to take something off something; to remove something such as dirt or dirty dishes. ☐ *Please clean the table off and put the dishes in the kitchen.* 🅃 *I'll clean off the table.*

clean something off ((of) something) to remove something from something. ☐ *Judy cleaned the writing off the wall.* 🅃 *I'm glad she cleaned off the writing.* ☐ *Sam cleaned it off.*

clean something out to remove dirt or unwanted things from the inside of something. □ *Someone has to clean the garage out.* T *I'll clean out the garage.*

clean up (on someone or something) to make a large profit from someone or some business activity. □ *We are really going to clean up on this product.* □ *We will clean up on Tom. He is buying everything we have.* □ *We are really going to clean up.*

clear out (of some place) to get out of some place. □ *Will you all clear out of here?* □ *Please clear out!*

clear something away to take something away. □ *Please clear the tea things away.* T *Would you clear away the dishes?*

clear something off ((of) something) to take something off something. (The *of* is colloquial.) □ *Please clear the dishes off the table.* T *I'll clear off the dishes.* □ *Please clear them off.*

clear something up **1.** to clarify something; to take away the confusion about something. □ *Let me take a few minutes to clear things up.* T *I would like to clear up this confusion for you.* **2.** to cure a disease. □ *I think I can clear this up with a salve.* T *Will this salve clear up the rash?*

clear up **1.** [for something] to become more understandable. □ *At about the middle of the very confusing lecture, things began to clear up.* □ *I was having trouble, but things are beginning to clear up.* **2.** [for a disease] to improve or become cured. □ *His cold cleared up after a couple of weeks.* □ *I'm sure your rash will clear up soon.* **3.** [for the sky] to become less cloudy. □ *Suddenly, the sky cleared up.* □ *When the sky cleared up, the breeze began to blow.*

clip something on((to) someone or something) to attach something to someone or something with a clip. □ *I clipped a little name tag onto him before I put him on the plane.* T *I clipped on a name tag.* □ *Liz clipped it on.*

clip something out (of something) to remove something from something by clipping or cutting. □ *Please clip the article out of the magazine.* T *Could you clip out the article?* □ *Sam clipped it out.*

clock in to record one's time of arrival, usually by punching a time clock. □ *What time did she clock in?* □ *She forgot to clock in today.*

clock out to record one's time of departure, usually by punching a time clock. ☐ *I will clock out just before I go home.* ☐ *Juan clocked out before the official closing time.*

clock someone in to observe and record someone's time of arrival. (*Someone* includes *oneself.*) ☐ *The manager says he clocked you in at noon. That's a bit late, isn't it?* 🅃 *Does she clock in everyone?* ☐ *Henry clocked himself in and went straight to work.*

clock someone out to observe and record someone's time of departure. (*Someone* includes *oneself.*) ☐ *The manager clocked him out at about midnight.* 🅃 *Does the manager clock out everyone?* ☐ *Jane clocked herself out and went home.*

clog something up [for something] to obstruct a channel or conduit. ☐ *The leaves clogged the gutters up.* 🅃 *They clogged up the gutter.*

clog up [for a channel or conduit] to become blocked. ☐ *The canal clogged up with leaves and mud.*

close down [for a business, office, shop, etc.] to close permanently or temporarily. ☐ *This shop will have to close down if they raise taxes.* ☐ *I am afraid that you will have to close down for a while because of the gas leak.*

close in (on someone or something) to move in on someone or something. ☐ *The cops were closing in on the thugs.* ☐ *They closed in quietly.*

close someone or something down to force someone or someone's business, office, shop, etc., to close permanently or temporarily. ☐ *The police closed the bookstore down.* 🅃 *They closed down the shop.* 🅃 *The recession closed down Tom, whose shop could just barely make it in good times.*

close someone or something up **1.** to close someone or someone's business, office, shop, etc., temporarily or permanently. ☐ *Tom's restaurant nearly went out of business when the health department closed him up.* 🅃 *The health department closed up the restaurant.* ☐ *Dave's shop was failing. The bank closed him up.* **2.** to close someone or something completely. (Said of a person being stitched up at the end of a surgical procedure.) ☐ *Fred, would you close her up for me?* 🅃 *Fred closed up the patient.* 🅃 *I closed up the box and put it on the shelf.*

close someone out of something to prevent someone from getting into something, such as a class, a room, a privilege, etc. ☐ *They closed me out of the class I wanted.*

close something out **1.** to sell off a particular kind of merchandise with the intention of not selling it in the future. ☐ *These are not selling. Let's close them out.* 🅃 *They closed out the merchandise that wouldn't sell.* **2.** to prevent further registration in something. ☐ *We are going to have to close this class out.* 🅃 *The registrar closed out the class.*

close up [for an opening] to close completely. ☐ *The door closed up and would not open again.* ☐ *The shop closed up and did not open until the next day.*

cloud up [for the sky] to fill with clouds. ☐ *By midmorning, the sky had clouded up.* ☐ *I hope it doesn't cloud up today.*

clown around (with someone) to join with someone in acting silly; [for two or more people] to act silly together. ☐ *The boys were clowning around with each other.* ☐ *The kids are having fun clowning around.*

clue someone in (on something) to inform someone about something. ☐ *Would you please clue me in on what you are talking about?* 🅃 *I will clue in everyone on this matter if you want.* ☐ *Please clue me in.*

clutter something up to mess something up; to fill something or some place up with too many things. ☐ *Heaps of newspapers cluttered the room up and made it a fire hazard.* 🅃 *Who cluttered up this house?*

coil something up to roll or twist something into a coil. ☐ *Maria coiled the strip of stamps up and put them in the little dispenser.* 🅃 *Please coil up the rope.*

collapse into something **1.** to fall down into something. ☐ *She was so tired, she collapsed into the chair.* ☐ *Juan collapsed into a chair and fell fast asleep.* **2.** [for someone] to fall into a particular kind of despair. ☐ *The poor man collapsed into a deep depression.* ☐ *Scott collapsed into his own personal brand of grieving.*

collapse under someone or something to cave in under the weight of someone or something. □ *The framework collapsed under the weight of the spectators.* □ *The bridge collapsed under the heavy traffic.*

comb something out to comb something and make it straight or neat. □ *She combed her hair out.* [T] *She combed out her hair every morning.*

comb something out (of something) to remove knots and snarls from something by combing. □ *I had to comb the gum out of her hair.* [T] *I had to comb out the gum.* □ *Maria combed it out.*

come about [for a boat] to change its angle against the wind; [for a boat] to change tack. □ *The boat will have to come about. The wind shifted.* □ *We came about and went back.*

come around **1.** to agree in the end; to agree finally. □ *I knew you would come around in the end.* □ *Finally, she came around and agreed to our terms.* **2.** to return to consciousness. □ *After we threw cold water in his face, he came around.* □ *Ken came around almost immediately after he had fainted.*

come away (from someone or something) to move away from someone or something. □ *Please come away from the fire. You will get burned if you don't.* □ *Come away from that filthy person!* □ *Come away!*

come back to return to an advantageous or favorable state or condition. □ *Walter practiced his singing every day, hoping to come back in a wave of glory.* □ *When will the good old days come back?*

come back (to someone or something) to return to someone or something. □ *Please come back to me. I'm lonely.* □ *Come back to your home!* □ *Please come back!*

come by something to find something; to get something. □ *I hope you came by this money honestly.* □ *I come by all my ideas from my own experience.*

come down with something to catch a disease. □ *Dan came down with chicken pox.* □ *I don't want to come down with the flu again.*

come in **1.** to enter. (Often a command or polite request.) □ *Please come in.* □ *If you will come in and have a seat, I will tell Betty that you are here.* **2.** to arrive; [for a shipment of something] to arrive. □ *New models come in almost every week.* □ *When do you expect a new batch to come in?* □ *The tomatoes will come in at the end of July.* □ *The election results came in early in the evening.*

come off to happen as planned; to come to fruition; to succeed. (Colloquial.) □ *When is this party going to come off?* □ *Did the concert come off okay?*

come off ((of) something) [for something] to become detached from something else. (The *of* is colloquial.) □ *This piece came off of the top, not the bottom.* □ *There is a broken place here. I think something came off.*

come on **1.** to hurry along after someone. (Usually a command.) □ *Come on! We'll be late.* □ *Don't linger behind. Come on!* **2.** [for electricity or some other device] to start operating. □ *After a while, the lights came on again.* □ *I hope the heat comes on soon.* **3.** to walk out and appear on stage. □ *You are to come on when you hear your cue.* □ *Juan did not come on when he was supposed to.* **4.** [for a pain] to begin hurting; [for a disease] to attack someone. □ *The pain began to come on again, and Sally had to lie down.* □ *As a fainting spell came on, Gerald headed for a chair.* **5.** to yield; to agree. (Usually a command.) □ *Come on! Do it!* □ *Come on, now! Be a sport!* **6.** [for a program] to be broadcast on radio or television. □ *When does the news come on?* □ *The news didn't come on until an hour later.*

come on((to) someone or something) to find someone or something by accident; to happen onto someone or something. □ *When I was out on my walk, I came on a little shop that sells leather goods.* □ *I came on an old friend of yours downtown today.*

come out **1.** to exit; to leave the inside of a place. □ *Please come out. We have to leave.* □ *When do you think they will all come out?* **2.** to result; to succeed; to happen. □ *I hope everything comes out okay.* □ *It will come out okay. Don't worry.* **3.** to come before the public; to be published; to be made public. □ *A new magazine has just come out.* □ *When will your next book come out?* **4.** to become visible or evident. □ *His pride came out in his refusal to accept help.* □ *The real reason finally came out, and it was not flattering.*

come out with something **1.** to publish something. ☐ *When are you going to come out with a new edition?* ☐ *The publisher decided not to come out with the book.* **2.** to express or utter something. ☐ *He came out with a strong dissenting opinion.* ☐ *It was over an hour before the president came out with an explanation.* **3.** to say or shout something. ☐ *My nephew comes out with the cleverest remarks.* ☐ *Who came out with that rude remark?*

come over to come for a visit. ☐ *Why don't you come over next week?* ☐ *I would love to come over.*

come over someone [for something] to affect a person, perhaps suddenly. ☐ *I just don't know what came over me.* ☐ *Something came over her just as she entered the room.*

come over someone or something to move over and above someone or something. ☐ *A cloud came over us and rained like fury.* ☐ *A storm came over the city and did what it had to.*

come over (to our side) to join up with our side; to become one of our group, party, etc. ☐ *Seven of the other team came over to our side.* ☐ *I hope that Lynn comes over.*

come over to something to change to something; to convert to something. ☐ *We are going to come over to gas next year.* ☐ *Why don't you come over to a diesel-powered car?*

come through to be approved; to be sanctioned. ☐ *The mortgage came through.* ☐ *If the loan comes through, the car is yours.*

come through (for someone or something) to produce or perform as promised for someone or a group. ☐ *You knew I would come through for you, didn't you?* ☐ *The team came through for the college again.* ☐ *I knew they would come through.*

come through (something) **1.** to survive something. ☐ *We were never sure we would come through the ordeal.* ☐ *I knew I would come through all right.* **2.** to pass through something. ☐ *Please chain the gate up again when you come through.* ☐ *Please come through now.*

come through (with something) to produce or deliver something as promised. ☐ *Finally, Bob came through with the money he had promised.* ☐ *I knew he would come through.*

come to to become conscious; to return to consciousness. □ *After just a few seconds, she came to.* □ *He came to just after fainting.*

come up **1.** to come from a lower place to a higher one. □ *You can come up now. They are gone.* □ *Come up and enjoy the view from the tallest rooftop in the county.* **2.** to come near; to approach. □ *He came up and began to talk to us.* □ *A heron came up while we were fishing, but it just ignored us.* **3.** to come to someone's attention. □ *The question of what time to be there never came up.* □ *The matter came up, but it was never dealt with.*

come up against someone or something to reach an obstacle in the form of someone or something. □ *I have come up against something I cannot handle.* □ *I have never come up against anyone like him before.*

come up something [for a tossed coin] to turn out to be either heads or tails. □ *We tossed a coin, and it came up heads.* □ *The coin came up tails.*

connect (up) to something to attach to something; to attach something to some electrical device. □ *When we finish the house, we will connect up to the utilities.* □ *We have to connect to the outside telephone lines ourselves.*

contract something out to make an agreement with someone to do a specific amount of work. (Rather than doing it oneself or in one's own place of business.) □ *I will contract this out and have it done by experts.* T *I contracted out this kind of job the last time.*

cook (something) out to cook food out of doors. □ *I will cook this out. It's too hot in the kitchen to cook there.* T *Shall we cook out chicken tonight?* □ *Yes, let's cook out.*

cook something up (with someone) to arrange or plan to do something with someone. (The *something* is usually the word *something*.) □ *I tried to cook something up with Karen for Tuesday.* T *I want to cook up something with John.* □ *Let's see if we can cook something up.*

cool down AND **cool off** **1.** to become cooler. □ *After the sun set, things began to cool down a bit.* □ *The evening began to cool off.* **2.** [for someone] to become less angry. □ *They were very angry at first, but then they cooled down.* □ *Cool off, you guys!*

cool off See the previous entry.

cool someone down AND **cool someone off** to make someone less angry. (*Someone* includes *oneself.*) □ *Things are less threatening now. That ought to cool him down.* □ *Time cooled them off a little.* □ *She meditated for a while to cool herself down.*

cool someone off See the previous entry.

cool someone or something down AND **cool someone or something off** to make someone or something less hot. (*Someone* includes *oneself.*) □ *Use ice to cool him down and reduce his fever.* □ *The refrigerator cooled the pudding off in a hurry.* □ *Here, have a cold drink. Cool yourself down.* T *The ice cooled down the feverish child.* T *We need to cool off the pudding in a hurry.*

cool someone or something off See the previous entry.

count down to count backwards to an event that will start when zero is reached. □ *The project manager was counting down, getting ready for the launch of the rocket.* □ *I can still hear the captain counting down: Five, four, three, two, one, zero, blastoff!*

count off [for a series of people, one by one] to say aloud the next number in a fixed sequence. □ *The soldiers counted off by threes.* □ *The sergeant told them to count off.*

count someone or something off to count people or things, to see if they are all there. □ *Let's count them off to see who's missing.* T *Count off each person, one by one.* □ *I counted each one off.*

count someone out (for something) to exclude someone from something. (*Someone* includes *oneself.*) □ *We are going to count you out for the party unless you pay in advance.* □ *Please don't count me out yet!* □ *I must count myself out for the nomination.*

count something in to include something in a count of something. □ *Did you count the tall ones in?* T *Did you count in the tall ones in the corner?*

count something out to give out things, counting them, one by one. □ *She counted the cookies out, one by one.* T *She counted out the cookies to each child.*

count (up)on someone or something to rely on someone or something. (*Upon* is formal and less commonly used than *on*.) □ *Can I count upon you to do the job?* □ *You can count on me.* □ *Can I count on the court to rule fairly?*

couple up (with someone) [for one person] to join another person. □ *I decided to couple up with Larry.* □ *Larry and I coupled up with each other.* □ *Larry and I coupled up.* □ *By midnight, they all had coupled up and were dancing.*

cover someone or something up to place something on someone or something for protection or concealment. (*Someone* includes *oneself*.) □ *Cover the pie up, so Terry won't see it.* 🅃 *Cover up the money, so they won't know we were gambling.* 🅃 *Cover up Jimmy so he doesn't get cold.* □ *Tom—hiding in the leaves—covered himself up so no one could see any part of him.*

cover something up to conceal a wrongdoing; to conceal evidence. □ *They tried to cover the crime up, but the broken lock gave them away.* 🅃 *She could not cover up her misdeeds.*

cover (up) for someone to conceal someone's wrongdoing by lying or working in someone's place. □ *Are you covering up for the person who committed the crime?* □ *I wouldn't cover for anyone.*

crack down (on someone or something) to put limits on someone or something; to become strict about enforcing rules about someone or something. □ *The police cracked down on the kids.* □ *They cracked down once last year too.*

crack someone or something up to damage someone or something. (*Someone* includes *oneself*.) 🅃 *Who cracked up my car? Who was driving?* □ *The accident cracked him up a little.* □ *She cracked herself up pretty badly in the accident.*

crash into someone or something to bump or ram into someone or something. □ *The student crashed into the teacher.* □ *The car crashed into a bus.*

crash through something to break through something. □ *The cows crashed right through the fence.* □ *Don't crash through the door. I'll open it as soon as I get it unlocked.*

creep by [for time] to pass slowly. □ *The minutes crept by as I awaited Mrs. Barron's telephone call.* □ *I know the days will creep by until we finally move into the new house.*

crop out to appear on the surface; [for something] to reveal itself in the open; to begin to show above the surface. □ *A layer of rock cropped out at the edges of the desert.* □ *A little anger began to crop out.*

crop up to appear without warning; to happen suddenly; [for something] to begin to reveal itself in the open. □ *A new crisis has cropped up.* □ *Some new problems cropped up at the last minute.*

cross someone or something off ((of) something) to eliminate the name of someone or something from a list or record. (*Someone* includes *oneself*. The *of* is colloquial.) □ *We will have to cross her off our list.* 🆃 *We crossed off Sarah.* □ *I crossed the sweater off of the list and gave it away.* □ *Looking at the length of the list, Alice was willing to cross herself off.*

cross someone or something out to draw a line through the name of someone or something on a list or record. (*Someone* includes *oneself*.) □ *You can cross me out. I'm not going.* 🆃 *Please cross out Sarah.* □ *I crossed the sweater out. It was an error.* □ *Alice crossed herself out without any argument.*

crouch down to stoop or huddle down. □ *Crouch down here, next to me.* □ *Suddenly, Tex crouched down and reached for his pistol.*

crowd in (on someone or something) to press or crush around someone or something. □ *Please don't crowd in on the guest of honor.* □ *Can you keep them back from me? I don't like it when they crowd in.* □ *The people crowded in on us and frightened us a little bit.* □ *Don't crowd in on the display case. It is an antique.*

crowd in(to some place) to push or squeeze into some place. □ *Please don't try to crowd into this place.* □ *Too many people are trying to crowd in.*

crowd together to pack tightly together. □ *The tenants crowded together in the lobby.* □ *All the kittens crowded together to keep warm.*

crumble something (up) (into something) to crunch up or break up something into pieces. □ *Now, crumble the dried bread up into crumbs.* 🅃 *Crumble up the bread into crumbs.* □ *Ed crumbled the soil up to make planting easier.*

crumple someone or something up to fold up or crush someone or something. □ *Walter crumpled the newspaper up and put it in the fireplace.* 🅃 *He crumpled up the paper.* □ *The accident crumpled the poor dog up, but it recovered.*

crunch someone or something up to break someone or something up into pieces. (Also without *up*, but not eligible as an entry.) □ *That machine will crunch you up. Stay away from it!* 🅃 *A number of blows with the hammer crunched up the rocks into pebbles.* □ *Try to crunch the larger chunks up.*

crush something out to put out a fire or flame by crushing. □ *She crushed her cigarette out and put the butt into the sink.* 🅃 *Please crush out your cigarette.*

crush something up to reduce the mass of something by crushing. □ *Crush this up and put it in the sauce.* 🅃 *Crush up a clove of garlic and put it in the sauce.*

crush something up (into something) **1.** to press something with great force until it is reduced to something smaller. □ *The chef crushed the almonds up into a powder and sprinkled them on the dessert.* 🅃 *Please crush up the almonds into a powder.* □ *I will crush them up.* **2.** to break something up into small pieces. □ *The machine crushed the glass up into chunks and sent them on to be recycled.* 🅃 *It crushed up all the glass into tiny bits.* □ *The machine crushed it up.*

crush (up) against someone or something to press hard against someone or something. □ *The crowd crushed up against the people standing in line.* □ *The eager theatergoers crushed against the lobby doors.*

cuddle up (to someone or something) to nestle or snuggle close to someone or something to get warm or to be intimate. □ *She cuddled up to him and went to sleep.* □ *Let's cuddle up to the warm wall, near the fireplace.*

cue someone in to give a signal or cue to someone at the right time, usually in a performance of some kind. ☐ *Be sure to cue me in when you want me to talk.* 🅃 *Cue in the lighting technician at the right time.*

curl something up to roll something up into a coil. ☐ *She curled the edges of the paper up while she spoke.* 🅃 *Why did she curl up the paper?*

curl up (in(to) something) **1.** to roll into a coil. ☐ *The snake curled up into a neat coil.* ☐ *It curled up so we couldn't get at it.* **2.** to roll into a coil in a resting place, such as a chair or a bed. ☐ *Colleen curled up in the chair and took a nap.* ☐ *She curled up and took a nap.*

cut back (on something) to reduce the use, amount, or cost of something. ☐ *You are all going to have to cut back on water usage.* ☐ *You simply must cut back.*

cut down (on something) to reduce the amount of something or of doing something; to use or buy less of something. ☐ *You will have to cut down on your use of water.* ☐ *They told us to cut down.* ☐ *The doctor told him to cut down on his drinking.* ☐ *It was hard for him to cut down.*

cut in (on someone) **1.** [for someone] to ask to replace one member of a dancing couple. ☐ *Excuse me, may I cut in?* ☐ *Please don't cut in.* **2.** [for someone] to interrupt someone who is talking. ☐ *While Gloria was telling us her story, Tom kept cutting in on her.* ☐ *I'm talking. Please don't cut in!*

cut in (on something) **1.** to interrupt something, especially some sort of electronic transmission. ☐ *I didn't mean to cut in on your announcement.* ☐ *Who cut in on my telephone call?* **2.** to join in something, even when not invited. ☐ *Can I cut in on this little party?* ☐ *Yes, do cut in.*

cut in (with something) to interrupt [someone] with a comment; to speak abruptly, interrupting what someone else is saying. ☐ *Jimmy cut in with a particularly witty remark.* ☐ *Must you always cut in while others are talking?*

cut off to turn off of a road, path, highway, etc. ☐ *This is the place where you are supposed to cut off.* ☐ *Cut off right here.*

cut someone or something off from something to isolate someone or something from some place or something. □ *They cut the cattle off from the wheat field.* □ *The road construction cut Jane off from her office.* 🅃 *The tanks cut off the troops from their camp.*

cut something away (from something) to separate something from something by cutting. □ *The doctor cut the wart away from the patient's foot.* 🅃 *She cut away the wart.* □ *Eric cut the bushes away from the front door.* □ *He cut the old surface roots away so no one would trip.*

cut something back to prune plants; to reduce the size of plants, bushes, etc. □ *Let's cut these bushes back. They're getting in the way.* 🅃 *Don't cut back my roses!* □ *They have been cut back already.*

cut something down **1.** to chop something down; to saw or cut at something until it is felled. □ *Stop cutting the trees down!* 🅃 *Don't cut down that tree!* **2.** to destroy someone's argument; to destroy someone's position or standing. □ *The lawyer cut the testimony down quickly.* 🅃 *The lawyer cut down the witness's story.* **3.** to reduce the price of something. (Also without *down*, but not eligible as an entry.) □ *They cut the prices down to sell the goods off quickly.* 🅃 *I wish they would cut down the prices in this store.*

cut something in(to something) to mix something into something else. (Colloquial.) □ *Carefully cut the butter into the flour mixture.* 🅃 *Now, cut in some more butter.* □ *Cut some more butter in.*

cut something off **1.** to shorten something. □ *Cut this board off a bit, would you?* 🅃 *Cut off this board a little, please.* **2.** to turn something off, such as power, electricity, water, the engine, etc. □ *Would you please cut that engine off?* 🅃 *Cut off the engine, Chuck.*

cut something out to stop doing something. (Colloquial. Usually a command. Typically: **Cut that out!**) □ *Cut that noise out!* 🅃 *Cut out that noise!* □ *Now, cut that out!*

cut something out (from something) See the following entry.

cut something out (of something) AND **cut something out (from something)** to cut a pattern or shape from cloth, paper, sheet metal, etc.; to remove something from something by cutting; to excise something from something. (When both *out* and *of* are used, no direct object can intervene.) □ *Sam cut a pig out from the paper.* □ *I cut the picture out of a magazine.* 🅃 *I cut out the shape of the moon from the paper.* □ *Cut the pictures out and pin them up.* □ *The doctor cut the tumor out.* 🅃 *She cut out the tumor.*

D

dab something on((to) something) to pat or paint carefully something onto something else. ☐ *Dab some medicine onto the scratch.* 🅃 *Dab on some medicine.* ☐ *Just dab some on.*

dam something up to erect a barrier in a river, stream, brook, etc. ☐ *We are going to have to dam this stream up to make a pond for the cattle.* 🅃 *Let's dam up this stream.* ☐ *Why is this river dammed up?*

dash off [for someone] to leave in a hurry. ☐ *I have to dash off. Good-bye.* ☐ *Ken dashed off and left me behind to deal with the angry customer.*

dash out (for something) [for someone] to leave a place in a hurry to get something. ☐ *Harry dashed out for some cigarettes.* ☐ *Excuse me. I just have to dash out.*

dash something off **1.** to make or do something quickly. ☐ *I will dash this off now and try to take more time with the rest of them.* 🅃 *I will see if I can dash off a cherry pie before dinner.* **2.** to write a note or letter quickly and send it off. ☐ *I have to dash this note off, then I will be with you.* 🅃 *I'll dash off a note to her.*

date back (to someone or something) to have origins that extend back to the time of someone or something. ☐ *This part of the palace dates back to Catherine the Great.* ☐ *This is old! It really must date back.* ☐ *Carl had an old rifle that dates back to the Civil War.*

dawn (up)on someone [for a fact] to become apparent to someone; [for something] to be realized by someone. (*Upon* is formal and less commonly used than *on*.) ☐ *Then it dawned upon me that I* *was actually going to have the job.* ☐ *It never dawned on me that that might be the case.*

deal something out to pass something out piece by piece, giving everyone equal shares. ☐ *The manager dealt the proposals out, giving each person an equal number to read.* 🅃 *I'll deal out some more proposals.*

decide (up)on someone or something to choose someone or something; to make a judgment about some aspect of someone or something. (*Upon* is formal and less commonly used than *on*.) ☐ *Will you please hurry up and decide upon someone?* ☐ *I decided on chocolate.*

deck someone or something out (in something) AND **deck someone or something out (with something)** to decorate someone or something with something. (*Someone* includes *oneself*.) ☐ *Sally decked all her children out for the holiday party.* 🅃 *She decked out her children in Halloween costumes.* ☐ *Tom decked the room out with garlands of flowers.* ☐ *He decked the hall out.* ☐ *She is all decked out for the party.* ☐ *She decked herself out in her finest clothes.*

deck someone or something out (with something) See the previous entry.

dent something up to mar or make depressions in something. ☐ *I don't want to dent my car up. It's still new.* 🅃 *He dented up my car!* ☐ *Wow, is this dented up!*

deposit something in(to) something to put something into something. ☐ *Please deposit your chewing gum into the wastebasket.* ☐ *You should deposit your money in the bank.*

die away to fade away. ☐ *The sound of the waterfall finally died away.* ☐ *When the applause died away, the tenor sang an encore.*

die back [for vegetation] to die partway back to the roots. ☐ *The hedge died back in the winter and had to be replaced in the spring.* ☐ *This kind of grass dies back every year.*

die down to fade to almost nothing; to decrease gradually. ☐ *The fire died down and went out.* ☐ *As the applause died down, a child came on stage with an armload of roses for the singer.*

die off [for living things] to perish one by one until there are no more. ☐ *Most of the larger lizards died off eons ago.* ☐ *It would be really bad if all the owls died off.* ☐ *The cucumber blossoms all died off.*

die on someone to perish while in someone's care. ☐ *"Don't die on me!" cried the emergency room nurse.* ☐ *We don't like for patients to die on us.*

die out **1.** [for a species or family] to perish totally because of the failure to produce offspring. ☐ *I am the last one in the family, so I guess it will die out.* ☐ *The owls might die out if you ruin their nesting area.* **2.** [for an idea, practice, style, etc.] to fade away through time. ☐ *That way of doing things died out a long time ago.* ☐ *It died out like the horse and buggy.*

dig down **1.** to excavate deeply. ☐ *They are really having to dig down to reach bedrock.* ☐ *We are not to the buried cable yet. We will have to dig down some more.* **2.** to be generous; to dig deep into one's pockets and come up with as much money as possible to donate to something. ☐ *Please dig down. We need every penny you can spare.* ☐ *Dig down deep. Give all you can.*

dig in(to something) **1.** to use a shovel to penetrate a mass of something. ☐ *He dug into the soft soil and made a hole for the roots of the bush.* ☐ *He grabbed a shovel and dug in where he thought the tree ought to go.* **2.** to begin to process something; to go to work on something. ☐ *I have to dig into all these applications today and process at least half of them.* ☐ *Jed got out the stack of applications and dug in.* **3.** to begin to eat food. (Slang.) ☐ *We dug into the huge pile of fried chicken.* ☐ *I stuck the corner of my napkin in my collar and dug in.*

dig out (of something) to channel or excavate one's way out of something. ☐ *The miner had to dig out of the cave-in.* ☐ *They were too exhausted to dig out.*

dig someone or something out (of something) to excavate in order to get someone or something out of something; to dig about in order to get someone or something out of something. (*Someone* includes *oneself*. Also figurative uses. See the examples.) ☐ *Let's dig the bones out of the sand and send them to the museum.* 🅃 *She dug out the bones.* ☐ *Jimmy found Tim and dug him out of the* *pile of leaves in which he had been hiding.* □ *The dog dug itself out of the rubble of the fallen building.*

dig something in(to something) to stab or jab something into something. □ *Dig your fork into that heavenly cake!* 🅃 *He dug in his fork.* □ *Jed dug his fork in and took a huge bite.*

dim out [for a light] to grow dim and go out altogether. □ *The lights dimmed out twice during the storm.* □ *I was afraid that the lights would dim out completely.*

dim something down to make lights dim; to use a dimmer to lower the lights. (A dimmer is a rheostat, variable transformer, or something similar.) □ *Why don't you dim the lights down and put on some music?* 🅃 *Let me dim down the lights and put on some music.*

dim something up to use a dimmer to make the lights brighter. (Theatrical. The expression, a seeming contradiction, is the opposite of *dim something down.*) □ *As the curtain rose, the electrician dimmed the lights up on a beautiful scene.* 🅃 *You dimmed up the lights too fast.*

din something in(to someone) to repeat something over and over to someone. (Figurative. As if one could "hammer" words into someone.) □ *The teacher dinned it into her constantly, but it did no good.* 🅃 *He dinned in the same message over and over.* □ *He needed to learn Spanish, so he bought a tape recorder and dinned it in day and night.*

dine in to eat at home rather than at a restaurant. □ *I think we will dine in tonight.* □ *I am tired of dining in. Let's go out.*

dine off something to make a meal of something; to make many meals of something. (Formal.) □ *Do you think we can dine off the leg of lamb for more than one meal?* □ *I hope we dine off the turkey only one more time.*

dine out to eat away from home. □ *I love to dine out so I don't have to cook.* □ *We both want to dine out tonight.*

dip in((to) something) **1.** to reach into a liquid. □ *I dipped into the dishwater, looking for the missing spoon.* □ *I dipped in and* *there it was.* **2.** to reach into a substance, usually to remove some of the substance. □ *I dipped into the sour cream with a potato chip and brought out an enormous glob.* □ *He grabbed the jar of peanut butter and dipped in.* **3.** to take out part of something one has been saving. (Figurative.) □ *I had to dip into my savings in order to pay for my vacation.* □ *I went to the bank and dipped in. There wasn't much left.*

dip something in((to) something) to put something into a substance in order to take some of it. □ *Tom dipped some of the bread into the cheese sauce.* 🅃 *Dip in the bread again and get some more cheese on it.* □ *I dipped the soap in to get it wet enough to work up a lather.*

dirty something up to get something dirty. □ *Those pants are brand-new! Don't dirty them up!* 🅃 *Don't dirty up your brand-new pants!*

dish something out (to someone) **1.** AND **dish something up (for someone)** to place food onto dishes for someone. □ *Please dish the lasagna out to everyone.* 🅃 *Todd dished out the lasagna to everyone.* □ *He dished it out.* □ *He dished some up for everyone.* □ *He dished some up.* **2.** to give out criticism or punishment to someone. □ *He really knows how to dish the punishment out, doesn't he?* □ *He can really dish it out, but can he take it?* 🅃 *The boys dished out too much criticism of the meal. They were sent from the room.*

dish something up (for someone) See the previous entry.

dive in(to something) **1.** to plunge into something; to jump into something headfirst. □ *Don't dive into that water! It's too shallow.* □ *Donna dived into the pool.* □ *David walked to the edge of the pool and dived in.* **2.** to plunge into some business or activity. (Figurative.) □ *I can't wait to dive into the next project.* □ *Clara dives into her work eagerly every morning.*

divide something in something See the following entry.

divide something into something **1.** AND **divide something in something** to separate something into parts. □ *I will divide it into two parts.* □ *I will divide the cake in half.* □ *If you divide the pie in fourths, the pieces will be too big.* **2.** to do mathematical division so that the divisor goes into the number that is to be divided. ☐ *Divide seven into forty-nine and what do you get?* ☐ *If seven is divided into forty-nine, what do you get?*

do someone or something in **1.** to wear someone or some creature out. (*Someone* includes *oneself.*) ☐ *All this walking will do me in.* 🅃 *The walking did in most of the hikers.* ☐ *The climbing did them in.* ☐ *I did myself in running the race.* **2.** to destroy or ruin someone or something. ☐ *Who did my car in?* 🅃 *Who did in my car?* ☐ *He lost all his money on the horses and did himself in.* **3.** to kill someone or some creature. (*Someone* includes *oneself.*) ☐ *Max tried to do Lefty in.* 🅃 *Max tried to do in Lefty.* ☐ *The speeding car did my cat in.* ☐ *Be careful or you'll do yourself in!*

do someone or something over to remodel or redecorate something; to redo someone's appearance. ☐ *I am going to have to do this room over. It is beginning to look drab.* 🅃 *Yes, you should do over this room.* ☐ *There's no need to do it over.* ☐ *The beauty consultant did Janet over, and now she looks like a model.*

do someone or something up to make someone or something attractive; to decorate or ornament someone or something. (*Someone* includes *oneself.*) ☐ *Sally did Jane up for the party.* 🅃 *She did up Jane nicely.* 🅃 *Would you do up this present for Jane? It's her birthday.* ☐ *She did herself up just beautifully.*

do something up **1.** to fasten, zip, hook, or button some item of clothing. ☐ *Would you do my buttons up in back?* 🅃 *Please do up my buttons.* **2.** to wrap up something, such as a package, gift, etc. ☐ *I have to do this present up before the party guests get here.* 🅃 *Do up the presents quickly. They are coming up the walk.* **3.** to arrange, fix, repair, cook, clean, etc., something. ☐ *I have to do the kitchen up before the guests get here.* 🅃 *Do up the kitchen now, please.*

do without (someone or something) to manage or get along without someone or something that is needed. ☐ *I guess I will have to do without dinner.* ☐ *Yes, you'll do without.*

dole something out (to someone) to distribute something to someone. ☐ *The cook doled the oatmeal out to each camper who held out a bowl.* 🅃 *Please dole out the candy bars, one to a customer.* ☐ *She doled it out fairly.*

doll someone up to dress someone up in fancy clothes. (*Someone* includes *oneself.*) □ *She dolled her children up for church each Sunday.* Ⓣ *She dolls up all her kids once a week.* □ *I just love it when you doll yourself up like that.*

double back (on someone) to follow one's own pathway back toward a pursuer. □ *The deer doubled back on us, and we lost its trail.* □ *The horse doubled back, eluding the dogs.*

double back (on something) to follow one's own pathway back toward where one started. □ *I doubled back on my own trail.* □ *The horse doubled back.*

double over to bend in the middle. □ *Suddenly, he doubled over and collapsed.* □ *The people in the audience doubled over with laughter.*

double someone over to cause someone to bend in the middle. □ *The blow to the back of the head doubled Steve over.* □ *The wind almost doubled Debbie over.*

double something over to fold something over. □ *Double the paper over twice, then press it flat.* □ *Double the cloth over a few times before you pack it away.*

double up (on someone or something) [for people] to deal with someone or something in pairs. □ *We are going to have to double up on this job.* □ *We will double up and get it done.*

double up (with someone) to share something with someone. □ *We don't have enough. You will have to double up with Sam.* □ *Let's double up and use the book together.* □ *We'll double up with each other.*

double up (with something) to bend in the middle with something such as laughter, howls, pain, etc. (Sometime figurative or an exaggeration.) □ *The man doubled up with laughter when he heard why we were there.* □ *He laughed so hard that he doubled up.*

doze off (to sleep) to slip away into sleep. □ *I dozed off to sleep during the second act of the opera.* □ *I was so comfortable that I just dozed off.*

drag behind to follow along behind someone. ☐ *His little brother came along, dragging behind.* ☐ *Stop dragging behind!*

drag on to go on slowly for a very long time; to last a very long time. ☐ *The lecture dragged on and on.* ☐ *Why do these things have to drag on so?*

drag out to last for a long time. ☐ *The lecture dragged out for nearly an hour.* ☐ *How much longer do you think this thing will drag out?*

drag someone or something in(to something) **1.** to haul or pull someone or something into something or some place. (*Someone* includes *oneself.*) ☐ *The child's mother dragged him into store after store, looking for new shoes.* 🆃 *She dragged in the child to get some shoes.* ☐ *Despite his broken leg, he dragged himself into the shelter.* **2.** to involve someone or a group in something. ☐ *Please don't drag me into your argument.* ☐ *Don't drag the committee into this argument.* ☐ *It is a mess. Please don't drag me into it.*

drag someone or something off (to someone or something) to haul someone or something away to someone, something, or some place. ☐ *The cops dragged her off to jail.* 🆃 *They dragged off the criminal to the judge.* ☐ *We dragged him off.*

drag someone up to force someone to come up or to come and stand nearby. (*Someone* includes *oneself.*) ☐ *He wouldn't come on his own, so I dragged him up.* ☐ *You will have to drag him up. He is too tired to walk by himself.* ☐ *I had to drag myself up to bed.*

drag something behind one to pull something that is behind one. ☐ *The child dragged the wooden toy behind him.* ☐ *What is that you are dragging behind you?*

drag something out to make something last for a long time. ☐ *Why does the chairman have to drag the meeting out so long?* 🆃 *Don't drag out the meetings so long!*

drag something out of someone to force someone to reveal something; to pull an answer or information out of someone laboriously. ☐ *Why don't you just tell me? Do I have to drag it out of you?* 🆃 *We had to drag out the information, but she finally told us.*

drain away [for something] to flow away. □ *All the water drained away, and the fish lay dead on the bottom of the pond.* □ *When the water drained away, we found three snapping turtles in the bottom of the pond.*

drain out to flow out or empty. □ *All the milk drained out of the container onto the bottom of the refrigerator.* □ *All the oil drained out of the crankcase.*

drain something away (from something) to channel some liquid away from something. □ *Drain all of the standing water away from the foundation of the house.* 🅃 *Drain away the water from the foundation.* □ *Please drain it away.*

drain something off (from something) to cause or permit something to flow out of something. □ *Drain some of the fat off the gravy before you serve it.* 🅃 *Please drain off the fat!* □ *Oh, yes! Drain it off, please!*

drain something off (of something) to cause or permit something to flow from the surface or top of something. □ *Drain some of the broth off the chicken.* 🅃 *Drain off the broth.* □ *Drain the fat off.*

drain something out of something to cause something to flow from something; to empty all of some liquid out of something. □ *She drained the last drop out of the bottle.* 🅃 *She drained out the last drop.*

draw away (from someone or something) to pull back or away from someone or something. □ *Please don't draw away from me. I won't bite.* □ *She drew away.*

draw back to pull back; to respond to being pulled back. □ *The main drape drew back, revealing a beautifully set stage.* □ *The cat drew back as the snake hissed at it.*

draw back (from someone or something) to pull back from someone or something; to recoil from someone or something. □ *The timid puppy drew back from my hand.* □ *She drew back from me, shocked.*

draw near [for a particular time] to approach. □ *The time to depart is drawing near.* □ *As the time drew near, Ann became more and more nervous.*

draw near (to someone or something) to come near to someone or something. □ *Draw near to me, and let me look at you.* □ *Draw near to the table and look at this.*

draw on someone or something to use someone or something in some beneficial way. □ *I may have to draw on your advice in order to complete this project.* □ *If there is some way you can draw on me to your advantage, let me know.*

draw oneself up (to something) to stand up straight and reach a certain height. □ *Walter drew himself up to his six-foot height and walked away.* □ *She drew herself up and walked away.* □ *Tom drew himself up to his full height.*

draw someone or something in(to something) **1.** to pull someone or something into something; to attract someone or something in. □ *She drew the child into the shoe store and plunked her down.* [T] *Liz opened the door and drew in the child.* □ *The advertisement drew a lot of people in.* **2.** to sketch a picture, adding someone or something into the picture. (*Someone* includes *oneself.*) □ *She drew a little dog into the lower corner of the picture.* □ *I drew the man in.* □ *She drew herself into the scene.* **3.** to involve someone or something in something. □ *Don't draw me into this argument.* □ *This is not the time to draw that argument into the discussion.*

draw someone or something out (of something) **1.** to lure someone or some creature out of something or some place. □ *I thought the smell of breakfast would draw him out of his reverie.* [T] *The good smells drew out the rest of the family.* □ *The warm sunlight drew the snake out of its lair.* **2.** to pull someone or something out of something or some place. □ *We drew him out of the slot in the wall where he lay hiding.* [T] *We drew out the concealed microphone.* □ *Tom drew the stowaway out of the locker.*

draw someone or something to(ward) someone or something to pull someone or something to someone or something. □ *She drew him toward her and kissed him.* □ *Todd drew the child toward the light.* □ *Kelly tried to draw the chair to the window.*

draw someone out (about someone or something) See the following entry.

draw someone out (on someone or something) AND **draw some-**

one out (about someone or something) to find out someone's private thoughts about someone or something. □ *I tried to draw him out on this matter, but he would not say any more.* 🅃 *I tried to draw out the speaker, but she was very careful about what she said.* 🅃 *Fred wanted to draw out information about the company's plans, but the controller had nothing to say.* □ *We were not able to draw her out as hard as we tried.*

draw someone together to make people seek one another for emotional support. □ *The accident drew them all together.* □ *Do you think the meeting will draw us together better?*

draw something off (from something) to remove a portion of a liquid from something; to cause something to flow from something. □ *The steward drew some wine off from the cask.* 🅃 *He drew off some wine.* □ *We drew some more off.*

draw something out **1.** to extend something in time. □ *Do we have to draw this thing out? Let's get it over with.* 🅃 *Stop drawing out the proceedings.* **2.** to lengthen something. □ *She drew the bubble gum out and made a long pink string.* 🅃 *Look at her drawing out that gum. What a mess!*

draw something out (of someone) to get some kind of information from someone. □ *He kept his mouth closed, and we couldn't draw anything out of him.* 🅃 *We were able to draw out the information we wanted.*

draw something up **1.** to pull something close by, such as a chair, stool, etc. □ *Draw a chair up and sit down.* 🅃 *She drew up a chair and sat down.* **2.** to draft a document; to prepare a document. □ *Who will draw a contract up?* 🅃 *I will draw up a contract for the work.*

draw up to pull up; to shrink up. □ *When they got wet, his trunks drew up and became very tight.* □ *This cheap underwear has a tendency to draw up.*

draw (up) alongside ((of) someone or something) to move up even with someone or something in motion. □ *The police officer drew up alongside us and ordered us to pull over.* □ *A car drew up alongside of us.* □ *Draw up alongside that car.*

dream about someone or something AND **dream of someone or something** to have mental pictures about someone or something, especially in one's sleep. □ *I dreamed about you all night last night.* □ *I dreamed of a huge chocolate cake.*

dream of someone or something See the previous entry.

dream something up to invent something; to fabricate something. (The *something* can be the word *something.*) □ *I don't know what to do, but I'll dream something up.* 🅃 *Please dream up a solution for this problem.*

dredge someone or something up **1.** to scoop someone or something up from underwater. □ *The workers dredged the lifeless body up from the cold black water.* 🅃 *They dredged up the lifeless body.* 🅃 *They were amazed to dredge up an equally surprised scuba diver.* **2.** to seek and find someone or something. (Slang.) □ *I will see if I can dredge a date up for Friday.* 🅃 *Can you dredge up a date for me?* □ *I don't have a wrench here, but I'll see if I can dredge one up.*

dress someone down to scold someone. □ *His mother dressed him down but good.* 🅃 *I hate to have to get mad and dress down some helpless kid.*

dress someone or something up to make someone or something appear fancier than is actually so. (*Someone* includes *oneself.*) □ *The publicity specialist dressed the actress up a lot.* 🅃 *They dressed up the actress so much that no one recognized her in person.* 🅃 *They dressed up the hall so it looked like a ballroom.* □ *Go dress yourself up for the party.*

dress someone or something (up) (in something) to clothe, decorate, or ornament someone or something in something. (*Someone* includes *oneself.*) □ *She dressed her dolls up in special clothing.* 🅃 *She dressed up her dolls in tiny outfits.* 🅃 *She dressed up all of them.* □ *Roger dressed his nephew up for the service.* □ *Dress yourself up in your finest.*

dress (up) as someone or something to dress in the manner of someone or something or to look like someone or something. □ *I am going to dress up as a ghost for Halloween.* □ *Larry will dress up as the pumpkin from Cinderella.* □ *Sam will dress as himself.*

drift back (to someone or something) to move back to someone or something slowly, on the surface of water. (Considerable metaphorical use.) ☐ *The canoe drifted back to shore.* ☐ *Finally he drifted back to her and they made up.*

drift in(to something) to move slowly and gradually into something. ☐ *The people drifted slowly into the hall.* ☐ *The boats drifted into the masses of pondweed.*

drift off to move slowly away. ☐ *The boat slowly drifted off and was gone.* ☐ *The clouds drifted off and were soon gone.*

drift out to move out of a place slowly. ☐ *After there was no more food, the people drifted out, one by one.* ☐ *The boat drifted out and almost got away.*

drift to(ward) someone or something to move slowly and gradually toward someone or something. ☐ *The clouds drifted toward us, and we could see that a storm was coming.* ☐ *As the clouds drifted to us, we could feel the humidity increase.*

drill into something to bore into or penetrate something. ☐ *The worker drilled into the wall in three places.* ☐ *Please don't drill into the wall here, where it shows.*

drill something in(to someone or something) to force knowledge into someone or something. (Figurative.) ☐ *Learn this stuff! Drill it into your brain.* 🅃 *Drill in this information so you know it by heart!* ☐ *Yes, I will drill it in.*

drink something down to drink something; to consume all of something by drinking it. (Also without *down*, but not eligible as an entry.) ☐ *Here, drink this down, and see if it makes you feel better.* 🅃 *Drink down this medicine.*

drink something in to absorb something; to take in information, sights, a story, etc. (Figurative.) ☐ *Terry and Amy drove up to the top of the hill to drink the sights in.* 🅃 *They drank in the beautiful view.*

drink something up to drink all of something. ☐ *Who drank all the root beer up?* 🅃 *I drank up the root beer.*

drink up to drink something; to drink all of something. □ *Drink up, and let's get going.* □ *Let's drink up and be on our way.*

drip something in(to something) to make something fall into something drop by drop. □ *Alice dripped a little candle wax into the base of the candlestick.* 🅃 *Don't pour it all into the jar. Drip in a little at a time.* □ *Don't just drip it in. Pour it all in at once.*

drive away to leave some place driving a vehicle. □ *They got in the car and drove away.* □ *They drove away and left us here.*

drive back to propel a vehicle back to where it started. □ *Mary drove back and parked the car where it had been when she started.* □ *You drive us there and I'll drive back.*

drive down (to some place) to run a vehicle to a relatively lower place or to a place in the south. □ *We are going to drive down to Houston for the weekend.* □ *We were going to fly, but it will be nice to drive down.*

drive off to leave somewhere, driving a vehicle. □ *She got in her car and drove off.* □ *Please don't drive off and leave me!*

drive on to continue driving; to continue with one's journey. □ *We drove on for a little while.* □ *The traffic jam is breaking up, so we can drive on.*

drive out (to some place) to propel a vehicle to a place that is away from the center of things. □ *We drove out to a little place in the country for a picnic.* □ *Why don't you drive out this weekend? We would love to have you here.*

drive over (to some place) to motor to some place that is neither close by nor far away. □ *Let's drive over to Larry's place.* □ *Yes, let's drive over. It's too far to walk.*

drive someone down (to some place) to transport someone to a relatively lower place or to a place in the south. (*Someone* includes *oneself*.) □ *We have to drive Andrew down to school in the fall.* □ *She drove herself down to the hospital.* □ *Would you drive Sally down when you come this weekend?*

drive someone on (to something) to make someone move

onward toward some kind of success. (*Someone* includes *oneself.*) □ *She said her parents drove her on to her great success.* □ *They drove their daughter on to accomplish great things.* □ *The thought of earning a large salary drove him on.* □ *He drove himself on, even when he was exhausted.*

drive someone or something (away) (from some place) to repel someone or some creature from some place. □ *We drove the monkeys away from the pineapples.* 🅃 *We drove away the monkeys from the fruit.* □ *Get out there and drive those deer out of my flowers!* □ *The gang's activity drove a lot of people away from the neighborhood.* 🅃 *His drinking drove away his family and his friends.*

drive someone or something back to force someone or something away; to force someone or something to retreat. □ *The infantry drove the attackers back into the desert.* 🅃 *They drove back the invading army.* □ *We drove them back.*

drive someone or something off to repel or chase away someone or something. □ *The campers drove the cows off before the animals trampled the tents.* 🅃 *They drove off the cows.* □ *They drove them off.*

drive someone or something out (of something) to force or chase someone or some creature out of something or some place. □ *We drove them all out of the country.* 🅃 *We drove out the troublesome kids.*

drive someone up (to some place) to transport someone to a place on a higher level or to a place in the north. □ *Ralph drove Sally up to the cabin.* □ *He was going to drive her up last week, but could not.*

drive something down to force the price of something down. □ *The lack of buyers drove the price down.* 🅃 *The lack of buyers drove down the price.*

drive something down (to some place) to transport a vehicle to a lower place or to the south by driving it there. □ *I will drive the car down to the college and leave it there for you.* 🅃 *I'll drive down the car and meet you.* □ *Do I have to drive the car down? Can't you fly up here?*

drive something up AND **force something up** to accelerate the price of something upwards. □ *Someone is buying a lot of this stuff and driving the price up.* 🅃 *They are driving up the price.* 🅃 *They forced up the price by cornering the market on these goods.*

drive through (something) to motor from one side of something to the other; to pass through something while driving. □ *We drove through some nice little towns on the way here.* □ *We didn't stop. We just drove through.*

drive up to something to motor up close to something; to pull a car up to something. □ *The car drove up to the curb and stopped.* □ *If you want to order fried chicken here, you drive up to the window and place your order.*

drizzle down (on someone or something) to rain on someone or something. □ *The light rain drizzled down on the garden.* □ *The rain drizzled down and soaked us because we had no umbrella.* □ *A light rain drizzled down all day.*

drone on to continue to make low-pitched noise or to speak in a dull and boring voice. □ *The professor droned on for what seemed like hours.* □ *Why does he drone on so? Is he asleep too?*

drone on (about someone or something) to lecture or narrate about someone or something in a low-pitched, dull, and boring manner. □ *The dull old professor droned on about Byron—or was it Keats?* □ *It was Shelley and, yes, he did drone on.*

drop away **1.** to fall off; to fall away. □ *The leaves were still dropping away from the trees in November.* □ *The dead branches dropped away from the tree.* **2.** to reduce in number over time. □ *His friends gradually dropped away.* □ *As the other contenders dropped away, Mary's chances improved.*

drop back **1.** to fall back to an original position. □ *His arm raised up and then dropped back.* □ *The lid dropped back to its original position as soon as we let go of it.* **2.** to go slowly and lose one's position in a march or procession. □ *He dropped back a bit and evened up the spacing in the line of marchers.* □ *He got tired and dropped back a little.*

drop behind (in something) to fail to keep up with a schedule. □ *I* *don't want to drop behind in my work.* ☐ *She is dropping behind and needs someone to help her.*

drop behind (someone or something) **1.** to reduce speed and end up after someone or something, such as a group, or at the back of a moving line. ☐ *I dropped behind the rest of the people, because I can't walk that fast.* ☐ *I dropped behind the speeding pack of cars and drove a little slower.* **2.** to fail to keep up with the schedule being followed by someone or a group. ☐ *My production output dropped behind what it should have been.* ☐ *I stayed later at work to keep from dropping behind.*

drop below someone or something to fall to a point lower than someone or something. ☐ *The gunman dropped below the cowboy's hiding place and got ready to take a shot.* ☐ *The temperature dropped below the freezing point.*

drop by (some place) AND **go by (some place)** to stop for a casual visit. (*Go by* means to stop at, not to pass by, in this expression.) ☐ *I hope you can drop by our house sometime.* ☐ *We really want you to drop by.* ☐ *We went by the house, but there was no one home.*

drop by the wayside AND **fall by the wayside** **1.** to leave a march or procession to rest beside the pathway. (The origin of the figurative usage in sense 2.) ☐ *A few of the marchers dropped by the wayside in the intense heat.* ☐ *They fell by the wayside, one by one.* **2.** to fail to keep up with others. (Figurative.) ☐ *Many of the students will drop by the wayside and never finish.* ☐ *Those who fall by the wayside will find it hard to catch up.*

drop down **1.** [for someone] to fall down or stoop down. ☐ *Suddenly, Ted dropped down, trying not to be seen by someone in a passing car.* ☐ *I dropped down as soon as I heard the loud sounds.* **2.** [for something] to fall from above. ☐ *The tiles on the ceiling dropped down, one by one, over the years.* ☐ *The raindrops dropped down and gave the thirsty plants a drink.*

drop in to come for a casual visit. ☐ *Please drop in when you get a chance.* ☐ *I hope you don't mind if I drop in for a while.*

drop in (on someone) to come for an unexpected, casual visit. ☐ *Guess who dropped in on us last night?* ☐ *I never thought Wally Wilson would drop in without calling first.*

drop in (to say hello) to come for a brief, friendly visit. ☐ *We just dropped in to say hello. How are you all?* ☐ *We just wanted to drop in and see you.*

drop off **1.** [for someone or something] to fall off something. ☐ *The leaves finally dropped off about the middle of November.* ☐ *When do the leaves normally drop off in Vermont?* **2.** [for a part of something] to break away and fall off. ☐ *The car's bumper just dropped off—honest.* ☐ *I lifted boxes until I thought my arms would drop off.* **3.** to decline. (Figurative.) ☐ *Attendance at the meetings dropped off after Martin became president.* ☐ *Spending dropped off as the recession became worse.*

drop out (of something) **1.** [for someone] to resign from or cease being a member of something; [for someone] to leave school. ☐ *Sally dropped out of school for some unknown reason.* ☐ *But why did she drop out?* **2.** to fall out of something. ☐ *One by one, the divers dropped out of the plane.* ☐ *The marshmallows dropped out of the bag.* **3.** [for the bottom of something] to break loose and drop. (Both literal and figurative.) ☐ *The bottom dropped out of the box, spilling everything everywhere.* ☐ *The bottom dropped out of the market, and we lost a lot of money.*

drop over to come for a casual visit. ☐ *We would love for you to drop over.* ☐ *I would really like to drop over soon.*

drop someone or something down to let someone or something fall. ☐ *He dropped his pants down, revealing the swimming trunks beneath.* 🅃 *The rescuer dropped down the baby to the doctor a few feet below.* ☐ *Sam went to the well and dropped a rock down.*

drop someone or something in(to something) to let someone or something fall into something. ☐ *He dropped a quarter into the slot and waited for something to happen.* 🅃 *He dropped in a quarter.* ☐ *Johnny Green dropped a cat into a well.* ☐ *He went to the well and dropped a cat in.*

drop someone or something off ((at) some place) **1.** to let someone or a group out of a vehicle at a particular place; to deliver someone or something some place. ☐ *Let's drop these shirts off at the cleaners.* 🅃 *Let's drop off Tom and Jerry at the hamburger joint.* 🅃 *Please drop off my shirts too.* ☐ *I'd be happy to drop them* *off.* **2.** to give someone or a group a ride to some place. ☐ *Can I drop you off somewhere in town?* 🅃 *I dropped off the kids at the party.* ☐ *I can't drop you off there because I'm not going there.*

drop someone or something off (of something) to let someone or something fall from something; to make someone or something fall from something. ☐ *They dropped the feather off the top of the building.* 🅃 *Jake dropped off a feather and it fell to the ground.* ☐ *Max took Lefty to the top of the building and threatened to drop him off.*

drop up (some place) to come for a visit to a place that is relatively higher or in the north. ☐ *Drop up and see us sometime.* ☐ *Please drop up when you can.*

drown someone or something out **1.** [for a flood] to drive someone or some creature away from home. ☐ *The high waters almost drowned the farmers out last year.* 🅃 *The water drowned out the rabbits.* ☐ *The flood almost drowned us out.* **2.** to make more noise than someone or something. ☐ *The noise of the passing train drowned our conversation out.* 🅃 *The noise of the passing train drowned out our conversation.* ☐ *The train drowned us out.*

drum some business up to create business or commerce in some item. ☐ *I'll go out and drum some business up.* 🅃 *Please go out and drum up some business.*

drum someone out of something to force someone to leave a position or an organization. ☐ *The citizens' group drummed the mayor out of office.* 🅃 *They drummed out the crooked politicians.*

drum something in(to someone) AND **drum something in(to someone's head)** to teach someone something intensely. (Figurative. As if one were pounding knowledge into someone's head.) ☐ *Her mother had drummed good manners into her.* 🅃 *She drummed in good manners day after day.* ☐ *The teacher drummed the multiplication tables into Tom's head.* ☐ *The teacher drummed them in.*

drum something in(to someone's head) See the previous entry.

drum something out to beat a rhythm, loudly and clearly, as if teaching it to someone. □ *Drum the rhythm out before you try to sing this song.* T *Drum out the rhythm first.*

dry out **1.** to become dry. □ *The clothes finally dried out in the wet weather.* **2.** to allow alcohol and the effects of drunkenness to dissipate from one's body. □ *He required about three days to dry out completely.* □ *He dried out in three days.*

dry someone or something off to remove the moisture from someone or something. (*Someone* includes *oneself.*) □ *Please dry your feet off before coming in.* T *Dry off your feet before you come in here!* □ *Todd dried the baby off and dressed him.* □ *I have to dry myself off before I catch cold.*

dry something out to make something become dry. □ *Dry this out and put it on immediately.* T *Dry out your jacket in the clothes dryer.*

dry something up **1.** to cause moisture to dry away to nothing. □ *Dry this spill up with the hair dryer.* T *Will the hair dryer dry up this mess?* **2.** to cure a skin rash by the use of medicine that dries. □ *Let's use some of this to try to dry that rash up.* T *This medicine will dry up your rash in a few days.*

dry up **1.** [for something] to become dry; [for something] to dry away to nothing. □ *Finally, the water on the roads dried up, and we were able to continue.* □ *When will the fields dry up so we can plant?* **2.** [for someone] to be quiet or go away. (Slang.) □ *Dry up, you jerk!* □ *I wish you would dry up!*

dub something in to mix a new sound recording into an old one. □ *The actor messed up his lines, but they dubbed the correct words in later.* T *They dubbed in his lines.*

duck down to stoop down quickly, as if to avoid being hit. □ *He ducked down when he heard the gunshot.* □ *Duck down and get out of the way.*

duck out (of some place) to sneak out of some place. □ *She ducked out of the theater during the intermission.* □ *When no one was looking, she ducked out.*

duck out of something to evade something; to escape doing something. ☐ *Are you trying to duck out of your responsibility?* ☐ *Fred tried to duck out of going to the dance.*

dust someone or something off to wipe or brush the dust off someone or something. (*Someone* includes *oneself.*) ☐ *Dust this vase off and put it on the shelf.* 🅃 *Please dust off this vase.* ☐ *Tom dusted Fred off and offered him a chair.* ☐ *He got up and dusted himself off.*

dust something out to brush the dust out of something. ☐ *Dust this cabinet out and put the china back in.* 🅃 *Please dust out this cabinet.*

E

ease away (from someone or something) to pull away from someone or something slowly and carefully. □ *The great ship eased away from the pier.* □ *The ship eased away slowly.*

ease back on something to move something back slowly and carefully. (Usually refers to a throttle or some other control on an airplane or other vehicle.) □ *Ann eased back on the throttle and slowed down.* □ *Please ease back on the volume control a little. You will deafen us.*

ease off [for something] to diminish. □ *The rain began to ease off.* □ *The storm seems to have eased off a little.*

ease off (from someone or something) to move away from someone or something, slowly and carefully. □ *Ease off carefully from the deer, so you don't frighten it.* □ *Ease off quietly.*

ease off (on someone or something) to let up doing something to someone or something; to diminish one's pressure or demands on someone or something. □ *Ease off on him. He's only a kid!* □ *Ease off! He's just a kid!*

ease out (of something) to move out of something, slowly and carefully; to retreat from something. □ *I eased out of the parking space with no trouble.* □ *I looked both ways and eased out.*

ease someone out (of something) **1.** to get someone out of something carefully. (*Someone* includes *oneself.*) □ *The paramedics eased the injured man out of the wreckage.* □ *Please ease me out carefully.* □ *The bystanders eased the injured child out of the wrecked car.* □ *I eased myself out of the chair and walked away.* **2.** to get someone out of an office or position quietly and without much embarrassment. (*Someone* includes *oneself*.) □ *We eased the sheriff out of office without a fight.* □ *We eased him out just before the election.* □ *He eased himself out of office, and no one was suspicious.*

ease up (on someone or something) to treat someone or something more gently. □ *Ease up on the guy! He can only do so much.* □ *Ease up on the gas! You want to kill us all?* □ *Please ease up! I'm tired.*

eat (away) at someone [for a problem] to trouble someone constantly. (Figurative.) □ *The nasty situation at work began to eat away at me.* □ *Nagging worries ate at me day and night.*

eat (away) at something **1.** to eat something eagerly and rapidly. □ *They ate away at the turkey until it was all gone.* □ *We just ate at it little by little.* **2.** to erode something. □ *The acid ate away at the metal floor.* □ *Fingers have a mild acid that eats at the metal of the doorknob.*

eat in to eat a meal at home. □ *I really don't want to eat in tonight.* □ *Let's eat in. I'm tired.*

eat in(to something) to erode into something; to etch something. □ *The acidic water ate into the rocks on the shore.* □ *The acid ate in and weakened the structure.*

eat out to eat a meal away from home. □ *I just love to eat out every now and then.* □ *Let's eat out tonight. I'm tired.*

eat out of someone's hand to do exactly as someone says; to grovel to someone. □ *I've got her eating out of my hand. She'll do anything I ask.* □ *He will be eating out of your hand before you are finished with him.*

eat someone up **1.** to consume a person. (Figurative.) □ *The whole idea of going to the South Pole was just eating her up.* □ *Juan's obsession almost ate him up.* **2.** [for insects] to bite a person all over. (Figurative.) □ *These mosquitoes are just eating me up!* □ *Don't let the bugs eat you up.*

eat something away to erode something; to consume something bit by bit. □ *The acid ate the finish away.* [T] *It ate away the finish.*

eat something off ((of) something) to erode something off a larger part. (The *of* is colloquial.) □ *The acidic rain ate the finish off the steeple.* T *The acid ate off the finish.* □ *It ate the chrome off.*

eat something out **1.** to eat a meal or a particular food away from home. □ *We eat fish out, but we don't cook it at home.* □ *We almost never eat breakfast out.* **2.** [for something or some creature] to consume the inside of something. □ *The ants ate the inside of the pumpkin out.* T *The ants ate out the pumpkin.*

eat (something) out of something to eat food directly from a container, such as a bag, box, can, etc. □ *You shouldn't eat out of the can.* □ *Maria was eating potato chips right out of the bag.*

eat something up **1.** to devour all of some food or some creature. □ *They ate the turkey up, and no one had to eat leftovers.* T *Please eat up the turkey.* **2.** [for someone] to believe something completely. (Figurative.) □ *Your story was really good. Everybody just ate it up.* T *They will eat up almost any lie.*

eat up to eat everything; to eat eagerly. (Usually a command to begin eating.) □ *Come on, let's eat up and get going.* □ *Eat up, you guys, and get back to work!*

echo back to something [for something] to recall something similar in the past. □ *This idea echoes back to the end of the last century, when people thought this way.*

edge away (from someone or something) to move cautiously away from someone or something. □ *We edged away from the dirty man in the ragged clothes.* □ *As others saw the gun, they edged away.*

egg someone on to incite someone to do something; to encourage someone to do something. □ *I want Richard to stop making up those horrible puns. Please don't egg him on.* □ *She does not need any encouragement. Don't egg her on.*

eke something out to extend something; to add to something. □ *He worked at two jobs in order to eke his salary out.* T *He managed to eke out a living.*

elbow (one's way) through something to push or drive oneself through something, such as a crowd, perhaps using one's elbows or arms to move people out of the way. ☐ *She elbowed her way through the crowd.* ☐ *Jerry elbowed through the people gathered at the door.*

elbow someone aside to push someone aside with one's arm. ☐ *She elbowed the other woman aside and there was almost a fight.* 🅃 *The rude woman elbowed aside all the other people.*

emblazon something on(to) something **1.** to decorate something with something. ☐ *The workers emblazoned wild decorations on the door.* ☐ *They emblazoned their name on the side of the building.* **2.** to put some writing or symbols that proclaim something onto something. ☐ *The knight emblazoned his name onto his shield.* ☐ *The craftsman emblazoned the knight's name on his shield.*

empty something out to remove or pour all of the contents from something. ☐ *Please empty this drawer out and clean it.* 🅃 *She emptied out the aquarium and cleaned it well.*

end something up to terminate something; to bring something to an end. ☐ *He ended his vacation up by going to the beach.* 🅃 *She ended up her speech with a poem.*

end up to come to an end. ☐ *When will all this end up?* ☐ *I think that the party will have to end up about midnight.*

end up at something to be at something or some place at the end. ☐ *The plane ended up at Denver airport because of a storm in Colorado Springs.* ☐ *We ended up at home for the evening because the car broke down.*

end up doing something to have to do something one has tried to get out of doing. ☐ *I refused to do it, but I ended up doing it anyway.* ☐ *Juan didn't want to end up going home alone.*

end up somehow to come to the end of something in a particular way. ☐ *I really didn't want to end up this way.* ☐ *I ended up broke when my vacation was over.*

end up something to become something at the end of everything. ☐ *I always knew I would end up a doctor.* ☐ *If I don't get a job, I will end up a beggar.*

engrave something on(to) something to cut symbols into the surface of something. □ *She engraved her initials onto the side of the tree.* □ *Ted engraved her name on the bracelet.*

engrave something (up)on something **1.** to cut letters or a design into the surface of something. □ *He asked them to engrave his initials upon the back of his watch.* □ *He engraved his name on the desktop.* **2.** to imprint something firmly on someone's mind. □ *I engraved the combination to the safe upon my brain.* □ *The teacher engraved the definition of a noun on my consciousness.*

enlarge (up)on something to add details to a report about something. □ *Would you care to enlarge upon your remarks?* □ *I enlarged on my original comments.*

enlist someone in something to recruit someone into something; to recruit someone into the armed services. □ *They tried to enlist me in the army, but I decided against it.* □ *David enlisted his brother in an organization that gave assistance to peasants in South America.*

enter in something to enroll as a participant in something, such as a contest, competition, etc. □ *She was not ready to enter in the competition.* □ *I can't enter in that contest. I'm not prepared.*

enter into something **1.** to get into something. □ *She entered into the house and immediately went to work.* □ *As the people entered into the cathedral, they became quiet.* **2.** to join in something. □ *I couldn't get him to enter into the spirit of the party.* □ *She just loves to enter into things and have a good time with people.*

enter someone or something in((to) something) to enroll someone or something in something; to make someone or something a competitor in something. (*Someone* includes *oneself.*) □ *I will enter you into the contest whether you like it or not.* □ *Ed entered his favorite horse in the race.* □ *She entered herself into the contest.*

enter (up)on something **1.** to come in at a particular point as marked by something. □ *We entered the theater upon the most delicate point of the story.* □ *We entered on the tail end of a live scene.* **2.** to begin something. □ *Todd entered upon a new phase of his life.* □ *He entered on the management of a new project.*

entomb someone or something in something 1. to place someone or something in a tomb. (*Someone* includes *oneself*.) ☐ *In the opera, they entombed Aida and her lover in a dusty place where they sang themselves to death.* ☐ *They accidentally entombed the queen's jewels in the vault with her.* ☐ *She entombed herself in her final resting place and waited for death.* 2. to imprison someone or some creature in a tomblike enclosure. ☐ *Please don't entomb me in that huge, cold office.* ☐ *Unknowingly, when they closed the door, they had entombed a tiny mouse within.*

erase something from something to delete or wipe something from something. ☐ *Please erase the writing from the blackboard.* ☐ *I will erase the incorrectly spelled word from my paper.*

erupt from something to burst out of something or some place. ☐ *A billow of smoke erupted from the chimney.* ☐ *A mass of ashes and gasses erupted from the volcano.*

erupt into something to become a serious problem suddenly; to blow up into something. (Figurative.) ☐ *The argument erupted into a terrible fight.* ☐ *They were afraid the fight would erupt into a riot.*

escalate into something to intensify into something; to increase gradually into something. ☐ *This argument is going to escalate into something serious very soon.* ☐ *These cases of the flu could escalate into a real epidemic.*

even something off to make something level or smooth. ☐ *Please even this surface off before you paint it.* Ⓣ *You need to even off this surface.*

even something out to make something level or level. ☐ *Please even the road out.* Ⓣ *They evened out the surface of the road.*

even something up to make something even, square, level, equal, balanced, etc. ☐ *I'll even the table up.* Ⓣ *See if you can even up the legs of this table. It wobbles.*

exact something from someone to demand something from someone; to take something from someone. ☐ *The bill collector sought to exact payment from them for a debt that had been paid off long ago.* ☐ *You cannot exact a single cent from me.*

exclude someone or something from something to leave someone or something out of something; to leave someone or something off a list. (*Someone* includes *oneself.*) □ *Did you mean to exclude me from the party?* □ *I excluded chocolate cake from the shopping list.* □ *I exclude myself from consideration for the nomination.*

exempt someone from something to release someone from the obligation to do something; to allow a person not to be affected by a rule or law. (*Someone* includes *oneself.*) □ *I cannot exempt anyone from this rule.* □ *The members of Congress exempted themselves from the wage freeze.*

expand into something to grow into something; to enlarge into something. □ *The little problem expanded into a big one in no time at all.* □ *In no time at all, the vegetable garden had expanded into a small farm.*

expand something into something to enlarge something into something; to make something grow into something. □ *She expanded her business into a national company.* □ *I would like to do something to expand this room into a more usable space.*

expand (up)on something to add detail to a report about something. □ *Would you please expand upon that last remark?* □ *May I expand on your remarks?*

experiment (up)on someone or something to use someone or something as the subject of an experiment. (*Upon* is formal and less commonly used than *on.*) □ *Do you think we should experiment upon people?* □ *The researchers were experimenting on a new drug that might cure rabies.*

explain something away to explain something so that it is no longer a problem. □ *You can try to explain it away if you want, but that won't solve the problem.* [T] *You can't just explain away all your problems.*

extend across something to spread across something. □ *The shadows extended across the whole land.* □ *The fog extended across the low-lying land.*

F

face off **1.** to begin a hockey game with two players facing one another. □ *They faced off and the match was on.* **2.** to prepare for a confrontation. (From sense 1.) □ *The opposing candidates faced off and the debate began.* □ *They faced off and I knew there was going to be a fight.*

face someone down to make a face-to-face stand with someone who eventually backs down. □ *Chuck succeeded in facing Tom down.* 🅃 *Facing down Tom wasn't difficult for Chuck.*

face up (to someone or something) to confront with courage someone or something representing a threat or unpleasantness. □ *You are simply going to have to face up to Fred.* □ *You must face up to the authorities if you have done something wrong.* □ *You will simply have to face up.*

fade away into something to diminish into something. □ *The light faded away into nothing.* □ *The sound of the drums faded away into the distance.*

fade down [for sound] to diminish. □ *The roar of the train faded down as it passed and fled into the night.* □ *As the thunder faded down, the sun began to break through the clouds.*

fall apart to break into pieces; to disassemble. (Both literal and figurative uses.) □ *The whole thing fell apart.* □ *Gerald's whole life began falling apart.*

fall back to move back from something; to retreat from something. □ *The gang members fell back, and I took that opportunity to get away.* □ *The troops fell back to regroup.*

fall back on(to) someone or something **1.** to fall backwards onto someone or something. □ *She stumbled and fell back onto the lady behind her.* □ *She fell back on the couch.* **2.** to begin to use someone or something held in reserve. (Figurative.) □ *We fell back on our savings to get us through the hard times.* □ *We had to fall back on our emergency generator.*

fall behind (in something) AND **fall behind (on something); fall behind (with something); get behind (in something); get behind (on something); get behind (with something)** to lag behind schedule in some kind of work or some other scheduled activity. □ *You are falling behind in your car payments.* □ *I tried not to get behind on them.* □ *Please don't fall behind with your payments.* □ *I won't fall behind again.*

fall behind (on something) See the previous entry.

fall behind (with something) See *fall behind (in something).*

fall by the wayside See *drop by the wayside.*

fall down to drop or topple. □ *The baby fell down.* □ *Walk carefully on this ice or you will fall down.*

fall down on the job to fail to do an efficient job. (Figurative.) □ *Henry has been falling down on the job.* □ *All of the workers tend to fall down on the job on Friday.*

fall (down) to something to fall or drop to something below. □ *The coconut fell down to the people below.* □ *It fell to the people shaking the tree.*

fall in to get into line and stand at attention. (Military. Often a command.) □ *The commander ordered that the troops fall in.* □ *If you don't fall in now, you'll all have to do a hundred push-ups.*

fall in love [for two people] to become enamored of each other. □ *They fell in love.* □ *When they fell in love, they thought it would last forever.*

fall in love (with someone or something) to become enamored of someone or something. □ *I simply fell in love with the dress. I had to have it.* □ *I fell in love with her.*

fall in(to) line (with someone or something) **1.** to get into a line with other people or a group. ☐ *I fell in line with the others and waited my turn.* ☐ *Please fall in line and stay there.* **2.** to behave in a manner similar to someone or something. (Figurative.) ☐ *You are expected to fall into line with the other people.* ☐ *We want you to fall in line and obey the rules.*

fall in(to) place to move into place; to fit into the correct place. (Both literal and figurative.) ☐ *At last, things began to fall into place, and life became livable again.* ☐ *In the end, everything fell in place.*

fall in(to step) to get into the same marching pattern as everyone else as regards which foot moves forward. (Everyone should be moving the same foot forward at the same time.) ☐ *I just can't seem to fall into step. I am very uncoordinated.* ☐ *Fall in! March with the others!*

fall off to decline. ☐ *At dawn, the horrible insect noises of the night began to fall off.* ☐ *As business began to fall off, so did my income.*

fall off ((of) something) to drop off something. (The *of* is colloquial.) ☐ *A button fell off my shirt.* ☐ *I fell off the log.* ☐ *The twigs fell off of him as he stood up.*

fall outside something to be beyond someone's power, responsibility, or jurisdiction. ☐ *This matter falls outside my bailiwick.* ☐ *Her offense fell outside of the manager's jurisdiction.*

fall over to topple over and fall down. ☐ *The fence fell over and dented the car.* ☐ *I felt faint and almost fell over.*

fall over backwards (to do something) to go to great extremes to do something; to endure all sorts of trouble to do something. (Figurative.) ☐ *She fell over backwards to make everyone comfortable.* ☐ *Just do your best. There is no need to fall over backwards.*

fall over someone or something to stumble over someone or something. ☐ *Sam came into the house and fell over a kitchen chair.* ☐ *Walter fell over Roger, who was napping on the floor.*

fall through [for something, such as plans] to fail. ☐ *Our party for next Saturday fell through.* ☐ *I hope our plans don't fall through.*

fall to to begin doing something. ☐ *She asked for help, and everyone fell to.* ☐ *Fall to, you guys!*

fall to pieces **1.** to break into pieces. ☐ *The road was so rough the car almost fell to pieces.* ☐ *I was afraid that my bicycle would fall to pieces before I got there.* **2.** to become emotionally upset. (Figurative.) ☐ *I was so nervous, I fell to pieces and couldn't give my speech.* ☐ *Roger fell to pieces and couldn't attend the sales meeting.*

fall to someone or something to become the responsibility of someone or a group. ☐ *It falls to you to go and tell Mrs. Wilson that you broke her window.* ☐ *The responsibility falls to the board of directors.*

fall (up)on someone (to do something) to become someone's responsibility to do something. ☐ *It falls upon you to explain this matter to her.* ☐ *It falls on you to fix the window.*

fan out (from some place) to spread or move outward from a particular area in the shape of a fan. ☐ *The paths seem to fan out from the wide trail that starts at the house.* ☐ *The trails fanned out and soon we were all separated.*

fan something out to spread something out so that all parts can be seen better. (As one opens a wood and paper fan.) ☐ *Todd fanned the cards out so we could see which ones he held.* 🅃 *He fanned out the cards.*

farm someone out **1.** [for someone in control] to send someone to work for someone else. ☐ *I have farmed my electrician out for a week, so your work will have to wait.* 🅃 *We farmed out the office staff.* **2.** to send a child away to be cared for by someone; to send a child to boarding school. ☐ *We farmed the kids out to my sister for the summer.* 🅃 *We farmed out the kids.*

farm something out **1.** to deplete the fertility of land by farming too intensely. ☐ *They farmed their land out through careless land management.* 🅃 *They farmed out their land.* **2.** to make money by renting out land or buildings. ☐ *I farmed the pasture out.* 🅃 *I farmed out the west pasture to Bill Franklin, who will graze his cattle there.* **3.** to send work to someone to be done away from one's normal place of business; to subcontract work. ☐ *We farmed the* *sewing out.* 🅃 *We always farm out the actual sewing together of the dresses.*

fasten something up to close something up, using buttons, a zipper, snaps, hooks, a clasp, or other things meant to hold something closed. ☐ *Please fasten this up for me. I can't reach the zipper.* 🅃 *Please fasten up my buttons in back.*

fasten (up)on someone or something **1.** to take firm hold of someone or something. ☐ *She fastened upon me and would not let me go until she finished speaking.* ☐ *I don't like people who fasten on you.* **2.** to fix one's attention on someone or something. (Figurative.) ☐ *He fastened upon the picture for a brief moment and then turned away.* ☐ *The baby fastened on the television screen and watched it for many minutes.*

fatten someone or something up (with something) to use something to make someone or some creature fat. (*Someone* includes *oneself.*) ☐ *We will fatten the calf up with corn.* 🅃 *I don't know why they keep fattening up their children with so much food.* ☐ *They keep fattening them up.* ☐ *I fattened myself up with lots of good food.*

feed off (of) something to regularly include something as a part of a diet. (The *of* is colloquial.) ☐ *This creature feeds off fallen fruit.* ☐ *Mosquitoes feed off of me!*

feed (up)on someone or something to eat someone or something. (*Upon* is formal and less commonly used than *on.*) ☐ *They say that some Bengal tigers feed upon people.* ☐ *They feed on anything that moves.*

feel for someone to feel the emotional pain that someone else is feeling; to empathize or sympathize with someone. ☐ *I really feel for you. I'm so sorry it turned out this way.* ☐ *Fred felt for Dave, but there was nothing he could do for him.*

feel out of something to feel alienated from something. ☐ *I feel out of things lately. Are people ignoring me?* ☐ *I feel a little out of it at this party, but I will try to join in the fun.*

feel someone out (about someone or something) to find out what someone thinks about someone or something. ☐ *I will feel* *him out about going to Florida.* 🅃 *Let me feel out the boss about this matter.* □ *I felt the boss out. The answer will be no, so don't ask.*

feel up to something to feel like doing something; to feel well enough to do something. □ *I'm sorry, but I don't feel up to going out.* □ *Do you feel up to playing a game of cards?*

fence someone or something off (from something) to separate someone or something from something else with a fence or barrier. (*Someone* includes *oneself.*) □ *We fenced the children's play area off from the rest of the yard.* 🅃 *Dave fenced off the play area.* 🅃 *We fenced off the children from the rest of the yard.* □ *He fenced himself off from the rest of the crowd.*

fence something in to enclose some creature or something within a fence or barrier. □ *We fenced the yard in to keep the dogs at home.* 🅃 *We had to fence in the dog.* □ *We fenced the garden in.*

fend someone or something off to hold someone or something off; to fight someone or something off. □ *We knew we could fend them off only a little while longer.* 🅃 *They could not fend off the attackers.* □ *Max fended Lefty off.*

fiddle around (with someone or something) to play around with someone or something. □ *I will fiddle around with this for a while and maybe I can fix it.* □ *I wish you would stop fiddling around and hire someone to fix it.*

fight against someone or something to battle against someone or something. □ *The boxer refused to fight against the challenger, who was much stronger.* □ *He fought against the disease to the very end.*

fight back (at someone or something) to defend oneself against someone or something; to retaliate against someone or something. □ *You are going to have to fight back at them. You can't expect us to defend you.* □ *It's hard for me to fight back.*

fight (one's way) back to something to struggle to return to something or some place. □ *She fought her way back to the head of the line.* □ *Jan fought back to good health.*

fight one's way out of something to struggle to get out of something or some place. ☐ *He fought his way out of the crowded room and out through the door.* ☐ *He couldn't fight his way out of a paper bag.*

fight (one's way) through something **1.** to struggle to get through something; to struggle to penetrate something. ☐ *I'll have to fight my way through all this crepe paper in order to reach the punch bowl.* ☐ *The room was filled with trash, and I had to fight through it to get to the other door.* **2.** to struggle to work through all of something. ☐ *I have to fight my way through this stack of papers by noon.* ☐ *I am tired of fighting through red tape.*

fight someone or something down to fight against and defeat someone or something. ☐ *We fought the opposition down and got our bill through the committee.* 🅃 *We had to fight down Fred, who wanted something entirely different.*

fight something down **1.** to struggle to hold something back; to struggle to keep from being overwhelmed by something. ☐ *She fought her anger down and managed to stay till the end.* 🅃 *She fought down the urge to buy the vase.* **2.** to struggle to swallow something; to fight to get something down one's throat. ☐ *It tasted terrible, but I managed to fight it down.* 🅃 *She fought down the medicine.*

fight something through (something) to force something through some sort of procedure or process. ☐ *The governor fought the bill through the legislature successfully.* 🅃 *She fought through the bill successfully.* ☐ *Our committee fought it through.*

figure on something to plan on something; to count on doing something. ☐ *We figured on going down to the country next weekend.* ☐ *Did you figure on doing the repair work yourself?*

figure someone or something in((to) something) to reckon someone or something into the total. (*Someone* includes *oneself.*) ☐ *I will figure the electric bill into the total.* 🅃 *We can figure in one more person.* ☐ *Did you figure David in?* ☐ *Did you figure yourself into the final total?*

figure someone or something out to comprehend someone or something; to understand someone or something better. (*Someone* includes *oneself.*) ☐ *I just can't figure you out.* 🅃 *I can't figure out quiet people readily.* ☐ *It will take a while for me to figure the instructions out.* ☐ *Well, I can't figure myself out. I don't know how you could either.*

figure something up to add up the amount of something. ☐ *Please figure the bill up. We have to go now.* 🅃 *I will figure up the bill right away.* 🅃 *I will figure up how many yards of material I need.*

file in((to) something) [for a line of people] to move into something or some place. ☐ *The people filed into the hall quietly.* ☐ *Everyone filed in quietly.*

file out (of something) [for a line of people] to move out of something or some place. ☐ *The people filed quietly out of the theater.* ☐ *They filed out at the end.*

file something away to put something away, usually in a file folder or file cabinet. ☐ *She filed the letter away for future reference.* ☐ *Please file this away. You will need it some day.*

fill in (for someone or something) to substitute for someone or something; to take the place of someone or something. ☐ *I will have to fill in for Wally until he gets back from his vacation.* ☐ *I don't mind filling in.*

fill out to become full; to gain weight. ☐ *About a month after her debilitating illness, Maggie began to fill out again.* ☐ *The fruit on the trees began to fill out, and we knew it was going to ripen soon.*

fill someone in (on someone or something) to tell someone the details about someone or something. ☐ *Please fill me in on what happened last night.* 🅃 *Please fill in the committee on the details.* ☐ *Please fill me in!*

fill something in **1.** to add material to an indentation, hole, etc., to make it full. ☐ *You had better fill the crack in with something before you paint the wall.* 🅃 *You should fill in the cracks first.* **2.** to write in the blank spaces on a paper; to write on a form. ☐ *Please fill this form in.* 🅃 *I will fill in the form for you.*

fill something out to complete a form by writing in the blank spaces. ☐ *Please fill this form out and send it back to us in the mail.* 🅃 *I will fill out the form as you asked.*

fill up 1. to become full. □ *The creek filled up after the heavy rain yesterday.* □ *The rain barrel began to fill up during the storm.* **2.** to fill one's gas tank. (Informal.) □ *I've got to stop and fill up. I'm running low.* □ *We will fill up at the next little town.*

find for someone or something [for a jury or a judge] to announce a decision in favor of one side of a case. □ *The judge found for Mrs. Franklin and that made everyone quite happy.* □ *The court found for the law firm and admonished the disgruntled client.*

finish someone or something up to finish doing something to someone or something. □ *The hairdresser had to work fast in order to finish Mrs. Wilson up by quitting time.* 🅃 *She finished up Fred in a short time.* □ *I will finish this typing up in a few minutes.*

finish something off to eat or drink up all of something; to eat or drink up the last portion of something. □ *Let's finish the turkey off.* 🅃 *You finish off the turkey. I've had enough.* 🅃 *Let's finish off this pot of coffee and I'll make some more.*

finish up to complete the doing of something. □ *When do you think you will finish up?* □ *I will finish up next week sometime.*

fire (something) back at someone or something to shoot a gun back at someone or something. □ *We fired about ten rounds back at them.* □ *The soldiers in the fort did not fire back at the attackers.*

firm something up 1. to make something more stable or firm. □ *We need to firm this table up. It is very wobbly.* 🅃 *You need to learn to firm up your meringues better.* **2.** to make a monetary offer for something more appealing and definite. □ *You will have to firm the offer up with cash today, if you really want the house.* 🅃 *Please firm up this offer if you still want the house.*

firm up 1. to become more stable or viable; to recover from or stop a decline. (Figurative.) □ *The economy will probably firm up soon.* □ *I hope that cattle prices firm up next spring.* **2.** to develop better muscle tone; to become less flabby. □ *I need to do some exercises so I can firm up.* □ *You really ought to firm up.*

fish someone or something out (of something) to pull someone or something out of something or some place. □ *She is down at the riverbank, fishing driftwood out of the water.* 🅃 *She fished out a lot of wood.* □ *We need more wood. Please fish it all out.*

fish something up (out of something) to pull or hoist something out of something. □ *The old shopkeeper fished a huge pickle up out of the barrel.* T *He fished up a huge pickle.* T *Please fish up another one.*

fit in((to) something) [for something] to be a suitable size to go into something. □ *This peg does not fit into this hole.* □ *It simply doesn't fit in.*

fit someone or something in((to) something) to manage to place someone or something into something. □ *I think I can fit you into my schedule.* T *I have fit in three people already today.* □ *The shelf is tight, but I think I can fit one more book in.*

fit someone or something out (for something) to equip someone or something for something; to outfit someone or something for something. (*Someone* includes *oneself.*) □ *We are going to fit our boat out so we can live on it during a long cruise.* T *We fit out the children in funny costumes for Halloween.* □ *We fit them all out and sent them off to their costume party.* □ *Let's fit ourselves out for the expedition.*

fit something on((to) something) to manage to place something onto something. □ *See if you can fit this lid onto that jar over there.* □ *Sorry, I can't fit it on.*

fix someone or something up to rehabilitate someone or something. □ *The doctor said he could fix me up with a few pills.* T *The doctor fixed up the hunter and sent him home.* □ *I fixed the car up so it was safe to travel in.* □ *Is the car fixed up yet?*

fix something over to redo something; to redecorate something. □ *I want to fix this room over next spring.* T *I really want to fix over this room.*

flag someone or something down to show a signal or wave, indicating that someone or something should stop. □ *Please go out and flag a taxi down. I'll be right out.* T *She went to flag down a taxi.* □ *The hitchhiker tried to flag us down.*

flame up **1.** [for something] to catch fire and burst into flames. □ *The trees flamed up one by one in the forest fire.* □ *Suddenly the car flamed up and exploded.* **2.** [for a fire] to expand and send out larger flames. □ *The raging fire flamed up and jumped to even more trees.* □ *As Bob opened the door and came in, the fire flamed up and brightened the room.*

flare up 1. [for something] to ignite and burn. □ *The flames flared up at last—four matches having been used.* **2.** [for a fire] to expand rapidly. □ *After burning quietly for a while, the fire suddenly flared up and made the room very bright.* **3.** [for a disease] to get worse suddenly. □ *My arthritis flares up during the damp weather.* **4.** [for a dispute] to break out or escalate into a battle. □ *A war flared up in the Middle East.* □ *We can't send the whole army every time a dispute flares up.*

flare up (at someone or something) to lose one's temper at someone or something. □ *I could tell by the way he flared up at me that he was not happy with what I had done.* □ *I didn't mean to flare up.*

flash back (on someone or something) to provide a glimpse of someone or something in the past. (In films, literature, and television.) □ *The next scene flashed back on Fred's murder.* □ *The story then flashed back, giving us information out of the past.*

flatten someone or something out to make someone or something flat. □ *If you fall under the steamroller, it will flatten you out.* 🅃 *Flatten out that dough a little more.* □ *Please flatten it out.*

flesh out to become more fleshy. □ *She began to flesh out at the age of thirteen.* □ *After his illness, Tom fleshed out and regained his strength.*

flesh something out (with something) to make the frame or skeleton of something complete; to add detail to the basic framework of something. □ *I will flesh this out with more dialogue and music here and there. Then we'll have a fine play.* 🅃 *We will flesh out the outline with more details later.* □ *Give me the outline, and I will flesh it out.*

flick something off to turn something off, using a toggle switch. □ *Mary flicked the light off and went out of the room.* □ *Please flick the light off as you go out the door.* 🅃 *Please flick off the light.*

flick something off ((of) someone or something) to brush or knock a speck of something off of someone or something. (The *of* is colloquial.) □ *She flicked a speck of lint off his collar.* 🅃 *She flicked off the lint.* □ *Harriet flicked it off.*

flick something on to turn something on, using a toggle switch. □ *Mary came into the room and flicked the light on.* □ *Please flick the light on as you go out the door.* 🅃 *Please flick on the light.*

flicker out [for a flame] to dwindle, little by little, until it goes out. □ *The candle flickered out, leaving us in total darkness.* □ *When the last flame flickered out, the room began to get cold.*

fling something off (of oneself) **1.** to yank something off of oneself hastily. □ *She flung the blanket off herself.* 🅃 *She flung off the blanket.* □ *Sarah flung the blankets off.* **2.** to pull or take off an article of clothing. □ *Larry flung his jacket off and went straight to the kitchen.* 🅃 *He flung off his jacket.* □ *Todd flung his jacket off.*

flip through something to go quickly through the leaves of a book, etc., page by page. □ *She flipped through the book, looking at the pictures.* □ *Don't just flip through it. Read it.*

flock in((to) some place) to move into some place in crowds. □ *People were flocking into the store where everything was on sale.* □ *They flocked in in droves.*

flock together to gather together in great numbers. (Typically said of birds and sheep.) □ *A large number of blackbirds flocked together, making a lot of noise.* □ *Do sheep really flock together in a storm?*

flood in(to something) to pour into something. (Both literally, with water, and figuratively.) □ *The people flooded into the hall.* □ *We opened the door, and the people flooded in.* □ *The water flooded in under the door.*

flood out (of something) to pour out of something or some place. (Both literal and figurative.) □ *The people flooded out of the theater, totally disgusted with the performance.* □ *Water flooded out of the break in the dam.* □ *Jimmy tipped over the jug of milk and the contents flooded out.*

flood someone or something out (of something) [for too much water] to force someone or something to leave something or some place. □ *The high waters flooded them out of their home.* 🅃 *The high waters flooded out a lot of people.* □ *The water flooded many raccoons out of the neighborhood.*

flow in(to something) to course into something; to pour into something. (Both literal and figurative.) □ *The strength flowed into my body, and I felt alive again.* □ *The water flowed in when I opened the door on the flood.*

flow out (of something) **1.** to course or pour out of something. □ *The apple juice flowed out of the press as we turned the crank.* □ *It stopped flowing out when we had crushed the apples totally.* **2.** to issue forth from something. □ *The people flowed out of the stadium exits.* □ *At the end of the game, the people flowed out in a steady stream.*

flush something away to wash something unwanted away. □ *Flush all this away and be done with it.* Ⓣ *Fred flushed away all the leaves on the sidewalk.*

fly by **1.** to soar past. □ *Three jet fighters flew by.* □ *A huge hawk flew by, frightening all the smaller birds.* **2.** [for time] to go quickly. (Figurative.) □ *The hours just flew by, because we were having fun.* □ *Time flew by so fast that it was dark before we knew it.*

fly in(to something) to arrive in an airplane at something or some place. □ *I flew into Denver on time.* □ *When did you fly in?*

fly off **1.** to take to flight quickly. □ *The stork flew off before we got a good look at it.* □ *The little birds flew off and things were quiet again.* **2.** to leave in a hurry. (Figurative.) □ *Well, it's late. I must fly off.* □ *She flew off a while ago.*

fob someone or something off (on(to) someone) to get rid of someone or something by transferring that someone or something to someone else. □ *Don't try to fob your girlfriend off on me!* Ⓣ *She fobbed off her brother onto her friend.* □ *I took him to my grandmother's house and fobbed him off.*

fog over [for something made of glass] to become covered over with water vapor. □ *The windshield fogged over because I forgot to turn on the defroster.* □ *The mirror fogged over, and I couldn't see to shave.*

fog something up to make something made of glass become covered with a film of water. □ *The moisture fogged the windshield up, and we had to stop to clean it off.* Ⓣ *The moisture fogged up the mirror in the bathroom.*

fog up [for something made of glass] to become partially or completely obscured by a film of water. □ *The glass fogged up, and we couldn't see out.*

fold something back to bend a sheet or flap of something back. □ *She very carefully folded the page back to mark her place in the book.* 🅃 *She folded back the page to mark her place in the book.* □ *The surgeon folded the flap of skin back, revealing the torn ligament.* 🅃 *He folded back his shirt cuffs carefully.*

fold something in(to something) to blend something, such as eggs, into batter. □ *Carefully, the chef folded the eggs into the other ingredients.* 🅃 *The chef folded in the eggs.* □ *Now fold the egg whites in carefully.*

fold something over to double something over; to make a fold in something. □ *I folded the paper over twice to make something I could fan myself with.* □ *Fold the cloth over a few times before you put it away.*

fold something up to double something over into its original folded position. □ *Please fold the paper up when you are finished.* 🅃 *Please fold up the paper.*

fold up **1.** [for something] to close by folding. □ *The table just folded up with no warning, trapping my leg.* □ *I would like to find a map that would fold up by itself.* **2.** [for a business] to cease operating. □ *Our shop finally folded up because of the recession.* □ *Tom's little candy shop folded up.* **3.** [for someone] to faint. □ *She folded up when she heard the news.* □ *I was so weak that I was afraid I was going to fold up.*

follow someone up AND **follow up (on someone)** to check on the work that someone has done. □ *I have to follow Sally up and make sure she did everything right.* 🅃 *I follow up Sally, checking on her.* □ *I'll follow up on her.* □ *Someone has to follow up.*

follow something through See *follow through (with something).*

follow something up AND **follow up (on something)** **1.** to check something out. □ *Would you please follow this lead up? It might be important.* 🅃 *Please follow up this lead.* □ *I'll follow up on it.* □ *Yes, please follow up.* **2.** to make sure that something was done the way it was intended. ☐ *Please follow this up. I want it done right.* 🅃 *Please follow up this business.* ☐ *I'll follow up on it.* ☐ *I'll follow up.*

follow through (on something) to supervise something to its completion; to oversee something to make sure it gets done properly. ☐ *I want someone to follow through on this project.* ☐ *It isn't enough to start a project; you've got to follow through.*

follow through (with something) AND **follow something through** to complete an activity, doing what was promised. ☐ *I wish you would follow through with the project we talked about.* ☐ *You never follow through!* ☐ *When you start a project, you should be prepared to follow it through.*

follow up (on someone) See *follow someone up.*

follow up (on something) See *follow something up.*

fool around to waste time doing something unnecessary or doing something amateurishly. ☐ *Stop fooling around.* ☐ *I wish you didn't spend so much time fooling around.*

force someone or something out (of something) to drive someone or something out of something or some place. ☐ *The citizen's group forced the governor out of office.* 🅃 *They forced out the governor.* ☐ *We forced him out.*

force something down to force oneself to swallow something. ☐ *I can't stand sweet potatoes, but I manage to force them down just to keep from making a scene.* 🅃 *She forced down the sweet potatoes.*

force something through something to press or drive something through resistance. ☐ *The president forced the bill through the legislature.* ☐ *We were not able to force the matter through the board of directors.*

force something up See *drive something up.*

fork money out for something to pay money for something. (Slang.) ☐ *Do you think I'm going to fork twenty dollars out for that little book?* 🅃 *I won't fork out any money for a cheap piece of garbage like that.*

fork something over (to someone) to give something to someone. (Slang. Usually refers to money.) □ *Come on! Fork the money over to me!* 🅃 *Fork over the money!* □ *Fork it over!*

freeze over [for a body of water] to get cold and form a layer of ice on top. □ *The pond froze over, so we went skating.*

freeze up **1.** [for something] to freeze and stop functioning. □ *The joint froze up and wouldn't move anymore.* **2.** [for someone] to become frightened and anxious, and be unable to continue with something. □ *I froze up and couldn't say anything more.*

freshen someone or something up to revive or restore the appearance or vitality of someone or something. (*Someone* includes *oneself.*) □ *What can we do to freshen this room up?* 🅃 *A cold shower freshened up the runner.* □ *Let me take a moment to freshen myself up before we go into the dining room.*

frighten someone or something away AND **frighten someone or something off** to scare someone or something away. □ *The noise frightened the burglar away.* 🅃 *Something frightened away the prowlers.* □ *The high prices frightened the shoppers off.* □ *You frightened the deer off!*

frighten someone or something off See the previous entry.

fuel up to fill one's tank with fuel. □ *Let's stop here and fuel up.* □ *I need to fuel up at the next little town.*

fuss (around) with someone or something to keep bothering with someone or something; to fiddle, mess, or tinker with someone or something. □ *Don't fuss around with it. We'll have to get a new one.* □ *Don't fuss with your children. They will get along just fine without all that attention.*

G

gamble on someone or something **1.** to make a wager on something concerning someone or something. □ *I wouldn't gamble on it happening.* □ *Don't gamble on Betty. You'll be sorry.* **2.** to run a risk by choosing or depending on someone or something. □ *I wouldn't gamble on Ted's being able to come. I don't think he can.* □ *Don't gamble on Ted. I'm almost sure he won't come.*

gang up (on someone or something) [for a group] to make an assault on someone or something. □ *They ganged up on us!* □ *We can't do it alone. We will have to gang up.*

gather something in **1.** to collect something and bring it in; to harvest something. □ *We gathered the pumpkins in just before Halloween.* 🅃 *We gathered in the pumpkins just in time.* **2.** to fold or bunch cloth together when sewing or fitting clothing. □ *Try gathering it in on each side to make it seem smaller.* 🅃 *I will have to gather in this skirt.*

gather something up to collect something; to pick something up. □ *Let's gather our things up and go.* 🅃 *Please gather up your things.*

gaze out on something to look out on something, such as a lovely view, from inside a building. □ *She gazed out on the flowering trees and knew that life would go on.* □ *Henry sat for hours, gazing out on the lake.*

get about AND **get around** to move around freely. □ *I can hardly get about anymore.* □ *It's hard for Aunt Mattie to get around.*

get across (something) to manage to cross something. □ *We finally got across the river where it was very shallow.* □ *Where the water was low, it was easy to get across.*

get after someone 1. to bother or nag someone about doing something. □ *I will get after Fred about his behavior.* □ *Please don't get after me all the time.* 2. to begin to chase someone. □ *The other boys got after him and almost caught him.* □ *Henry got after Bill and almost caught up with him.*

get along with someone or something to manage with someone or something; to manage with only something. □ *I can't get along with only one assistant.* □ *Mary said she could not get along with the old computer.*

get along without someone or something to manage without someone or something. □ *I don't think I can get along without you.* □ *Laura can't get along without her dictionary.*

get around See *get about.*

get at someone or something 1. to manage to lay hands on someone or something; to get someone or something. □ *Just wait till I get at Charlie J. Wilson!* □ *I want to get at that chocolate cake.* 2. to manage to attack someone or something. □ *The dog was chained up, so it couldn't get at us.* □ *The army was unable to get at the munitions storage area.*

get at something to arrive at a point of discussion; to work toward stating a point of discussion or an accusation. □ *What are you trying to get at?* □ *We were trying to get at the basis of the problem.*

get away (from someone or something) 1. to go away from someone or something. □ *Please get away from me!* □ *Get away from that cake!* 2. to escape from someone, something, or some place. □ *Max did get away from the police but not away from Lefty.* □ *Mary couldn't get away from the telephone all morning.*

get back (at someone) to get revenge on someone. □ *I will get back at her someday, somehow.* □ *I'll get back, don't worry.*

get back on one's feet 1. to recover from an illness and leave one's sickbed. (Both literal and figurative.) □ *I will go back to work as soon as I get back on my feet.* □ *I want to get back on my feet as soon as possible.* 2. to recover from anything, especially financial problems. (Figurative.) □ *I can't afford to buy a car until I get a job and get back on my feet.* □ *I'll get back on my feet and start living normally.*

get back (some place) to manage to return to some place. ☐ *I can't wait till we get back home.* ☐ *When will we get back? Is it much farther?*

get back to someone or something to return to dealing with someone or something. ☐ *I will have to get back to you. I can't deal with this matter now.* ☐ *I want to get back to my work.*

get behind (in something) See *fall behind (in something).*

get behind (on something) See *fall behind (in something).*

get behind someone or something to back or support someone or something; to put oneself into a position to "push" or promote someone or something. ☐ *Let's all get behind Andrew for president!* ☐ *I want all of you to get behind the committee and support their efforts.*

get behind (with something) See *fall behind (in something).*

get by (on something) to survive with only something; to survive by relying on something. ☐ *I can't get by on that much money.* ☐ *That is a very small salary to live on. No one could get by.*

get by without someone or something to survive without someone or something. ☐ *I can't get by without you.* ☐ *We can probably get by without two cars.*

get down to something to reach the point of dealing with something; to begin to work on something seriously. (Especially with *business, brass tacks, work, cases.*) ☐ *Now, let's get down to business.* ☐ *It's time to get down to brass tacks.*

get off easy AND **get off lightly** to receive little or no punishment for doing something wrong. ☐ *She really got off easy, considering what she did.* ☐ *You got off lightly in court. She is a hard judge.*

get off lightly See the previous entry.

get off ((of) something) to stop discussing the topic that one is supposed to be discussing [and start discussing something else]; to stray from the topic at hand. (The *of* is colloquial.) ☐ *I wish you wouldn't get off the subject so much.* ☐ *This writer gets off his topic all the time.*

get on to get along; to thrive. ☐ *Well, how are you two getting on?* ☐ *We are getting on okay.*

get on with someone to get along with someone. ☐ *How does Colleen get on with Tracy?* ☐ *I hear that Mary gets on with Henry quite well.*

get on with something to continue doing something. ☐ *Let's get on with the game!* ☐ *We need to get on with our lives.*

get on without someone or something to survive and carry on without someone or something. ☐ *I think we can get on without bread for a day or two.* ☐ *Can you get on without your secretary for a while?*

get on(to) someone (about something) to remind someone about something. ☐ *I'll have to get onto Sarah about the deadline.* ☐ *I'll get on Gerald right away.*

get out [for something] to become publicly known. ☐ *We don't want the secret to get out.* ☐ *The word soon got out that he had a prison record.*

get out (of something) **1.** to escape from something. ☐ *I've got to get out of here.* ☐ *Max wanted to get out of jail, but didn't know how.* ☐ *He doubted that he would get out alive.* **2.** to get free of the responsibility of doing something. ☐ *Are you trying to get out of this job?* ☐ *You agreed to do it, and you can't get out of it!*

get over someone or something **1.** to move or climb over someone or something. ☐ *Fred was slumped ahead of me in the trench. I managed to get over him and moved on toward the big gun at the other end.* ☐ *I couldn't get over the huge rock in the path, so I went around it.* **2.** to recover from difficulties regarding someone or something. ☐ *I almost never got over the shock.* ☐ *Sharon finally got over Tom. He had been such a pest.*

get over something to recover from a disease. ☐ *It took a long time to get over the flu.* ☐ *I thought I would never get over the mumps.*

get someone down to make someone depressed or sad. ☐ *Now, now, don't let this matter get you down.* ☐ *All of this is beginning to get me down.*

get someone in(to something) to manage to get someone enrolled into something; to manage to get someone accepted into something. (*Someone* includes *oneself.*) □ *Somehow, we managed to get Jody into a fine private school.* □ *We got her in at last!* □ *Well, I managed to get myself into the class I wanted.*

get someone on(to) someone or something to assign someone to attend to someone or something. □ *Get someone onto the injured man in the hall right now.* □ *Get someone on the telephone switchboard at once!*

get someone up (for something) to get someone into peak condition for something; to prepare someone for something. □ *I hope we can get Walter up for the race.* □ *Sharon was not quite prepared for the race, and the trainer did everything possible to get her up.*

get something across (to someone) to make someone understand something. (Especially if the details are difficult to understand or if the person being explained to understands poorly.) □ *I hope I can get this across to you once and for all.* □ *Try as I may, I just can't get this theory across.* □ *She doesn't pay any attention, and I don't think I am getting it across.*

get something down (on paper) to write some information down on paper; to capture some information in writing. □ *This is important. Please get it down on paper.* □ *Please speak slowly. I want to get this down.*

get something off (to someone or something) to send something to someone or something. □ *I have to get a letter off to Aunt Mary.* 🅃 *Did you get off all your packages?* □ *I have to get this parcel off to the main office.*

get something out **1.** to remove or extricate something. □ *Please help me get this splinter out.* 🅃 *Would you help me get out this splinter?* □ *The tooth was gotten out without much difficulty.* **2.** to manage to get something said. □ *He tried to say it before he died, but he couldn't get it out.* □ *I had my mouth full and couldn't get the words out.*

get something out of someone to cause or force someone to give specific information. □ *We will get the truth out of her yet.* □ *The detective couldn't get anything out of the suspect.* □ *They got a confession out of him by beating him.*

get something out of someone or something to remove something from someone or something. □ *He probably will be okay when they get the tumor out of him.* □ *Please get that dog out of the living room.*

get something over (to someone) **1.** to deliver something to someone. □ *Get these papers over to Mr. Wilson's office right away.* □ *He needs it now, so try to get it over as soon as you can.* **2.** to make someone understand something; to succeed in explaining something to someone. □ *I finally got it over to him.* □ *He tries to understand what I'm talking about, but I can't get it over.*

get something up to organize, plan, and assemble something. □ *Let's get a team up and enter the tournament.* 🅃 *I think we can get up a team quite easily.* 🅃 *She got up a party on very short notice.*

get through (something) **1.** to complete something; to manage to finish something. □ *I can't wait till I get through school.* □ *I'll get through in five years instead of four.* **2.** to penetrate something. □ *We couldn't get through the hard concrete with a drill, so we will have to blast.* □ *The hardest drill bit we have couldn't get through.*

get through to someone or something **1.** to make contact, usually on the telephone, with someone or a group. □ *I could not get through to her until the end of the day.* □ *Harry couldn't get through to his office.* **2.** to manage to get one's message, feelings, desires, etc., understood by someone or a group. □ *I am really angry! Am I getting through to you?* □ *Nancy really wanted to get through to the bank, but they just seemed to ignore her.*

get through with someone or something **1.** to finish with someone or something. □ *I can't wait to get through with this lecture.* □ *Every student was anxious to get through with the professor.* **2.** to manage to transport someone or something through difficulties or barriers. □ *Customs was a mess, but we got through with all our baggage in only twenty minutes.* □ *I got through with my aged father without any trouble.*

get worked up (about someone or something) AND **get worked up (over someone or something)** to get excited or angry about someone or something. □ *I hate to get worked up about this kind of thing.* □ *Now, now, don't get worked up over Sam.* □ *There's no need to get worked up.*

get worked up (over someone or something) See the previous entry.

give in to cave in; to push in. □ *The rotting door gave in when we pushed, and we went inside.* □ *The wall gave in where I kicked it.*

give in (to someone or something) to give up to someone or something; to capitulate to someone or something. □ *Why do I always have to give in to you?* □ *I'm the one who always gives in.*

give out 1. to wear out and stop; to quit operating. □ *My old bicycle finally gave out.* □ *I think that your shoes are about ready to give out.* **2.** to be depleted. □ *The paper napkins gave out, and we had to use paper towels.* □ *The eggs gave out, and we had to eat pancakes for breakfast for the rest of the camping trip.*

give someone or something back (to someone or something) to return someone or something to someone or something. □ *Please give it back to me.* □ *You took Gloria away from me. You had better give her back.* □ *She gave the pencil back to the carpenter.*

give someone or something up (to someone) to hand someone or something over to someone; to relinquish claims on someone or something in favor of someone else. □ *We had to give the money we found up to the police.* 🆃 *We gave up the money to the police.* □ *Mary still wanted it, but she had to give it up.*

give something away (to someone) 1. to donate to, or bestow something upon, someone. □ *I gave the old clothing away to Tom.* 🆃 *I gave away my coat to Tom.* □ *Don't just give it away!* **2.** to tell a secret to someone. □ *Please don't give the surprise away to anyone.* 🆃 *Don't give away my secret.* □ *I had planned a surprise party but Donna gave it away.* **3.** to reveal the answer to a question, riddle, or problem to someone. □ *Don't give the answer away to them!* 🆃 *Don't give away the answer!* □ *Carla would have figured it out, but the audience gave it away.*

give something out 1. to distribute something; to pass something out. □ *The teacher gave the test papers out.* 🆃 *The teacher gave out the papers.* **2.** to make something known to the public. □ *When will you give the announcement out?* 🆃 *The president gave out the news that the hostages had been released.*

give something over (to someone or something) to hand something over to someone or something. □ *Please give the money over to Sherri, who handles the accounts.* □ *She is waiting at the front office. Just go there and give it over.*

give up to quit; to quit trying. □ *I give up! I won't press this further.* □ *Are you going to give up or keep fighting?*

give up (on someone or something) to give up trying to do something with someone or something, such as being friendly, giving advice, managing, etc. □ *I gave up on jogging. My knees went bad.* □ *Gloria tried to be friendly with Kelly, but finally gave up.*

glance back (at someone) **1.** to look quickly again at someone. □ *He glanced back at Mary, so he could remember her smile.* □ *She saw him briefly but never even glanced back.* **2.** to look quickly at someone who is behind you. □ *Dan glanced back at the man chasing him and ran on even faster.* □ *He glanced back and ran faster.*

glance down (at something) to look quickly downward at something. □ *Sherri glanced down at her watch and then pressed on the accelerator.* □ *She glanced down and hurried off.*

glance off ((of) someone or something) to bounce off someone or something. (The *of* is colloquial.) □ *The bullet glanced off the huge boulder.* □ *The baseball glanced off of Tom and left a bruise on his side where it had touched.* □ *The stone glanced off the window glass without breaking it.*

glance over someone or something to examine someone or something very quickly. □ *I only glanced over the papers. They look okay to me.* □ *The doctor glanced over the injured woman and called for an ambulance.*

glance through something to look quickly at the contents of something. □ *I glanced through the manuscript, and I don't think it is ready yet.* □ *Would you glance through this when you have a moment?*

gnaw (away) at someone to worry someone; to create constant anxiety in someone. □ *The thought of catching some horrible disease gnawed away at her.* □ *A lot of guilt over his behavior gnawed at him day and night.*

gnaw (away) at someone or something to chew at someone or something. ☐ *I hear a mouse gnawing away at the wall.* ☐ *The mosquitoes are gnawing at me something awful.*

gnaw on something to chew on something. (Usually said of an animal.) ☐ *The puppy has been gnawing on my slippers!* ☐ *This slipper has been gnawed on!*

go after someone or something **1.** to pursue someone or something. ☐ *The dogs went after the burglar.* ☐ *I went after the gang that took my wallet.* **2.** to charge or attack someone or some creature. ☐ *The bear went after the hunters and scared them to death.* ☐ *Then the bear went after the hunting dogs and killed two.*

go against someone or something to disfavor someone or something; to turn against someone or something; to oppose someone or something. ☐ *When did the trial go against us?* ☐ *The weather went against the cruise on the second day out.*

go along with someone or something **1.** to agree with someone or agree to something. ☐ *I will go along with you on that matter.* ☐ *I will go along with Sharon's decision, of course.* **2.** to consent on the choice of someone or something. ☐ *I go along with Jane. She would be a good treasurer.* ☐ *Sharon will probably go along with chocolate. Everyone likes chocolate!*

go around to serve a need; to serve all who have a need. ☐ *There's not enough coffee to go around.* ☐ *Will there be enough chocolates to go around?*

go around someone to avoid dealing with someone. (Figurative.) ☐ *I try to go around Steve. He can be very difficult.* ☐ *We will want to go around the boss. He will say no if asked.*

go away to leave. (Often a command.) ☐ *Go away and leave me alone.* ☐ *Please go away!*

go away with someone or something **1.** to leave in the company of someone or something. ☐ *I saw him go away with Margie.* ☐ *She went away with the others.* **2.** to take someone, some creature, or a group away with one. ☐ *He went away with the baby in his arms.* ☐ *He went away with the package.*

go back to return to the place of origin. □ *That's where I came from, and I'll never go back.* □ *I don't want to go back.*

go back on something to reverse one's position on something, especially one's word or a promise. □ *You went back on what you promised! Can't I trust you?* □ *I don't want to go back on my word, but there has been an emergency.* □ *I hope she doesn't go back on her word.*

go behind someone's back **1.** to move behind someone; to locate oneself at someone's back. □ *The mugger went behind my back and put a gun to my spine.* □ *Bob went behind my back and pushed me through the opening.* **2.** to do something that is kept a secret from someone. (Figurative.) □ *I hate to go behind her back, but she makes so much trouble about things like this.* □ *Please don't try to go behind my back again!*

go below to go beneath the main deck of a ship. (Nautical.) □ *I will have to go below and fiddle with the engine.* □ *The captain went below to escape the worst of the storm.*

go by (some place) See *drop by (some place).*

go down **1.** to sink below a normal or expected level or height. □ *The plane went down in flames.* □ *The ship went down with all hands aboard.* **2.** to descend to a lower measurement. □ *Her fever went down.* □ *The price of the stock went down yesterday.* **3.** to be swallowed. □ *The medicine went down without any trouble at all.* □ *The food simply would not go down. The puppy was going to starve.* **4.** to fall or drop down, as when struck or injured. □ *Sam went down when he was struck on the chin.* □ *The deer went down when it was hit with the arrow.*

go in for something to enjoy doing something; to be fond of something. □ *Laurie goes in for skating and skiing.* □ *We don't go in for that kind of thing.*

go in with someone (on something) to join efforts with someone on a project; to pool financial resources with someone to buy something. □ *I would be happy to go in with you on the charity ball. I'll find a hall.* □ *Yes, we can pool our money. I'll go in with you.* □ *Let's go in with Sally on a gift for Walter.*

go in((to) something) to enter something; to penetrate something. ☐ *The needle went into the vein smoothly and painlessly.* ☐ *It went in with no trouble.*

go off **1.** [for an explosive device] to explode. ☐ *The fireworks all went off as scheduled.* ☐ *The bomb went off and did a lot of damage.* **2.** [for a sound-creating device] to make its noise. ☐ *The alarm went off at six o'clock.* ☐ *The siren goes off at noon every day.* **3.** [for an event] to happen or take place. ☐ *The party went off as planned.* ☐ *Did your medical examination go off as well as you had hoped?*

go off (by oneself) to go into seclusion; to isolate oneself. ☐ *She went off by herself where no one could find her.* ☐ *I have to go off and think about this.*

go off with someone to go away with someone. ☐ *Tom just now went off with Maggie.* ☐ *I think that Maria went off with Fred somewhere.*

go on **1.** to continue. ☐ *Please go on.* ☐ *Can I go on now?* **2.** to hush up; to stop acting silly. (Always a command. No tenses.) ☐ *Go on! You're crazy!* ☐ *Oh, go on! You don't know what you are talking about.* **3.** to happen. ☐ *What went on here last night?* ☐ *The teacher asked what was going on.*

go on (and on) about someone or something to talk endlessly about someone or something. ☐ *She just went on and on about her new car.* ☐ *Albert went on about the book for a long time.*

go on at someone to rave at someone. ☐ *He must have gone on at her for over an hour—screaming and waving his arms.* ☐ *I wish you would stop going on at me.*

go (on) before (someone) **1.** to precede someone. ☐ *Please go on before me. I will follow.* ☐ *She went on before.* **2.** to die before someone. (Euphemism.) ☐ *Uncle Herman went on before Aunt Margaret by a few years.* ☐ *He went before her, although we had all thought it would be the other way around.*

go out **1.** to leave one's house. ☐ *Call me later. I'm going out now.* ☐ *Sally told her father that she was going out.* **2.** to become extinguished. □ *The fire finally went out.* □ *The lights went out and left us in the dark.*

go out for someone or something to leave in order to bring back someone or something. □ *Albert just went out for a newspaper.* □ *Fran went out for Bob, who was on the back porch, smoking a cigarette.*

go out (for something) to try out for a sports team. □ *Walter went out for football in his junior year.* □ *Did you ever go out for any sports?*

go out with someone to go on a date with someone; to date someone on a regular basis. □ *Will you go out with me next Saturday?* □ *Do you want to go out with Alice and Ted tomorrow night?* □ *Mary's parents are upset because she's going out with someone they don't approve of.*

go through to be approved; to pass examination; to be ratified. □ *I hope the amendment goes through.* □ *The proposal failed to go through.*

go through someone to work through someone; to use someone as an intermediary. □ *I can't give you the permission you seek. You will have to go through our manager.* □ *I have to go through the treasurer for all expenditures.*

go through something **1.** to search through something. □ *She went through his pants pockets, looking for his wallet.* □ *He spent quite a while going through his desk, looking for the papers.* **2.** to use up all of something rapidly. □ *We have gone through all the aspirin again!* □ *How can you go through your allowance so fast?* **3.** [for something] to pass through an opening. □ *The piano wouldn't go through the door.* □ *Do you think that such a big truck can go through the tunnel under the river?* **4.** to pass through various stages or processes. □ *The pickles went through a number of processes before they were packed.* □ *Johnny is going through a phase where he wants everything his way.* **5.** to work through something, such as an explanation or story. □ *I went through my story again, carefully and in great detail.* □ *I would like to go through it again, so I can be sure to understand it.* **6.** to experience or endure something. □ *You can't believe what I've gone through.* □ *Mary has gone through a lot lately.* **7.** to rehearse something; to practice something for performance. □ *They went through the second act a number of times.* □ *We need to go through the whole play a few more times.*

go under **1.** to sink beneath the surface of the water. □ *After capsizing, the ship went under very slowly.* □ *I was afraid that our canoe would go under in the rapidly moving water.* **2.** [for something] to fail. □ *The company went under exactly one year after it opened.* □ *We tried to keep it from going under.* **3.** to become unconscious from anesthesia. □ *After a few minutes, she went under and the surgeon began to work.* □ *Tom went under and the operation began.*

go without (someone) to manage without a particular type of person. □ *I can't go without a doctor much longer.* □ *I need a doctor now. I simply can't go without.*

go without (something) to manage without something. □ *We can go without food for only so long.* □ *I simply can't go without.*

grab on(to someone or something) to grasp someone or something; to hold onto someone or something. □ *Here, grab onto this rope!* □ *Grab on and hold tight.*

grade someone or something down to lower the ranking, rating, or score on someone or something. □ *I had to grade you down because your paper was late.* 🅃 *I graded down the paper because it was late.*

graduate from something to earn and receive a degree from an educational institution. □ *I graduated from a large midwestern university.* □ *Bill intends to graduate from the institute in the spring.*

graze on something **1.** [for animals] to browse or forage in a particular location. □ *The cattle are grazing on the neighbor's land.* □ *I wish they wouldn't graze on other people's land.* **2.** [for animals] to browse or forage, eating something in particular. □ *The deer are grazing on my carrots!* □ *The cows were grazing on the meadow grasses for weeks.*

grind someone down to wear someone down by constant requests; to wear someone down by constant nagging. □ *If you think you can grind me down by bothering me all the time, you are wrong.* 🅃 *The constant nagging ground down the employees at last.*

grind something away to remove something by grinding. ☐ *Grind the bumps away and make a smooth wall.* 🅃 *Please grind away the bumps.*

grind something down to make something smooth or even by grinding. ☐ *Grind this down to make it smooth.* 🅃 *Please grind down this rough spot.*

grind something out **1.** to produce something by grinding. ☐ *Working hard, he ground the powder out, a cup at a time.* 🅃 *He ground out the powder, a cup at a time.* **2.** to produce something in a mechanical or perfunctory manner. ☐ *The factory just keeps grinding these toys out, day after day.* 🅃 *The factory grinds out toys all day long.*

grind something up to pulverize or crush something by crushing, rubbing, or abrasion. ☐ *Please grind the fennel seeds up.* 🅃 *Grind up the fennel seeds and sprinkle them on the top.*

H

hack something down to chop something down. □ *Who hacked this cherry tree down?* 🅃 *Who hacked down this cherry tree?*

hack something up **1.** to chop something up into pieces. □ *Hack all this old furniture up, and we'll burn it in the fireplace.* 🅃 *Hack up this stuff, and we'll burn it.* **2.** to damage or mangle something. □ *Who hacked my windowsill up?* 🅃 *Who hacked up my windowsill?*

ham something up to perform in something in an exaggerated and exhibitionist manner. □ *Stop hamming it up! This is a serious drama.* 🅃 *She really hammed up her part in the play.*

hammer (away) at someone to interrogate someone; to ask questions endlessly of someone. (Figurative.) □ *The cops kept hammering away at Max until he told them everything they wanted to know.* □ *They hammered at Max for hours.*

hammer something down to pound something down, even with the surrounding area. □ *Hammer all the nails down so that none of them will catch on someone's shoe.* 🅃 *Hammer down all these nails!*

hammer something in(to someone) AND **pound something in(to someone)** to teach something to someone intensively, as if one were driving the information in by force. (Figurative.) □ *Her parents had hammered good manners into her head since she was a child.* 🅃 *They hammered in good manners every day.* □ *They pounded proper behavior into the children.* □ *The teacher held a review session on the material and really pounded the stuff in.*

hammer something in(to something) AND **pound something in(to something)** to drive something into something as with a hammer.

☐ *Todd hammered the spike into the beam.* 🅃 *He hammered in the spike.* ☐ *He hammered it in with two hard blows.* ☐ *The carpenter pounded the nail into the board.* 🅃 *The carpenter pounded in the nail.*

hand something down [for a court] to issue a ruling. (Legal.) ☐ *The appeals court handed a negative opinion down.* 🅃 *The court has not yet handed down a ruling.*

hand something down from someone to someone to pass something down through many generations. ☐ *We can make it a tradition to hand this down from generation to generation.* 🅃 *I will hand down this watch from generation to generation.* ☐ *It is a family tradition to hand this book down from mother to daughter.*

hand something down (to someone) to pass on something to a younger person, often a younger relative. ☐ *I will hand this down to my grandson also.* 🅃 *I will hand down this dress to my niece.* ☐ *When I am finished with this, I will hand it down.*

hand something off (to someone) to give something directly to someone else. ☐ *Roger handed the ball off to Jeff.* 🅃 *He handed off the contract.* ☐ *Tim handed it off.*

hand something out (to someone) to pass something, usually papers, out to people. ☐ *The teacher handed the tests out to the students.* 🅃 *Please hand out these papers.* ☐ *Hand them out, if you would.*

hang around (some place) to loiter some place; to be in a place or in an area, doing nothing in particular. ☐ *Why are you hanging around my office?* ☐ *It's comfortable here. I think I'll hang around here for a while.* ☐ *Stop hanging around and get a job.*

hang around with someone to spend time doing nothing in particular with someone. ☐ *You spend most of your day hanging around with your friends.* ☐ *I like to hang around with people I know.*

hang back (from someone or something) to lag back behind someone or something; to stay back from someone or something, perhaps in avoidance. ☐ *Why are you hanging back from the rest of the group?* ☐ *Come on! Don't hang back!*

hang on 1. to wait awhile. ☐ *Hang on a minute. I need to talk to you.* ☐ *Hang on. Let me catch up with you.* ☐ *Please hang on. I'll call her to the phone.* 2. to survive for awhile. (Figurative.) ☐ *I think we can hang on without electricity for a little while longer.* ☐ *We can't hang on much longer.* 3. to linger or persist. ☐ *This cold has been hanging on for a month.* ☐ *This is the kind of flu that hangs on for weeks.*

hang on (to someone or something) AND **hold on (to someone or something)** 1. to grasp someone or something. ☐ *She hung on to her husband to keep warm.* ☐ *She sat there and hung on, trying to keep warm.* ☐ *Jane held on to Jeff to keep from slipping on the ice.* 2. to keep someone or something. ☐ *Please hang on to Tom. I need to talk to him.* ☐ *If you have Ted there, hang on. I need to talk to him.* ☐ *Hold on to your money. You will need it later.*

hang out (with someone or something) to associate with someone or a group on a regular basis. ☐ *She hangs out with Alice too much.* ☐ *I wish you would stop hanging out with that crowd of boys.* ☐ *Kids hang out too much these days.*

hang together 1. [for something or a group of people] to hold together; to remain intact. ☐ *I hope our bridge group hangs together until we are old and gray.* ☐ *I don't think that this car will hang together for another minute.* 2. [for a story] to flow from element to element and make sense. ☐ *This story simply does not hang together.* ☐ *Your novel hangs together quite nicely.* 3. [for people] to spend time together. ☐ *We hung together for a few hours and then went our separate ways.* ☐ *The boys hung together throughout the evening.*

hang up 1. [for a machine or a computer] to grind to a halt; to stop because of some internal complication. ☐ *Our computer hung up right in the middle of the job.* ☐ *I was afraid that my computer would hang up permanently.* 2. to replace the telephone receiver after a call. ☐ *I said good-bye and hung up.* ☐ *Please hang up and place your call again.*

happen (up)on someone or something to find someone or something, as if by accident. ☐ *I just happened upon a strange little man in the street who offered to sell me a watch.* ☐ *Andrew happened on a book that interested him, so he bought it.*

harp on someone or something to criticize someone or something constantly. □ *I wish you would quit harping on Jeff all the time. He couldn't be all that bad.* □ *Stop harping on my mistakes and work on your own.*

hash something over (with someone) to discuss something with someone. □ *I need to hash this matter over with you.* 🅃 *I've hashed over this business enough.* □ *We need to get together with Rachel and hash this over.*

haul someone in [for an officer of the law] to take someone to the police station. □ *The officer hauled the boys in and booked every one of them.* 🅃 *He hauled in the young boys.*

have it out (with someone) to settle something with someone by fighting or arguing. □ *Finally, John had it out with Carl, and now they are speaking to one another again.* □ *Elaine had been at odds with Sam for a long time. She finally decided to have it out.*

have something out to have something, such as a tooth, stone, tumor, removed surgically. □ *You are going to have to have that tumor out.* □ *I don't want to have my tooth out!*

head back (some place) to start moving back to some place. □ *I walked to the end of the street and then headed back home.* □ *This is far enough. Let's head back.*

head someone or something off to intercept and divert someone or something. □ *I think I can head her off before she reaches the police station.* 🅃 *I hope we can head off trouble.* □ *We can head it off. Have no fear.*

head something up **1.** to get something pointed in the right direction. (Especially a herd of cattle or a group of covered wagons.) □ *Head those wagons up—we're moving out.* 🅃 *Head up the wagons!* **2.** to be in charge of something; to be the leader of some organization. □ *I was asked to head the new committee up for the first year.* 🅃 *Will you head up the committee for me?*

heal over [for the surface of a wound] to heal. □ *The wound healed over very quickly, and there was very little scarring.* □ *I hope it will heal over without having to be stitched.*

heal up [for an injury] to heal. □ *The cut healed up in no time at all.*

heap something up to make something into a pile. □ *He heaped the mashed potatoes up on my plate, because he thought I wanted lots.* 🅃 *Heap up the leaves in the corner of the yard.*

heap something (up)on someone or something **1.** to pile something up on someone or something. (*Upon* is formal and less commonly used than *on.*) □ *Please don't heap so much trouble upon me!* □ *Wally heaped leaves on the flower bed.* **2.** to give someone too much of something, such as homework, praise, criticism, etc. (Figurative. *Upon* is formal and less commonly used than *on.*) □ *Don't heap too much praise on her. She will get conceited.* □ *The manager heaped criticism on the workers.*

hear someone out **1.** to hear all of what someone has to say. □ *Please hear me out. I have more to say.* □ *Hear him out. Don't jump to conclusions.* **2.** to hear someone's side of the story. □ *Let him talk! Hear him out! Listen to his side!* 🅃 *We have to hear out everyone in this matter.*

heat up **1.** to get warmer or hot. □ *It really heats up in the afternoon around here.* □ *How soon will dinner be heated up?* **2.** to grow more animated or combative. □ *The debate began to heat up near the end.* □ *Their argument was heating up, and I was afraid there would be fighting.*

help out some place to help [with the chores] in a particular place. □ *Would you be able to help out in the kitchen?* □ *Sally is downtown, helping out at the shop.*

help out (with something) to help with a particular chore. □ *Would you please help out with the dishes?* □ *I have to help out at home on the weekends.* □ *I'll come over and help out before the party.*

help someone back (to something) to help someone return to something or some place. □ *The ushers helped him back to his seat.* □ *When she returned, I helped her back.*

help someone off with something to help someone take off an article of clothing. □ *Would you please help me off with my coat?*

☐ *We helped the children off with their boots and put their coats in the hall.*

help (someone) out to help someone do something; to help someone with a problem. ☐ *I am trying to raise this window. Can you help me out?* 🅃 *I'm always happy to help out a friend.* ☐ *This calculus assignment is impossible. Can you help out?*

hide out (from someone or something) to hide oneself so that one cannot be found by someone or something. ☐ *Max was hiding out from the police in Detroit.* ☐ *Lefty is hiding out too.*

hide someone or something away (some place) to conceal someone or something somewhere. (*Someone* includes *oneself.*) ☐ *Please hide Randy away where no one can find him.* ☐ *Rachel hid the cake away, hoping to save it for dessert.* 🅃 *Mary hid away the candy so the kids wouldn't eat it all.* ☐ *He hid himself away in his study until Mrs. Bracknell had gone.*

hike something up to raise something, such as prices, interest rates, a skirt, pants legs, etc. ☐ *The grocery store is always hiking prices up.* 🅃 *She hiked up her skirt so she could wade across the creek.*

hinge (up)on someone or something to depend on someone or something; to depend on what someone or something does. (*Upon* is formal and less commonly used than *on.*) ☐ *The success of the project hinges upon you and how well you do your job.* ☐ *It all hinges on the weather.*

hire someone away (from someone or something) [for one] to get someone to quit working for someone or something and begin working for one. ☐ *We hired Elaine away from her previous employer, and now she wants to go back.* 🅃 *The new bank hired away all the tellers from the old bank.* ☐ *They tried to hire them all away.*

hit back (at someone or something) to strike someone or something back. ☐ *Tom hit Fred, and Fred hit back at Tom.* ☐ *I have to hit back when someone hits me.*

hit it off (with someone) to start a good and friendly relationship with someone from the first meeting. ☐ *I really hit it off with my* *new boss.* ☐ *From the moment I met her, we really hit it off.* ☐ *They hit it off with each other from the start.*

hit someone (up) for something to ask someone for the loan of money or for some other favor. (Colloquial.) ☐ *The tramp hit me up for a dollar.* ☐ *My brother hit me for a couple of hundred bucks.*

hit something off to begin something; to launch an event. ☐ *The mayor hit the fair off by giving a brief address.* 🅃 *She hit off the fair with a speech.*

hit (up)on someone or something **1.** to discover someone or something. ☐ *I think I have hit upon something. There is a lever you have to press in order to open this cabinet.* ☐ *I hit on Tom in an amateur play production. I offered him a job in my nightclub immediately.* **2.** to strike or pound on someone or something. (Colloquial. *Upon* is formal and less commonly used than *on*.) ☐ *Jeff hit upon the mugger over and over.* ☐ *I hit on the radio until it started working again.*

hold back (on something) to withhold something; to give only a limited amount. ☐ *Hold back on the gravy. I'm on a diet.* ☐ *That's enough. Hold back. Save some for the others.*

hold forth (on someone or something) to speak at great length about someone or something. ☐ *Sadie held forth on the virtues of home cooking.* ☐ *Sharon is holding forth, and everyone is paying close attention.*

hold off ((from) doing something) to avoid doing something; to postpone doing something. ☐ *Can you hold off from buying a new car for another few months?* ☐ *I will hold off firing him until next week.*

hold on **1.** to wait. ☐ *Hold on a minute! Let me catch up!* ☐ *Hold on till I get there.* ☐ *Hold on. I'll call her to the phone.* **2.** to be patient. ☐ *Just hold on. Everything will work out in good time.* ☐ *If you will just hold on, everything will probably be all right.*

hold on (to someone or something) See *hang on (to someone or something).*

hold out to survive; to last. □ *I don't know how long we can hold out.* □ *They can probably hold out for another day or two.*

hold out (against someone or something) to continue one's defense against someone or something. □ *We can hold out against them only a little while longer.* □ *Dave can hold out forever.*

hold out (for someone or something) to strive to wait for someone or something. □ *I will hold out for someone who can do the job better than your last suggestion.* □ *I want to hold out for a better offer.*

hold someone or something down **1.** to keep someone, something, or some creature down. □ *The heavy beam held him down, and he could not rise.* □ *The hunter held the animal down until the porters arrived.* □ *Hold him down until I get out my handcuffs.* **2.** to prevent someone or something from advancing. □ *I had a disability that held me down in life.* □ *The company had a lot of debt that held it down, even in prosperous times.*

hold someone or something off **1.** to make someone or something wait. □ *I know a lot of people are waiting to see me. Hold them off for a while longer.* 🅃 *See what you can do to hold off the reporters.* **2.** AND **keep someone or something off** to stave someone or something off. □ *Tom was trying to rob us, but we managed to hold him off.* 🅃 *We held off the attackers.* 🅃 *I couldn't keep off the reporters any longer.*

hold someone or something out (of something) **1.** to keep someone or something out of something. □ *We held the kids out of the party room as long as we could.* □ *We couldn't hold them out any longer.* **2.** to set someone or something aside from the rest; to prevent someone or a group from participating. □ *Her parents held her out of sports because of her health.* □ *The school board held the team out of competition as punishment for something.* 🅃 *They held out every player.*

hold someone or something over to keep a performer or performance for more performances. (Because the performance is a success.) □ *The manager held Julie over for a week because she was so well received.* □ *They held our act over too.*

hold someone or something up **1.** to keep someone or something upright. □ *Johnny is falling asleep. Please hold him up until I pre-*

pare the bed for him. ☐ *Hold the window up while I prop it open.* **2.** to rob someone or a group. ☐ *Some punk tried to hold me up.* 🅃 *The mild-looking man held up the bank and shot a teller.* **3.** to delay someone or something. ☐ *Driving the kids to school held me up.* ☐ *We were stuck in traffic, and I couldn't see what was holding us up.* 🅃 *An accident on Main Street held up traffic for thirty minutes.*

hold something out (to someone) to offer something to someone. ☐ *I held an offer of immunity out to her.* 🅃 *I held out an offer of immunity from prosecution to her, but she would not cooperate.* 🅃 *The court held out an offer of leniency, but the defendant turned it down.*

hold up (for someone or something) to wait; to stop and wait for someone. ☐ *Hold up for Wallace. He's running hard to catch up to us.* ☐ *Hold up a minute.*

hold up (on someone or something) to delay or postpone further action on someone or something. ☐ *I know you are getting ready to choose someone, but hold up on Tom. There may be someone better.* ☐ *Hold up on the project, would you?* ☐ *We need to hold up for a while longer.*

hollow something out to make the inside of something hollow. ☐ *Martha hollowed the book out and put her money inside.* 🅃 *She hollowed out a book.*

home in (on someone or something) to aim directly at someone or something. ☐ *She came into the room and homed in on the chocolate cake.* ☐ *She saw the cake and homed in.*

home on(to something) to aim directly at something; to fix some type of receiver on a signal source. ☐ *The navigator homed onto the radio beam from the airport.* ☐ *The navigator located the beam and homed on.*

hook in(to something) to connect into something. ☐ *We will hook into the water main tomorrow morning.* ☐ *We dug the pipes up and hooked in.*

hook someone or something up (to someone or something) AND **hook someone or something up (with someone or something)**

to attach someone or something to someone or something. (*Someone* includes *oneself*.) □ *The nurse hooked the patient up to the oxygen tubes.* 🅃 *They hooked up the patient with the tubes.* □ *Let's hook the dog up to the post.* □ *We hooked the dog up.* □ *She hooked herself up to the machine and began her biofeedback session.*

hook someone or something up (with someone or something) See the previous entry.

hook something into something to connect something to something. □ *I want to hook another communication line into the system.* □ *Is it possible to hook my computer into your network?*

hook something up to set something up and get it working. (The object is to be connected to electricity, gas, water, telephone lines, etc.) □ *Will it take long to hook the telephone up?* 🅃 *As soon as they hook up the telephone, I can call my friends.*

hop in(to something) to jump into something; to get into something. □ *Hop into your car and drive over to my house.* □ *I hopped in and drove off.*

huddle (up) (together) to bunch up together. □ *The children huddled up together to keep warm.* □ *They huddled up to keep warm.* □ *The newborn rabbits huddled together and squirmed hungrily.*

hunch up to squeeze or pull the parts of one's body together. □ *He hunched up in a corner to keep warm.* □ *Why is that child hunched up in the corner?*

hunt someone or something down **1.** to chase and catch someone or something. □ *I don't know where Amy is, but I'll hunt her down. I'll find her.* 🅃 *I will hunt down the villain.* **2.** to locate someone or something. □ *I don't have a big enough gasket. I'll have to hunt one down.* 🅃 *I have to hunt down a good dentist.*

hunt someone or something out to find someone or something even if concealed. □ *We will hunt them all out and find every last one of those guys.* 🅃 *We will hunt out all of them.* 🅃 *They hunted out the murderer.*

hunt someone or something up to seek someone or something. □ *I don't know where Jane is. I'll hunt her up for you, though.* 🅃 *I'll help you hunt up Jane.* 🅃 *Will someone please hunt up a screwdriver?*

hunt through something to search through the contents of something; to search among things. □ *Joel hunted through his wallet for a dollar bill.* □ *I will have to hunt through my drawers for a pair of socks that match.*

hurl someone or something down to throw or push someone or something downward to the ground. (*Someone* includes *oneself*.) □ *Roger hurled the football down and it bounced away wildly.* Ⓣ *He hurled down the football in anger.* □ *The angry player hurled the ball down.* □ *Fred hurled himself down and wept at the feet of the queen.*

hurry away AND **hurry off** to leave in a hurry. □ *I have to hurry away. Excuse me, please. It's an emergency.* □ *Don't hurry off. I need to talk to you.*

hurry back (to someone or something) to return to someone or something immediately or as fast as possible. □ *Oh, please hurry back to me as soon as you can.* □ *Hurry back!*

hurry off See *hurry away.*

hurry on See *hurry up.*

hurry someone or something in(to something) to make someone or something go into something fast. □ *She hurried the chickens into the coop and closed the door on them for the night.* □ *It was beginning to rain, so Jerry hurried the children in.* □ *Please don't hurry me into a decision.*

hurry someone or something up to make someone or something go or work faster. □ *Please hurry them all up. We are expecting them very soon.* □ *See if you can hurry this project up a little.*

hurry up AND **hurry on** to move faster. □ *Hurry up! You're going to be late.* □ *Please hurry on. We have a lot to do today.*

hush someone or something up to make someone or something be quiet. □ *Please hush the children up. I have a telephone call.* □ *Can you hush that radio up, please?*

hush something up to keep something from public knowledge. □ *The company moved quickly to hush the bad news up.* Ⓣ *They wanted to hush up the bad financial report.*

hush up to be quiet; to get quiet; to stop talking. □ *You talk too much. Hush up!* □ *I want you to hush up and sit down!*

I

ice over [for water] to freeze and develop a covering of ice. ☐ *I can't wait for the river to ice over so we can do some ice fishing.*

ice something down to cool something with ice. ☐ *They are icing the champagne down now.* [T] *They are icing down the champagne now.*

ice up to become icy. ☐ *Are the roads icing up?*

identify someone or something with someone or something to associate people and things, in any combination. (*Someone* includes *oneself.*) ☐ *I tend to identify Wally with big cars.* ☐ *We usually identify green with grass.* ☐ *We tend to identify big cars with greedy people.* ☐ *We always identify Tom with the other kids from Toledo.*

idle something away to waste one's time in idleness; to waste a period of time, such as an afternoon, evening, or one's life. ☐ *She idled the afternoon away and then went to a party.* [T] *Don't idle away the afternoon.*

immunize someone against something to vaccinate someone against some disease; to do a medical procedure that causes a resistance or immunity to a disease to develop in a person. ☐ *They wanted to immunize all the children against the measles.* ☐ *Have you been immunized against polio?*

implant something in(to) someone or something to embed something into someone or something. ☐ *The surgeon implanted a pacemaker into Fred.* ☐ *They implanted the device in Fred's chest.*

implicate someone in something to say that someone is involved in something. (*Someone* includes *oneself.*) ☐ *Dan implicated Ann in the crime.* ☐ *Ted refused to implicate himself in the affair.*

impose something (up)on someone to force something on someone. (*Upon* is formal and less commonly used than *on.*) ☐ *Don't try to impose your ideas upon me!* ☐ *The colonists tried to impose their values on the indigenous peoples.*

impose (up)on someone to make a bothersome request of someone. (*Upon* is formal and less commonly used than *on.*) ☐ *I don't mean to impose upon you, but could you put me up for the night?* ☐ *Don't worry, I won't let you impose on me.*

impress someone with someone or something to awe someone with someone or something. ☐ *Are you trying to impress me with your wisdom?* ☐ *She impressed him with her friend, who was very tall.*

impress something (up)on someone to make someone fully aware of something. (*Upon* is formal and less commonly used than *on.*) ☐ *You must impress these facts upon everyone you meet.* ☐ *She impressed its importance on me.*

imprint something into something See *imprint something on(to) something.*

imprint something on(to) something **1.** to print something onto something. ☐ *We imprinted your name onto your stationery and your business cards.* ☐ *Please imprint my initials on this watch.* **2.** AND **imprint something into something** to record something firmly in the memory of someone. ☐ *The severe accident imprinted a sense of fear onto Lucy's mind.* ☐ *Imprint the numbers into your brain and never forget them!* **3.** AND **imprint something into something** to make a permanent record of something in an animal's brain. (As with newly hatched fowl, which imprint the image of the first moving creature into their brains.) ☐ *The sight of its mother imprinted itself on the little gosling's brain.* ☐ *Nature imprints this information into the bird's memory.*

imprison someone in something to lock someone up in something. ☐ *The authorities imprisoned him in a separate cell.* ☐ *Bob imprisoned Timmy in the closet for an hour.*

improve (up)on something to make something better. (*Upon* is formal and less commonly used than *on*.) ☐ *Do you really think you can improve upon this song?* ☐ *No one can improve on my favorite melody.*

improvise on something [for a musician] to create a new piece of music on an existing musical theme. ☐ *For an encore, the organist improvised on "Mary Had a Little Lamb."* ☐ *She chose to improvise on an old folk theme.*

incarcerate someone in something to imprison someone in something. ☐ *The sheriff incarcerated Lefty in the town jail.* ☐ *He had wanted to incarcerate Max in the jail too.*

incline toward someone or something **1.** to lean or slant toward someone or something. ☐ *The piece of scenery inclined toward Roger very slowly and stopped its fall just in time.* ☐ *The tree inclined toward the flow of the wind.* **2.** to favor or "lean" toward choosing someone or something. ☐ *I don't know which to choose. I incline toward Terri but I also favor Amy.* ☐ *I'm inclining toward chocolate.*

include someone in (something) to invite someone to participate in something. (*Someone* includes *oneself*.) ☐ *Let's include Terri in the planning session.* ☐ *I will include her in.* ☐ *Without asking, Henry included himself in the group going on a picnic.*

incorporate someone or something in(to) something to build someone or something into something; to combine someone or something into something. (*Someone* includes *oneself*.) ☐ *We want to incorporate you into our sales force very soon.* ☐ *The prince had incorporated himself into the main governing body.*

inoculate someone against something to immunize someone against a disease. ☐ *We need to inoculate all the children against whooping cough.* ☐ *Have you been inoculated against measles?*

inscribe something on(to) something to write or engrave certain information on something. (Emphasis is on the message that is inscribed.) ☐ *The jeweler inscribed Amy's good wishes onto the watch.* ☐ *I inscribed my name on my tools.*

inscribe something with something to engrave something with a message. ☐ *Could you please inscribe this trophy with the infor-*

mation on this sheet of paper? □ *I inscribed the bracelet with her name.*

insist (up)on something to demand something. (*Upon* is formal and less commonly used than *on*.) □ *I want you here now! We all insist upon it!* □ *I insist on it too.*

instill something in(to) something to add something to a situation. □ *The presence of the mayor instilled a legitimacy into the proceedings.* □ *Sharon sought to instill a little levity in the otherwise dull meeting.*

intervene in something to get involved in something. □ *I will have to intervene in this matter. It's getting out of hand.* □ *I want to intervene in this before it gets out of hand.*

introduce someone to someone to make someone acquainted with someone else. (*Someone* includes *oneself*.) □ *I would like to introduce you to my cousin, Rudolph.* □ *Allow me to introduce myself to you.*

intrude (up)on someone or something to encroach on someone or something or matters that concern only someone or something else. (*Upon* is formal and less commonly used than *on*.) □ *I didn't mean to intrude upon you.* □ *Please don't intrude on our meeting. Please wait outside.*

invest in someone or something to put resources into someone or something in hopes of increasing the value of the person or thing. (The emphasis is on the act of investing.) □ *We invested in Tom, and we have every right to expect a lot from him.* □ *She invested in junk bonds heavily.*

invite someone in(to some place) to bid or request someone to enter a place. (*Someone* includes *oneself*.) □ *Don't leave Dan out there in the rain. Invite him into the house!* T *Oh, do invite in the visitors!* □ *Yes, invite them in.* □ *To my horror, he invited himself in.*

invite someone out to ask someone out on a date. □ *I would love to invite you out sometime. If I did, would you go?* □ *Have you been invited out this week?*

invite someone over (for something) to bid or request someone to come to one's house for something, such as a meal, party, chat, cards, etc. □ *Let's invite Tony and Nick over for dinner.* 🅃 *Let's invite over some new people.* □ *I will invite Amy over for a talk.*

iron something out **1.** to use a flatiron to make cloth flat or smooth. □ *I will iron the drapes out, so they will stay flat.* 🅃 *I ironed out the drapes.* **2.** to ease a problem; to smooth out a problem. (Figurative. Here *problem* is synonymous with *wrinkle.*) □ *It's only a little problem. I can iron it out very quickly.* 🅃 *We will iron out all these little matters first.*

J

jazz something up to make something more exciting or livelier. ☐ *Let's jazz this musical number up a bit.* 🅃 *We will jazz up the number.*

jerk something away (from someone or something) to snatch something away or pull something back from someone or something. ☐ *I jerked the bone away from the dog.* ☐ *Kelly jerked the ant poison away from the child.* ☐ *Mary jerked her hand away from the fire.*

jerk something off ((of) someone or something) to snatch something off someone or something. (The *of* is colloquial.) ☐ *Alice jerked the top off the box and poured out the contents.* 🅃 *She jerked off the box top.* ☐ *She jerked the socks off of Jimmy and put clean ones on him.*

jerk something out (of someone or something) to pull something out of someone or something, quickly. ☐ *The doctor jerked the arrow out of Bill's leg.* 🅃 *He jerked out the arrow.* ☐ *Ted jerked the sword out of Max and wiped it off.*

jerk something up **1.** to pull something up quickly. ☐ *He jerked his belt up tight.* 🅃 *He jerked up the zipper to his jacket.* **2.** to lift up something, such as ears, quickly. ☐ *The dog jerked its ears up.* 🅃 *The dog jerked up its ears when it heard the floor creak.* ☐ *The soldier jerked his binoculars up to try to see the sniper.*

jockey someone or something into position to manage to get someone or something into a chosen position. (*Someone* includes *oneself.*) ☐ *The rider jockeyed his horse into position.* ☐ *Try to jockey your bicycle into position so you can pass the other riders.*

☐ *With much effort, she jockeyed herself into position to peek over the transom.*

join up to become part of some organization. ☐ *The club has opened its membership rolls again. Are you going to join up?* ☐ *I can't afford to join up.*

join ((up) with someone or something) to bring oneself into association with someone or something. ☐ *I decided to join up with the other group.* ☐ *Our group joined with another similar group.*

jolt someone out of something to startle someone out of inertness. (*Someone* includes *oneself.*) ☐ *The cold water thrown in her face was what it took to jolt Mary out of her deep sleep.* ☐ *At the sound of the telephone, he jolted himself out of his stupor.*

jot something down to make a note of something. ☐ *This is important. Please jot this down.* 🅃 *Jot down this note, please.*

jump in((to) something) to leap into something, such as water, a bed, a problem, etc. ☐ *She was so cold she just jumped into bed and pulled up the covers.* ☐ *I jumped in and had a refreshing swim.*

jump off ((of) something) to leap off something. (The *of* is colloquial.) ☐ *Rachel lost her balance and jumped off the diving board instead of diving.* ☐ *Better to jump off than to fall off.*

jump off the deep end (over someone or something) to get deeply involved with someone or something. (Often refers to romantic involvement.) ☐ *Jim is about to jump off the deep end over Jane.* ☐ *Jane is great, but there is no need to jump off the deep end.*

jump out of something to leap from something. ☐ *A mouse jumped out of the cereal box.* ☐ *I jumped out of bed and ran to answer the telephone.*

jump over something to leap over or across something. ☐ *The fellow named Jack jumped over a candle placed on the floor.* ☐ *Puddles are to be jumped over, not waded through.*

jump to conclusions to move too quickly to a conclusion; to form a conclusion from too little evidence. (Idiomatic.) □ *Please don't jump to any conclusions because of what you have seen.* □ *There is no need to jump to conclusions!*

jump up (on someone or something) to leap upward onto someone or something. □ *A spider jumped up on me and terrified me totally.* □ *The cat jumped up on the sofa.*

jut out (from something) to stick outward from something. □ *The flagpole juts out from the side of the building.* □ *His nose juts out sharply.*

jut out (into something) to stick outward into an area. □ *The back end of the truck jutted out into the street.* □ *The back end jutted out.*

jut out (over someone or something) to stick out over someone or something. □ *The roof of the house jutted out over the patio.* □ *I'm glad the roof jutted out and kept us dry during the brief storm.*

K

keel over to fall over; to capsize. ☐ *The boat keeled over.* ☐ *Tom was so surprised he nearly keeled over.*

keep after someone (about something) to nag someone about something. ☐ *I'll have to keep after him about getting the roof repaired.* ☐ *He'll get it done if you keep after him.*

keep at someone (about something) to harass someone about something. ☐ *I will keep at Megan about the meeting until she sets it up.* ☐ *You will have to keep at her if you want to get anything done.*

keep at something to continue to do something; to continue to try to do something. ☐ *Keep at it until you get it done.* ☐ *I have to keep at this.*

keep away (from someone or something) to avoid someone or something; to maintain a physical distance from someone or something. ☐ *Please keep away from me if you have a cold.* ☐ *Keep away from the construction site, Timmy.*

keep back (from someone or something) to continue to stay in a position away from someone or something. ☐ *You must keep back from the edge of the crater.* ☐ *Keep back! It's really dangerous.*

keep off ((of) something) to remain off something; not to trespass on something. (The *of* is colloquial.) ☐ *Please keep off the grass.* ☐ *This is not a public thoroughfare! Keep off!*

keep on someone (about something) to nag someone about something. ☐ *We will have to keep on him about the report until he turns it in.* ☐ *Don't worry. I'll keep on him.*

keep on (something) to work to remain mounted on something, such as a horse, bicycle, etc. □ *It's really hard for me to keep on a horse.* □ *It's hard to keep on when it's moving all over the place.*

keep on something to pay close attention to something. □ *Keep on that story until everything is settled.* □ *This is a problem. Keep on it until it's settled.*

keep out (of something) **1.** to remain uninvolved with something. □ *Keep out of this! It's my affair.* □ *It's not your affair. Keep out!* **2.** to remain outside something or some place. □ *You should keep out of the darkroom when the door is closed.* □ *The door is closed. Keep out!*

keep someone at something to make sure someone continues to work at something. (*Someone* includes *oneself.*) □ *Please keep Walter at his chores.* □ *I was so sick I couldn't keep myself at my work.*

keep someone back **1.** to hold a child back in school. □ *We asked them to keep John back a year.* □ *John was kept back a year in school.* **2.** to keep someone from advancing in life. □ *I think that your small vocabulary is keeping you back.* □ *Her vocabulary kept her back in life.*

keep someone down to prevent someone from advancing or succeeding. □ *His lack of a degree will keep him down.* □ *I don't think that this problem will keep her down.*

keep someone on to retain someone in employment longer than is required or was planned. □ *She worked out so well that we decided to keep her on.* □ *Liz was kept on as a consultant.*

keep someone or something back to hold someone or something in reserve. □ *Keep some of the food back for an emergency.* □ *We are keeping Karen back until the other players have exhausted themselves.*

keep someone or something off See *hold someone or something off.*

keep someone or something out (of something) **1.** to prevent someone or something from getting into something or some place.

(*Someone* includes *oneself*.) □ *Keep your kids out of my yard.* □ *Please keep the loose papers out of the room.* □ *She just couldn't keep herself out of the cookie jar.* **2.** to keep the subject of someone or something out of a discussion. (*Someone* includes *oneself*.) □ *Keep the kids out of this! I don't want to talk about them.* □ *They kept Dorothy out of the discussion.*

keep someone up **1.** to hold someone upright. □ *Try to keep him up until I can get his bed turned down.* □ *Keep her up for a few minutes longer.* **2.** to prevent someone from going to bed or going to sleep. □ *I'm sorry, was my trumpet keeping you up?* □ *We were kept up by the noise.*

keep something on to continue to wear an article of clothing. □ *I'm going to keep my coat on. It's a little chilly in here.* 🅃 *I'll keep on my coat, thanks.*

keep something up **1.** to hold or prop something up. □ *Keep your side of the trunk up. Don't let it sag.* 🅃 *Keep up your side of the trunk.* **2.** to continue doing something. □ *I love your singing. Don't stop. Keep it up.* 🅃 *Please keep up your singing.* **3.** to maintain something in good order. □ *I'm glad you keep the exterior of your house up.* 🅃 *You keep up your house nicely.*

kick back (at someone or something) to kick at someone or something in revenge. □ *She kicked at me, so I kicked back at her.* □ *If you kick me, I'll kick back.*

kick something back (to someone or something) to move something back to someone, something, or some place by kicking. □ *I kicked the ball back to Walter.* □ *He kicked it to me, and I kicked it back.*

kick something down to break down something by kicking. □ *I was afraid they were going to kick the door down.* 🅃 *Don't kick down the door!*

kick something in to break through something by kicking. □ *Tommy kicked the door in and broke the new lamp.* 🅃 *He kicked in the door by accident.*

kick something out (of something) to move something out of something or some place by kicking. □ *The soccer player kicked the* *ball out of the tangle of legs.* 🅃 *She got into the fracas and kicked out the ball.* □ *It looked trapped, but Todd kicked it out.*

kill someone or something off to kill all of a group of people or creatures. □ *Lefty set out to kill Max and his boys off.* 🅃 *Something killed off all the dinosaurs.*

kneel down (before someone or something) to show respect by getting down on one's knees in the presence of someone or something. □ *We were told to kneel down in front of a statue of a golden calf.* □ *I'm too old to kneel down comfortably.*

knock it off to stop talking; to be silent. (Usually a rude command.) □ *Shut up, you guys! Knock it off!* □ *Knock it off and go to sleep!*

knock someone or something down to thrust someone or something to the ground by force. □ *The force of the blast knocked us down.* 🅃 *It knocked down everyone in the room.* □ *The wind knocked the fence down.*

knock someone out **1.** to knock someone unconscious. (*Someone* includes *oneself.*) □ *Max knocked Lefty out and left him there in the gutter.* 🅃 *Max knocked out Lefty.* □ *She fell and knocked herself out.* **2.** to make someone unconsciousness. (*Someone* includes *oneself.*) □ *The drug knocked her out quickly.* 🅃 *The powerful medicine knocked out the patient.* **3.** to wear someone out; to exhaust someone. (*Someone* includes *oneself.*) □ *All that exercise really knocked me out.* □ *The day's activities knocked the kids out, and they went right to bed.*

knock someone over to surprise or overwhelm someone. (Figurative.) □ *His statement simply knocked me over.* □ *When she showed me what happened to the car, it nearly knocked me over.*

knock (up) against someone or something to bump against someone or something. □ *The loose shutter knocked up against the side of the house.* □ *The large branch knocked against the garage in the storm.* □ *The child's bicycle knocked up against me.*

L

lace into someone or something to set to work on someone or something; to "attack" someone or something. □ *Todd laced into Ralph and scolded him severely.* □ *Elaine laced into the job with the intention of finishing it within an hour.*

lag behind (someone or something) to linger behind someone or something; to fall behind someone or something. □ *Come on up here. Don't lag behind us or you'll get lost.* □ *Please don't lag behind the donkeys. Come up here with the rest of the hikers.* □ *Don't lag behind too much.*

land (up)on someone or something to light on someone or something. (*Upon* is formal and less commonly used than *on.*) □ *A bee landed upon her and frightened her.* □ *A butterfly landed on the cake and ruined the icing.*

lap over (something) [for something] to extend or project over the edge or boundary of something. □ *The lid lapped over the edge of the barrel, forming a little table.* □ *The blanket did not lap over enough to keep me warm.*

lap something up **1.** [for an animal] to lick something up. □ *The dog lapped the ice cream up off the floor.* 🅃 *The dog lapped up the ice cream.* **2.** [for someone] to accept or believe something with enthusiasm. (Figurative.) □ *Of course, they believed it. They just lapped it up.* 🅃 *They lapped up the lies without questioning anything.*

lap (up) against something [for waves] to splash gently against something. □ *The waves lapped up against the shore softly.* □ *The waves lapped against the shore all night long, and I couldn't sleep.*

last something out to endure until the end of something. □ *Ed said that he didn't think he could last the opera out and left.* 🅃 *He couldn't last out the first act.*

laugh someone or something down to cause someone to quit or cause something to end by laughing in ridicule. □ *Her singing career was destroyed when the audience laughed her down as an amateur.* 🅃 *The cruel audience laughed down the amateur singer.* 🅃 *They laughed down the magic act also.*

laugh something off to treat a serious problem lightly by laughing at it. □ *Although his feelings were hurt, he just laughed the incident off as if nothing had happened.* 🅃 *He laughed off the incident.*

launch into something to start in doing something. □ *Now, don't launch into lecturing me about manners again!* □ *Tim's mother launched into a sermon about how to behave at a concert.*

lay off ((from) something) to cease doing something. □ *Lay off from your hammering for a minute, will you?* □ *That's enough! Please lay off.*

lay off ((of) someone or something) to stop doing something to someone or something; to stop bothering someone or something. (The *of* is colloquial.) □ *Lay off of me! You've said enough.* □ *Please lay off the chicken. I cooked it as best I could.*

lay over (some place) to wait somewhere between segments of a journey. □ *We were told we would have to lay over in New York.* □ *I don't mind laying over if it isn't for very long.*

lay someone away to bury someone. (Euphemism.) □ *Yes, he has passed. We laid him away last week.* 🅃 *He laid away his uncle in a simple ceremony.*

lay someone off (from something) to put an end to someone's employment at something. □ *The automobile factory laid five hundred people off from work.* 🅃 *They laid off a lot of people.* □ *We knew they were going to lay a lot of people off.*

lay something away (for someone) to put something in storage for someone to receive at a later time. (Often said of a purchase that is held by the business until it is paid for.) □ *Please lay this away* *for me. I'll pay for it when I have the money.* 🅃 *Please lay away this coat until I can get the money together.* ☐ *I will lay it away for you.*

lay something away (for something) to set something aside or put something in storage for a special occasion or purpose. ☐ *She laid the lovely dress away for the next party.* 🅃 *She laid away the dress.* ☐ *Hoping there would be a chance to use it, she laid it away.*

lay something in to build up a supply of something. ☐ *We had better lay some firewood in for the winter.* 🅃 *I will lay in a supply.*

lay something out to explain something; to go over details of a plan carefully. ☐ *They laid the sales campaign out after many meetings.* 🅃 *She laid out exactly what she had been thinking so they all could discuss it.*

lay something out for someone or something See the following entry.

lay something out on someone or something AND **lay something out for someone or something** to spend an amount of money on someone or something. ☐ *We laid out nearly ten thousand dollars on that car.* 🅃 *We laid out a fortune on the children.* ☐ *I won't lay out another cent for that car!*

lay something up **1.** to acquire and store something. ☐ *Try to lay as much of it up as you can.* 🅃 *I am trying to lay up some firewood for the winter.* **2.** [for something] to disable something. ☐ *The ship was laid up by engine trouble and a number of other defects.* 🅃 *The accident laid up the ship for repairs.*

lead back (to some place) [for a pathway] to return to a place. ☐ *This path leads back to the camp.* ☐ *I hope it leads back. It seems to be going the wrong way.*

lead down to something [for a pathway or other trail] to run downward to something. ☐ *The trail led down to a spring at the bottom of the hill.* ☐ *These stairs lead down to the furnace room.*

lead off to be the first one to go or leave. ☐ *You lead off. I'll follow.* ☐ *Mary led off and the others followed closely behind.*

lead off (with someone or something) to begin with someone or something. □ *The musical revue led off with a bassoon trio.* □ *Sharon, the singer, will lead off tonight.*

lead someone on to guide someone onward. □ *We led him on so he could see more of the gardens.* □ *Please lead Mary on. There is lots more to see here.*

lead up to something **1.** to aim at or route movement to something. □ *A narrow path led up to the door of the cottage.* □ *This road leads up to the house at the top of the hill.* **2.** to prepare to say something; to lay the groundwork for making a point. (Typically with the present participle.) □ *I was just leading up to telling you what happened when you interrupted.* □ *I knew she was leading up to something, the way she was talking.*

leaf out [for a plant or tree] to open its leaf buds. □ *Most of the bushes leaf out in mid-April.* □ *The trees leafed out early this year.*

leaf through something to look through something, turning the pages. □ *Jan leafed through the catalog, looking for a suitable winter coat.* □ *Leaf through this and see if there is anything you like.*

leak in(to something) [for a fluid] to work its way into something. □ *Some of the soapy water leaked into the soil.* □ *The rainwater is leaking in!*

leak out [for information] to become known. □ *I hope that news of the new building does not leak out before the contract is signed.* □ *When the story leaked out, my telephone would not stop ringing.*

leak out (of something) [for a fluid] to seep out of something or some place. □ *Some of the brake fluid leaked out of the car and made a spot on the driveway.* □ *Look under the car. Something's leaking out.*

leak something out to permit [otherwise secret] information to become publicly known. □ *Please don't leak this out. It is supposed to be a secret.* 🅃 *Someone leaked out the report.*

lean back (against someone or something) to recline backwards, putting weight on someone or something. □ *Just lean back against* *me. I will prevent you from falling.* ☐ *Relax and lean back. Nothing bad is going to happen.*

lean over **1.** to bend over. ☐ *Lean over and pick the pencil up yourself! I'm not your servant!* ☐ *As Kelly leaned over to tie her shoes, her chair slipped out from under her.* **2.** to tilt over. ☐ *The fence leaned over and almost fell.* ☐ *As the wind blew, the tree leaned over farther and farther.*

lean toward someone or something **1.** to incline toward someone or something. ☐ *Tom is leaning toward Randy. I think he is going to fall on him.* ☐ *The tree is leaning toward the edge of the cliff. It will fall eventually.* **2.** to tend to favor [choosing] someone or something. ☐ *I am leaning toward Sarah as the new committee head.* ☐ *I'm leaning toward a new committee.*

leap for joy to jump up because one is happy; to be very happy. (Usually figurative.) ☐ *Tommy leapt for joy because he had won the race.* ☐ *We all leapt for joy when we heard the news.*

leave someone or something out (of something) to neglect to include someone or something in something. ☐ *Please leave me out of it.* ☐ *Can I leave John out this time?* 🅃 *Don't leave out Fred's name.*

leave something on **1.** to allow something [that can be turned off] to remain on. ☐ *Who left the radio on?* 🅃 *Please leave on the light for me.* **2.** to continue to wear some article of clothing. ☐ *I think I will leave my coat on.* 🅃 *It's chilly in here. I'll leave on my coat.*

leave something up to someone or something to allow someone or something to make a decision about something. ☐ *We will try to leave that decision up to you.* ☐ *Can we leave this up to the committee?*

legislate against something to prohibit something; to pass a law against something. ☐ *You can't just legislate against something. You have to explain to people why they shouldn't do it.* ☐ *The Congress has just legislated against insolvent banks.*

legislate for something to pass a law that tries to make something happen. ☐ *The candidate pledged to legislate for tax relief.* ☐ *We support your efforts to legislate for lower taxes.*

let down to relax one's efforts or vigilance. □ *Now is no time to let down. Keep on your guard.* □ *After the contest was over, Jane let down a bit so she could relax.*

let on (about someone or something) to confirm or reveal something about someone or something. □ *You promised you wouldn't let on about Sally and her new job!* □ *I didn't let on. She guessed.*

let out [for an event that includes many people] to end. (The people are then permitted to come out.) □ *What time does the movie let out? I have to meet someone in the lobby.* □ *The meeting let out at about seven o'clock.* □ *School lets out in June.*

let out (with) something **1.** to state or utter something loudly. □ *The man let out with a screaming accusation about the person whom he thought had wounded him.* □ *She let out a torrent of curses.* **2.** to give forth a scream or yell. □ *She let out with a blood-curdling scream when she saw the snake in her chair.* □ *They let out with shouts of delight when they saw the cake.*

let someone off (with something) to give someone a light punishment [for doing something]. □ *The judge let the criminal off with a slap on the wrist.* Ⓣ *The judge would not let off the criminal with a small fine.* □ *This judge lets too many of these petty crooks off.*

let someone or something down to fail someone or something; to disappoint someone or a group. □ *Please don't let me down. I am depending on you.* Ⓣ *I let down the entire cast of the play.* □ *I'm sorry I let you down.*

let something out **1.** to reveal something; to tell about a secret or a plan. □ *It was supposed to be a secret. Who let it out?* Ⓣ *Who let out the secret?* **2.** to enlarge the waist of an article of clothing. □ *She had to let her shirts out because she had gained some weight.* Ⓣ *I see you have had to let out your trousers.*

let something out (to someone) to rent something to someone. □ *I let the back room out to a college boy.* Ⓣ *I let out the back room to someone.*

let up **1.** to diminish. □ *I hope this rain lets up a little soon.* □ *When the snow lets up so I can see, I will drive to the store.* **2.** to stop [doing something] altogether. □ *The rain let up about noon, and the sun came out.*

let up (on someone or something) to reduce the pressure or demands on someone or something. ☐ *You had better let up on Tom. He can't handle any more work.* ☐ *Please let up on the committee. It can only do so much.* ☐ *Do let up. You are getting too upset.*

level off [for variation or fluctuation in the motion of something] to diminish; [for a rate] to stop increasing or decreasing. ☐ *The plane leveled off at 10,000 feet.* ☐ *After a while the work load will level off.* ☐ *Things will level off after we get through the end of the month.*

level out [for something that was going up and down] to assume a more level course or path. ☐ *The road leveled out after a while and driving was easier.* ☐ *As we got down into the valley, the land leveled out and traveling was easier.*

level something off to make something level or smooth. ☐ *You are going to have to level the floor off before you put the carpet down.* 🅃 *Please level off the floor.*

level something out to cause something to assume a more level course or path. ☐ *Level this path out before you open it to the public.* 🅃 *They have to level out this roadway.*

lie down to recline. ☐ *Why don't you lie down for a while?* ☐ *I need to lie down and have a little snooze.*

lie in [for a woman] to lie in bed awaiting the birth of her child. ☐ *The child is due soon, and the mother is lying in at the present time.* ☐ *All the women in that particular hospital are lying in.*

lift off [for a plane or rocket] to move upward, leaving the ground. ☐ *The rocket lifted off exactly on time.* ☐ *What time will the next one lift off?*

lift something off (of) someone or something to raise something and uncover or release someone or something. (The *of* is colloquial.) ☐ *Lift the beam off of him and see if he is still breathing.* 🅃 *Please lift off the heavy lid.*

light someone or something up to shine lights on someone or something. ☐ *We lit Fred up with the headlights of the car.* 🅃 *Light up the stage and let's rehearse.*

light up **1.** to become brighter. ☐ *Suddenly, the sky lit up like day.* ☐ *The room lit up as the fire suddenly came back to life.* **2.** [for someone] to become interested and responsive in something. ☐ *We could tell from the way Sally lit up that she recognized the man in the picture.* ☐ *She lit up when we told her about our team's success.*

light (up)on someone or something **1.** to land on someone or something; to settle on someone or something. (*Upon* is formal and less commonly used than *on*.) ☐ *Three butterflies lit on the baby, causing her to shriek with delight.* ☐ *The bees lit on the clover blossom and pulled it to the ground.* ☐ *Her glance lit upon a dress in the store window.* **2.** to arrive at something by chance; to happen upon something. (Figurative. Close to sense 1.) ☐ *The committee lit upon a solution that pleased almost everyone.* ☐ *We just happen to light upon this idea as we were talking to each other.*

line someone or something up **1.** to put people or things in line. (*Someone* includes *oneself*.) ☐ *Line everyone up and march them onstage.* 🅃 *Line up the kids, please.* ☐ *Please line these books up.* ☐ *Hey, you guys! Line yourselves up!* **2.** to schedule someone or something [for something]. ☐ *Please line somebody up for the entertainment.* 🅃 *We will try to line up a magician and a clown for the party.* 🅃 *They lined up a chorus for the last act.*

line someone or something up (in something) to put people or things into some kind of formation, such as a row, column, ranks, etc. (*Someone* includes *oneself*.) ☐ *The teacher lined the children up in two rows.* 🅃 *Please line up the children in a row.* ☐ *Yes, line them up.* ☐ *Let's line ourselves up into two columns.*

line up to form a line; to get into a line. ☐ *All right, everyone, line up!* ☐ *Please line up.*

line up for something to form or get into a line and wait for something. ☐ *Everyone lined up for a helping of birthday cake.* ☐ *Let's line up for dinner. The doors to the dining room will open at any minute.*

line up in(to) something to form or get into a line, row, rank, column, etc. ☐ *Please line up in columns of two.* ☐ *I wish you would all line up into a nice straight line.*

linger on (after someone or something) AND **stay on (after someone or something)** to outlast someone or something; to live longer than someone else or long after an event. ☐ *Aunt Sarah lingered on only a few months after Uncle Herman died.* ☐ *She lingered on and was depressed for a while.* ☐ *She stayed on after her husband for a short time.*

link up to someone or something AND **link (up) with someone or something** to join up with someone or something. ☐ *I have a computer modem so I can link up to Bruce.* ☐ *Now my computer can link up with a computer bulletin board.*

link (up) with someone or something See the previous entry.

listen in (on someone or something) **1.** to join someone or a group as a listener. ☐ *The band is rehearsing. Let's go listen in on them.* ☐ *It won't hurt to listen in, will it?* **2.** to eavesdrop on someone. ☐ *Please don't try to listen in on us. This is a private conversation.* ☐ *I am not listening in. I was here first. You are conversing carelessly.*

live off (of) someone or something to obtain one's living or means of survival from someone or something. (The *of* is colloquial.) ☐ *You can't live off your uncle all your life!* ☐ *I manage to live off of my salary.*

live something down to overcome some embarrassing or troublesome problem or event. ☐ *It was so embarrassing! I will never live it down.* 🅃 *I will never live down this incident.*

live through something to endure something; to survive an unpleasant or dangerous time of one's life. ☐ *I almost did not live through the operation.* ☐ *I know I can't live through another attack.*

live up to something to be equal to expectations or goals. ☐ *The dinner did not live up to my expectations.* ☐ *We will live up to your first impressions of us.*

live with something to put up with something. (Does not mean "to dwell with.") ☐ *That is not acceptable. I can't live with that. Please change it.* ☐ *Mary refused to live with the proposed changes.*

live within something **1.** to live within certain boundaries. ☐ *Do you think you can live within your space, or are we going to argue over the use of square footage?* ☐ *Ted demanded again that Bill live within his assigned area.* **2.** to keep one's living costs within a certain amount, especially within one's budget, means, etc. ☐ *Please try to live within your budget.* ☐ *You must learn to live within your means.*

live without something to survive, lacking something. ☐ *I just know I can't live without my car.* ☐ *I am sure we can live without vegetables for a day or two.*

liven something up to make something more lively or less dull. ☐ *Some singing might liven things up a bit.* 🅃 *The songs livened up the evening.*

load someone or something into something to put someone or something into something. ☐ *Load all the boxes into the truck.* ☐ *Would you load the dishes into the dishwasher?* ☐ *Let's load the kids into the car and go to the zoo.*

load up (with something) to take or accumulate a lot of something. ☐ *Don't load up with cheap souvenirs. Save your money.* ☐ *Whenever I get into a used bookstore, I load up.*

lobby against something to solicit support against something, such as a piece of legislation or a government regulation. ☐ *We sent a lot of lawyers to the state capital to lobby against the bill, but it passed anyway.* ☐ *They lobbied against the tax increase.*

lobby for something to solicit support for something among the members of a voting body, such as the Congress. ☐ *Tom is always lobbying for some bill or other.* ☐ *The manufacturers lobbied for tax relief.*

lock someone or something up (somewhere) to lock someone or something within something or some place. (*Someone* includes *oneself.*) ☐ *The captain ordered the sailor locked up in the brig until the ship got into port.* 🅃 *The sheriff locked up the crook in a cell.* ☐ *Don't lock me up.* ☐ *She locked herself up in her office where no one could get to her.*

lock something in to take action to fix a rate or price at a certain figure. □ *I can lock the price in for a week.* 🅃 *If you put down a deposit now, I can lock in the price for you for a week.*

lodge something against someone to place a charge against someone. □ *The neighbors lodged a complaint against us for parking on their grass.* □ *I want to lodge an assault charge against Max.*

lodge something against something to place or prop something against something. □ *We lodged the chest against the door, making it difficult or impossible to open.* □ *Let's lodge the stone against the side of the barn to help support it.*

log off AND **log out** to record one's exit from a computer system. (This action may be recorded, or logged, automatically in the computer's memory.) □ *I closed my files and logged off.* □ *What time did you log out?*

log on to attach oneself up to use a computer system. (This action may be recorded, or logged, automatically in the computer's memory.) □ *What time did you log on to the system this morning?* □ *I always log on before I get my first cup of coffee.*

log out See *log off*.

look away (from someone or something) to turn one's gaze away from someone. □ *She looked away from him, not wishing her eyes to give away her true feelings.* □ *In embarrassment, she looked away.*

look back (at someone or something) AND **look back (on someone or something)** **1.** to gaze back and try to get a view of someone or something. □ *She looked back at the city and whispered a good-bye to everything she had ever cared for.* □ *I went away and never looked back.* **2.** to think about someone or something in the past. □ *When I look back on Frank, I do remember his strange manner, come to think of it.* □ *When I look back, I am amazed at all I have accomplished.*

look back (on someone or something) See the previous entry.

look down (at someone or something) **1.** to turn one's gaze downward at someone or something. □ *She looked down at me and* *giggled at the awkward position I was in.* ☐ *She looked down and burst into laughter.* **2.** AND **look down on someone or something** to view someone or something as lowly or unworthy. ☐ *She looked down on all the waiters and treated them badly.* ☐ *They looked down on our humble food.*

look down on someone or something See *look down (at someone or something).*

look in (on someone or something) to check on someone or something. ☐ *I will look in on her from time to time.* ☐ *I looked in and everything was all right.*

look into something **1.** to gaze into the inside of something. ☐ *Look into the box and make sure you've gotten everything out of it.* ☐ *Look into the camera's viewfinder at the little red light.* **2.** to investigate something. ☐ *I will look into this matter and see what I can do about it.* ☐ *Please ask the manager to look into it.*

look on to be a spectator. ☐ *The beating took place while a policeman looked on.* ☐ *While the kittens played, the mother cat looked on contentedly.*

look on (with someone) to share and read from someone else's notes, paper, book, music, etc. ☐ *I don't have a copy of the notice, but I will look on with Tom.* ☐ *Carla has a copy of the music. She doesn't mind if I look on.*

look out to be careful; to think and move fast because something dangerous is about to harm one. (Usually a command.) ☐ *Look out! Don't trip over that board!* ☐ *Look out!*

look out for someone or something **1.** to be watchful for the appearance of someone or something. ☐ *Look out for Sam. He is due any minute.* ☐ *Look out for the bus. We don't want to miss it.* **2.** to be alert to the danger posed by someone or something. ☐ *Look out for that last step. It's loose.* ☐ *Look out for that truck!*

look someone or something over to examine someone or something. (*Someone* includes *oneself.*) ☐ *I think you had better have the doctor look you over.* 🅃 *Please look over these papers.* ☐ *They looked themselves over and declared themselves beautiful.*

look someone or something up 1. to seek someone, a group, or something out. ☐ *I lost track of Sally. I'll try to look her up and get in touch with her.* 🅃 *I am going to look up an old friend when I am in Chicago.* ☐ *I am going to look that old gang up.* 🅃 *Ted came into town and looked up his favorite pizza place.* **2.** to seek information about someone or something in a book or listing. (*Someone* includes *oneself.*) ☐ *I don't recognize his name. I'll look him up and see what I can find.* 🅃 *I'll look up this person in a reference book.* 🅃 *Can I use the directory to look up an address?* ☐ *She looked herself up in the telephone book to make sure her name was spelled correctly.*

look through something 1. to gaze through something. ☐ *Look through the window at what the neighbors are doing.* ☐ *Look through the binoculars and see if you can get a better view.* **2.** to examine the parts, pages, samples, etc., of something. ☐ *Look through this report and see what you make of it.* ☐ *I will look through it when I have time.*

look up to show promise of improving. ☐ *My prospects for a job are looking up.* ☐ *Conditions are looking up.*

look up to someone to admire someone. ☐ *We all look up to Roger. He's authoritative but kind.* ☐ *I am glad they look up to me.*

look (up)on someone or something as something to view someone or something as something; to consider someone or something to be something. ☐ *I look upon Todd as a fine and helpful guy.* ☐ *I look on these requests as an annoyance.*

loom out of something to appear to come out of or penetrate something. ☐ *A truck suddenly loomed out of the fog and just missed hitting us.* ☐ *A tall building loomed out of the mists.*

loom up to appear to rise up [from somewhere]; to take form or definition, usually threatening to some degree. ☐ *A great city loomed up in the distance. It looked threatening in the dusky light.* ☐ *A ghost loomed up, but we paid no attention, since it had to be a joke.* ☐ *The recession loomed up, and the stock market reacted.*

loosen someone or something up 1. to make someone's muscles and joints move more freely by exercising them. (*Someone* includes *oneself.*) ☐ *The exercise loosened me up quite nicely.* 🅃 *It loosened* *up my legs.* ☐ *I have to do some exercises to loosen myself up.* **2.** to make someone or a group more relaxed and friendly. (*Someone* includes *oneself.*) ☐ *I told a little joke to loosen the audience up.* 🅃 *I loosened up the audience with a joke.* ☐ *Loosen yourself up. Relax and try to enjoy people.*

loosen something up to make something less tight. ☐ *Loosen the freshly oiled hinges up by swinging the door back and forth.* 🅃 *Try to loosen up those hinges.*

loosen up to become loose or relaxed. ☐ *Loosen up. Relax.* ☐ *We tried to get Mary to loosen up, but she did not respond.*

lose out to lose in competition; to lose one's expected reward. ☐ *Our team lost out because our quarterback broke his leg.* ☐ *I ran my best race, but I still lost out.* ☐ *I was hoping for a promotion, but I lost out because of my bad attendance record.*

lose out (on something) to miss enjoying something; to miss participating in something. ☐ *I would hate to lose out on all the fun.* ☐ *We'll lose out if we don't get there on time.*

lose out to someone or something to lose in a competition to someone or something. ☐ *I didn't want to lose out to the other guys.* ☐ *Our firm lost out to the lowest bidder.*

lounge around (some place) to lie about some place. ☐ *I am going to lounge around the house this morning.* ☐ *Don't lounge around all day.*

lunch out to eat lunch away from one's home or away from one's place of work. ☐ *I think I'll lunch out today. I'm tired of carrying lunches.* ☐ *I want to lunch out today.*

lure someone or something in(to something) to entice someone or something into something or a place. ☐ *The thief tried to lure the tourist into an alley to rob him.* ☐ *The thief led the tourist to an alley and lured him in.* 🅃 *Using an old trick, the thief lured in the tourist.*

M

make a check out (to someone or something) to write a check to someone or a group. □ *Please make the check out to Bill Franklin.* 🅃 *Make out a check to me.* □ *Please make a check out to the bank.*

make off with someone or something to leave and take away someone or something. □ *The kidnappers made off with the baby in the night.* □ *Max made off with Lady Bracknell's jewels.*

make (out) after someone or something to run after someone or something; to start out after someone or something. □ *Paul made out after Fred, who had taken Paul's hat.* □ *The police officer made after the robber.*

make (out) for someone or something to run toward someone, something, or some place. □ *They made out for Sam as soon as they saw him coming.* □ *The boys made for the swimming pool as soon as the coach blew the whistle.*

make out (with someone or something) to manage satisfactorily with someone or something. □ *I know you are negotiating with George on that Franklin deal. How are you making out with him?* □ *How are you making out with school?* □ *He is making out okay.*

make over someone or something to pay a lot of attention to someone or something. □ *Why does she make over your sister so much?* □ *Aunt Em made over the wedding gifts as if they were for her instead of Susan.*

make someone or something over to convert someone or something into a new or different person or thing. (*Someone* includes *oneself.*) □ *The hairstylist tried to make Carla over, but she want-*

ed to be the way she has always been. 🅃 *She made over Carla.* □ *I would really like to make this house over.*

make someone up to put makeup on someone. (*Someone* includes *oneself.*) □ *You have to make the clowns up before you start on the other characters in the play.* 🅃 *Did you make up the clowns?* □ *He made himself up for the play.*

make something off (of) someone or something to make money from someone or something. (The *of* is colloquial.) □ *Are you trying to make your fortune off of me?* □ *We think we can make some money off the sale of the house.*

make something out to see, read, or hear something well enough to understand it. □ *What did you say? I couldn't quite make it out.* 🅃 *Can you make out what he is saying?* 🅃 *I could just make out the ship in the fog.*

make something up 1. to make a bed. □ *We have to make all the beds up and then vacuum all the rooms.* 🅃 *Did you make up the beds?* **2.** to fabricate something, such as a story or a lie. □ *That's not true. You are just making that up!* 🅃 *You made up that story!* **3.** to redo something; to do something that one has failed to do in the past. □ *Can I make the lost time up?* 🅃 *Can I make up the test that I missed?*

map something out to plot something out carefully, usually on paper. □ *I have a good plan. I will map it out for you.* 🅃 *I will map out the plan for you.*

march on [for time] to continue. □ *Time marches on. We are all getting older.* □ *As the day marches on, try to get everything completed.*

mark something down 1. to reduce the price of something. □ *We are going to mark all this merchandise down next Monday.* 🅃 *We marked down the merchandise.* **2.** to write something down on paper. □ *She marked the number down on the paper.* 🅃 *She marked down the number.*

mark something up 1. to make marks all over something. □ *Who marked my book up?* 🅃 *I did not mark up the book.* **2.** to raise the price of something. □ *I think that they mark everything up once a* *week at the grocery store.* 🅃 *They marked up the prices again last night.* **3.** to raise the wholesale price of an item to the retail level. □ *How much do you mark cabbage up?* 🅃 *They marked up the cabbage too much.*

mash something up to crush something into a paste or pieces. □ *Mash the potatoes up and put them in a bowl.* 🅃 *Mash up the potatoes and put them on the table.*

match up [for things or people] to match, be equal, or be complementary. □ *These match up. See how they are the same length?* □ *Sorry, but these two parts don't match up.*

measure something off **1.** to determine the length of something. □ *He measured the length of the room off and wrote down the figure in his notebook.* 🅃 *Fred measured off the width of the house.* **2.** to distribute something in measured portions. 🅃 *He measured off two feet of the wire.* □ *Fred measured a few feet of string off, and cut it with a knife.*

measure up (to someone or something) to compare well to someone or something. □ *He just doesn't measure up to Sarah in intelligence.* □ *He measures up fairly well.*

melt down **1.** [for something frozen] to melt. □ *The glacier melted down little by little.* □ *When the ice on the streets melted down, it was safe to drive again.* **2.** [for a nuclear reactor] to become hot enough to melt through its container. □ *The whole system was on the verge of melting down.*

melt into something to melt and change into a different physical state. □ *All the ice cream melted into a sticky soup.* □ *The candles melted into a pool of colored wax in the heat last summer.*

melt something down to cause something frozen to become a liquid; to cause something solid to melt. □ *The sun melted the candle down to a puddle of wax.* 🅃 *The heat melted down the ice.*

melt something into something to cause something to change its physical state when melting. □ *The heat melted the frozen juice into a cold liquid that we could drink.* □ *We melted the fat into a liquid that we could deep-fry in.*

mesh together to fit together. □ *The various gears mesh together perfectly.* □ *Their ideas don't mesh together too well.*

mesh with something to fit with something. □ *Your idea just doesn't mesh with my plans.* □ *Currently, things don't mesh at all well with our long-range planning.*

mess someone or something up **1.** to put someone or something into disarray; to make someone or something dirty or untidy. (*Someone* includes *oneself.*) □ *A car splashed water on me and really messed me up.* 🅃 *The muddy water messed up my shirt.* 🅃 *Don't mess up the living room.* □ *I messed myself up when I fell.* **2.** to interfere with someone or something; to misuse or abuse someone or something. □ *You really messed me up. I almost got fired for what happened.* 🅃 *The new owners messed up the company.* 🅃 *Dropping out of school really messed up my life.* □ *Mess him up good so he won't double-cross us again.*

miss out (on something) not to do something because one is unaware of the opportunity; to fail to or neglect to take part in something. □ *I hope I don't miss out on the January linen sale.* □ *I really don't want to miss out.*

mix in (with someone or something) to mix or combine with people or substances. □ *The band came down from the stage and mixed in with the guests during the break.* □ *The eggs won't mix in with the shortening!*

mix someone or something in(to something) to combine someone or something into something. □ *We will try to mix the new people into the group.* 🅃 *We will mix in the new people a few at a time.* □ *Ted mixed the flour into the egg mixture slowly.* □ *The cook mixed it in slowly.*

mix someone up to confuse someone. (*Someone* includes *oneself.*) □ *Please don't mix me up!* 🅃 *You mixed up the speaker with your question.* □ *I was so tired I mixed myself up as I spoke.*

mix someone up with someone to confuse one person with another. □ *I'm sorry. I mixed you up with your brother.* 🅃 *I mixed up Ted with his brother.*

mix something up (with something) to mix or stir something with a mixing or stirring device. □ *He mixed the batter up with a spoon.*

[T] *Please mix up the batter with a spoon.* □ *I will mix it up, if you wish.*

mop something down to clean a surface with a mop. □ *Please mop this floor down now.* [T] *Please mop down this floor.*

mop something off to wipe the liquid off something. □ *Please mop the counter off.* [T] *Mop off the counter.*

mop something up (with something) to clean up something, such as a spill, with a mop or with a mopping motion. □ *Please mop this mess up.* [T] *I will mop up this mess.* [T] *She will mop up the mess with the rag.*

motion someone aside to give a hand signal to someone to move aside. □ *He motioned her aside and had a word with her.* [T] *I motioned aside the guard and asked him a question.*

motion someone away from someone or something to give a hand signal to someone to move away from someone or something. □ *She motioned me away from Susan.* □ *The police officer motioned the boys away from the wrecked car.*

mount up **1.** to get up on a horse. □ *Mount up and let's get out of here!* □ *Please mount up so we can leave.* **2.** [for something] to increase in amount or extent. □ *Expenses really mount up when you travel.* □ *Medical expenses mount up very fast when you're in the hospital.*

move away (from someone or something) **1.** to withdraw from someone or something. □ *Please don't move away from me. I like you close.* □ *I have to move away from the smoking section.* □ *There was too much smoke there, so I moved away.* **2.** to move, with one's entire household, to another residence. □ *Timmy was upset because his best friend had moved away.* □ *They moved away just as we were getting to know them.*

move back (from someone or something) to move back and away. (Often a command.) □ *Please move back from the edge.* □ *Please move back!*

move in (for something) to get closer for some purpose, such as a kill. □ *The big cat moved in for the kill.* □ *As the cat moved in, the mouse scurried away.*

move in (on someone or something) **1.** to move closer to someone or something; to make advances or aggressive movements toward someone or something. (Both literal and figurative senses.) ☐ *The crowd moved in on the frightened guard.* ☐ *They moved in slowly.* **2.** to attempt to take over or dominate someone or something. ☐ *The police moved in on the drug dealers.* ☐ *Max tried to move in on Lefty's territory.* ☐ *So, you're trying to move in?*

move in(to something) **1.** [for someone] to come to reside in something or some place. ☐ *I moved into a new apartment last week.* ☐ *When did the new family move in?* **2.** to enter something or some place. ☐ *The whole party moved into the house when it started raining.* ☐ *All the children just moved in and brought the party with them.* **3.** to begin a new line of activity. ☐ *After failing at real estate, he moved into house painting.* ☐ *It looked like an area where he could make some money, so he moved in.*

move off (from someone or something) to move away from someone or something. ☐ *The doctor moved off from the patient, satisfied with her work.* ☐ *The officer stopped for a minute, looked around, and then moved off.*

move on to continue moving; to travel on; to move away and not stop or tarry. ☐ *Move on! Don't stop here!* ☐ *Please move on!* ☐ *There was no more for him to do in Adamsville, and so he reluctantly moved on.*

move on something to do something about something. ☐ *I will move on this matter only when I get some time.* ☐ *I have been instructed to move on this and give it the highest priority.*

move on (to something) to change to a different subject or activity. ☐ *Now, I will move on to a new question.* ☐ *That is enough discussion on that point. Let's move on.*

move out (of some place) **1.** to leave a place; to begin to depart. (Especially in reference to a large number of persons or things.) ☐ *The crowd started to move out of the area about midnight.* ☐ *They had moved out by one o'clock.* **2.** to leave a place of residence permanently. ☐ *We didn't like the neighborhood, so we moved out of it.* ☐ *We moved out because we were unhappy.*

move someone up to advance or promote someone. ☐ *We are ready to move you up. You have been doing quite well.* ☐ *How long will it be before they can move me up?*

move up (to something) to advance to something; to purchase a better quality of something. ☐ *We are moving up to a larger car.* ☐ *There are too many of us now for a small house. We are moving up.* ☐ *Isn't it about time that I move up? I've been an office clerk for over a year.* ☐ *I had hoped that I would move up faster than this.*

mow someone or something down to cut, knock, or shoot someone or something down. ☐ *The speeding car almost mowed us down.* 🅃 *The car mowed down the pedestrian.* 🅃 *The lawn mower mowed down the tall grass.* ☐ *Machine guns mowed the attackers down.*

muddle through (something) to manage to get through something awkwardly. ☐ *We hadn't practiced the song enough, so we just muddled through it.* ☐ *We didn't know what we were meant to do, so we muddled through.*

mull something over to think over something; to ponder something. ☐ *Let me mull this over a little while.* 🅃 *Mull over this matter for a while and see what you think.*

multiply by something to use the arithmetic process of multiplication to expand numerically a certain number of times. ☐ *To get the amount of your taxes, multiply by .025.* ☐ *Can you multiply by sixteens?*

multiply something by something to use the arithmetic process of multiplication to expand numerically a particular number a certain number of times. ☐ *Multiply the number of dependents you are claiming by one thousand dollars.* ☐ *Multiply 12 by 16 and tell me what you get.*

muscle in (on someone or something) to interfere with someone or something; to intrude on someone or something. ☐ *Max tried to muscle in on Lefty, and that made Lefty's gang really mad at Max.* ☐ *You're not trying to muscle in, are you?*

muscle someone out (of something) to force someone out of something; to push someone out of something. ☐ *Are you trying to* *muscle me out of my job?* ▣ *The younger people are muscling out the older ones.* □ *Lefty "Fingers" Moran had had enough competition, and he wanted to muscle Max out.*

mushroom into something to grow suddenly into something large or important. □ *The question of pay suddenly mushroomed into a major matter.* □ *The unpaid bill mushroomed into a nasty argument and, finally, a court battle.*

N

nag at someone (about someone or something) to pester someone about someone or something. □ *Don't keep nagging at me about her.* □ *Stop nagging at me!*

nail someone down (on something) See *pin someone down (on something).*

nail something up **1.** to put something up, as on a wall, by nailing. □ *Please nail this up.* [T] *I'll nail up this picture for you.* **2.** to nail something closed; to use nails to secure something from intruders. □ *Sam nailed the door up so no one could use it.* [T] *Who nailed up the door? I can't get in!*

narrow something down (to people or things) to reduce a list of possibilities from many to a selected few. □ *We can narrow the choice down to green or red.* [T] *We narrowed down the choice to you or Paul.* □ *We can't seem to narrow the choice down.*

nestle down (in something) to settle down in something; to snuggle into something, such as a bed. □ *They nestled down in their warm bed.* □ *Please nestle down and go to sleep.*

nestle (up) against someone or something AND **nestle up (to someone or something)** to lie close to someone or something; to cuddle up to someone or something. □ *The kitten nestled up against its mother.* □ *It nestled up to Kathy.* □ *Kathy nestled against the back seat of the car.*

nestle up (to someone or something) See the previous entry.

nose someone or something out to defeat someone or something by a narrow margin. (Alludes to a horse winning a race "by a nose.")

☐ *Karen nosed Bobby out in the election for class president.* 🅃 *Our team nosed out the opposing team in last Friday's game.*

number off (by something) to say a number in a specified sequence when it is one's turn. ☐ *Please number off by tens.* ☐ *Come on, number off!*

number someone off to provide people with numbers. ☐ *I had to number the children off.* 🅃 *I numbered off the contestants.*

nurse someone through (something) to care for a sick person during the worst part of a sickness or recovery. ☐ *There was no one there to nurse him through the worst part of his illness.* ☐ *It was a horrible ordeal, but John nursed her through.*

O

open (out) on(to) something [for a building's doors] to exit toward something. ☐ *The French doors opened out onto the terrace.* ☐ *The doors opened on a lovely patio.*

open something up **1.** to open something that was closed. ☐ *They opened Peru's border up recently.* 🅃 *They opened up the border.* **2.** to begin working on something for which there are paper records, such as a case, investigation, file, etc. ☐ *I'm afraid we are going to have to open the case up again.* 🅃 *They opened up the case again.*

open something up (to someone) to make something available to someone; to permit someone to join something or participate in something. ☐ *We intend to open the club up to everyone.* 🅃 *We will open up our books to the auditors.* ☐ *We had to open the books up.*

open up (to someone) **1.** to tell [everything] to someone; to confess to someone. ☐ *If she would only open up to me, perhaps I could help her.* ☐ *She just won't open up. Everything is "private."* ☐ *After an hour of questioning, Thomas opened up.* **2.** [for opportunities] to become available to someone. (Figurative.) ☐ *After Ann's inquiries, doors began to open up to me.* ☐ *An agent helps. After I got one, all sorts of doors opened up.*

open up (to someone or something) **1.** [for doors] to become open so someone, something, or some creature can enter; to open for someone or something. ☐ *The doors to the supermarket opened up to me, so I went in.* ☐ *The automatic doors opened up to the dog, and it came into the store.* **2.** [for someone] to become more accepting of someone or something. ☐ *Finally, he opened up to the suggestion that he should leave.* ☐ *Finally the boss opened up to Tom as a manager.*

operate on someone to perform a surgical operation on someone. ☐ *They decided not to operate on her.* ☐ *She wasn't operated on after all.*

order someone in(to something) to command someone to get into something. ☐ *The officer ordered Ann into the wagon.* ☐ *She didn't want to go, but the cop ordered her in.*

order something in to have something, usually food, brought into one's house or place of business. ☐ *Do you want to order pizza in?* 🅃 *Shall I order in pizza?*

own up to someone to confess or admit something to someone. ☐ *Finally, he owned up to his boss.* ☐ *We had hoped he would own up to us sooner.*

own up to something to admit something; to confess to something. ☐ *He refused to own up to doing it.* ☐ *I will own up to my mistakes.*

P

pace something out **1.** to deal with a problem by pacing around. ☐ *When she was upset, she walked and walked while she thought through her problem. When Ed came into the room, she was pacing a new crisis out.* 🅃 *She usually paced out her anxiety.* **2.** to measure a distance by counting the number of even strides taken while walking. ☐ *He paced the distance out and wrote it down.* 🅃 *He paced out the distance from the door to the mailbox.*

pack something up (in something) to prepare something to be transported by placing it into a container. ☐ *Gerry will pack the dishes up in a strong box, using lots of crumpled paper.* 🅃 *Please pack up the dishes carefully.*

pack up to prepare one's belongings to be transported by placing them into a container; to gather one's things together for one's departure. ☐ *If we are going to leave in the morning, we should pack up now.* ☐ *I think you should pack up and be ready to leave at a moment's notice.* ☐ *He didn't say good-bye. He just packed up and left.*

paint over something to cover something up with a layer of paint. ☐ *Sam painted over the rusty part of the fence.* ☐ *The work crew was told to paint over the graffiti.*

paint something out to cover something up or obliterate something by applying a layer of paint. ☐ *The worker painted the graffiti out.* 🅃 *They had to paint out the graffiti.*

pair up (with someone) to join with someone to make a pair. ☐ *Sally decided to pair up with Jason for the dance contest.* ☐ *Sally and Jason paired up with each other.* ☐ *Sally and Jason paired up.* ☐ *All the kids paired up and gave gifts to one another.*

pal around (with someone) to associate with someone as a good friend. ☐ *I like to pal around with my friends on the weekends.* ☐ *They like to pal around.* ☐ *They often palled around with each other.*

pan in (on someone or something) See *zoom in (on someone or something).*

parade someone or something out to bring or march someone or some creature out in public. ☐ *He parades his children out every Sunday as they go to church.* 🅃 *He paraded out all his children.* ☐ *The owners paraded their dogs out, and the judge got ready to choose the best one.*

pass away to die. (Euphemistic.) ☐ *Uncle Herman passed away many years ago.* ☐ *He passed away in his sleep.*

pass on to die. (Euphemistic.) ☐ *When did your uncle pass on?* ☐ *Uncle Herman passed on nearly thirty years ago.*

pass on (to someone or something) to leave the person or thing being dealt with and move on to another person or thing. ☐ *I am finished with Henry. I will pass on to Jerry.* ☐ *I will pass on when I am finished.*

pass over (someone or something) **1.** to skip over someone or something; to fail to select someone or something. ☐ *I was next in line for a promotion, but they passed over me.* ☐ *I passed over the bruised apples and picked out the nicest ones.* **2.** to pass above someone or something. ☐ *A cloud passed over our group, cooling us a little.* ☐ *The huge blimp passed over the little community.*

pass someone or something up **1.** to fail to select someone or something. ☐ *The committee passed Jill up and chose Kelly.* 🅃 *They passed up Jill.* ☐ *We had to pass your application up this year.* **2.** to travel past someone or something. ☐ *We had to pass her up, thinking we could visit her the next time we were in town.* 🅃 *We passed up a hitchhiker.* 🅃 *You passed up a nice restaurant near the edge of town when you left.*

pass something along (to someone) **1.** to give or hand something to someone. ☐ *Would you kindly pass this along to Hillary?* 🅃 *Please pass along my advice to Wally over there.* ☐ *I would be* *happy to pass it along.* **2.** to relay some information to someone. ☐ *I hope you don't pass this along to anyone, but I am taking a new job next month.* [T] *Could you pass along my message to Fred?* ☐ *I will pass it along as you ask.*

pass something back (to someone) to return something by hand to someone. ☐ *Kelly passed the pictures back to Betty.* ☐ *They weren't Betty's and she passed them back to Beth.*

pass something down (to someone) AND **pass something on (to someone)** **1.** to send something down a line of people to someone. (Each person hands it to the next.) ☐ *Please pass this down to Mary at the end of the row.* [T] *Pass down this box to Mary.* ☐ *Mary wants this. Please pass it down.* ☐ *Mary is expecting this. Please pass it on.* **2.** to will something to someone. ☐ *My grandfather passed this watch down to me.* [T] *He passed on the watch to me.* ☐ *I have always wanted it and I'm so glad he passed it down.*

pass something on (to someone) See the previous entry.

pass something out (to someone) to distribute something to someone. ☐ *Please pass these out to everyone.* [T] *Pass out these papers to everyone.* ☐ *Please pass them out.*

pass something over (to someone) to send something to someone farther down in a line of people. (Each person hands it to the next.) ☐ *Please pass this paper over to Jane.* [T] *Would you pass over this paper to Jane?* ☐ *I would be happy to pass it over.*

paste something up **1.** to repair something with paste. ☐ *See if you can paste this book up so it will hold together.* [T] *Paste up the book and hope it holds together for a while.* **2.** to assemble a complicated page of material by pasting the parts together. ☐ *There is no way a typesetter can get this page just the way you want it. You'll have to paste it up yourself.* [T] *Paste up this page again and let me see it.*

patch something together (with something) to use something to repair something hastily or temporarily. ☐ *I think I can patch the exhaust pipe together with some wire.* ☐ *See if you can patch this engine together well enough to run for a few more hours.*

patch something up to repair something in a hurry; to make something temporarily serviceable again. ☐ *Can you patch this up so I can use it again?* [T] *I'll patch up the hose for you.*

pay off to yield profits; to result in benefits. □ *My investment in those stocks has really paid off.* □ *The time I spent in school paid off in later years.*

pay someone back **1.** to return money that was borrowed from a person. □ *You owe me money. When are you going to pay me back?* □ *You must pay John back. You have owed him money for a long time.* **2.** to get even with someone [for doing something]. (Figurative.) □ *I will pay her back for what she said about me.* □ *Max will pay Lefty back. He bears a grudge for a long time.*

pay something back (to someone) to repay someone. □ *I paid the money back to Jerry.* 🅃 *Can I pay back the money to George now?* □ *Please pay the money back now.*

pay something down **1.** to make a deposit of money on a purchase. □ *You will have to pay a lot of money down on a car that expensive.* 🅃 *I only paid down a few thousand dollars.* **2.** to reduce a bill by paying part of it, usually periodically. □ *I think I can pay the balance down by half in a few months.* 🅃 *I will pay down the balance a little next month.*

pay something in(to something) to pay an amount of money into an account. □ *Mary paid forty dollars into my account by mistake.* 🅃 *She paid in a lot of money.* □ *I have an account here and I want to pay something in.*

pay something off to pay the total amount of a bill; to settle an account by paying the total sum. □ *You should pay the total off as soon as possible to avoid having to pay more interest.* 🅃 *I will pay off the entire amount.*

pay something out to unravel or unwind wire or rope as it is needed. □ *One worker paid the cable out, and another worker guided it into the conduit.* 🅃 *The worker paid out the cable.*

pay something out (for someone or something) to disburse money for someone or something. □ *We have already paid too much money out for your education.* 🅃 *We paid out too much money.* □ *How much did you pay out?*

pay something out (to someone) to pay money to someone. □ *The grocery store paid one hundred dollars out to everyone who* *had become ill.* 🅃 *They paid out money to people who claimed illness.* ☐ *Alice, the cashier, paid the money out as it was requested.*

pay something up to pay all of whatever is due; to complete all the payments on something. ☐ *Please pay all your bills up.* 🅃 *Would you pay up your bills, please?* ☐ *Your dues are all paid up.*

peal out [for bells or voices] to sound forth musically. ☐ *The bells pealed out to announce that the wedding had taken place.* ☐ *All six of the bells seemed to peal out at once.*

peek in (on someone or something) to glance quickly into a place to see someone or something. ☐ *Would you please peek in on the baby?* ☐ *Yes, I'll peek in in a minute.*

peel something off from something See the following entry.

peel something off ((of) something) AND **peel something off from something** to remove the outside surface layer from something. (The *of* is colloquial.) ☐ *She carefully peeled the skin off the apple.* 🅃 *She peeled off the apple's skin.* ☐ *Please peel the skin off from the potato.*

peer in(to something) to stare into something; to look deep into something. ☐ *I peered into the room, hoping to get a glimpse of the lovely furnishings.* ☐ *I only had time to peer in.*

peer out at someone or something to stare out at someone or something. ☐ *A little puppy peered out at them from the cage.* ☐ *When I looked under the box, Timmy peered out at me with a big smile.*

pelt down (on someone or something) [for something] to fall down on someone or something. (Typically rain, hail, sleet, stones, etc.) ☐ *The rain pelted down on the children as they ran to their school bus.* ☐ *The ashes from the volcanic eruption pelted down on the town, covering the houses in a gray shroud.*

pen someone or something in (some place) to confine someone or some creature in a pen. ☐ *We penned all the kids in in the backyard while we got the party things ready in the house.* 🅃 *We had to pen in the kids to keep them away from the traffic.* ☐ *Alice penned her dog in.*

pen someone or something up to confine someone or something to a pen. (Implies more security than the previous entry.) □ *He said he didn't want them to pen him up in an office all day.* 🅃 *They penned up the dog during the day.*

pencil someone or something in to write in something with a pencil. (Implies that the writing is not final.) □ *I will pencil you in for a Monday appointment.* □ *This isn't the final answer, so I will just pencil it in.* 🅃 *I penciled in a tentative answer.*

perk up to be invigorated; to become more active. □ *After a bit of water, the plants perked up nicely.* □ *About noon, Andy perked up and looked wide-awake.*

permit someone out (of something) to allow someone to go out of something or some place. □ *His mother won't permit him out of his room all weekend.* □ *I didn't do anything, but she won't permit me out!*

pick someone or something out (for someone or something) to choose someone or something to serve as someone or something. □ *I picked one of the new people out for Santa Claus this year.* 🅃 *I picked out several large potatoes for the stew.* 🅃 *Sally picked out a ripe one.* □ *I picked her out myself.*

pick someone or something out (of something) **1.** to lift or pull someone or something out of something. □ *The mother picked her child out of the fray and took him home.* 🅃 *I picked out the mushrooms before eating the soup.* □ *Larry fell off the boat into the water, and I picked him out.* **2.** to select someone or something out of an offering of selections. □ *I picked Jerry out of all the boys in the class.* 🅃 *I picked out Jerry.* □ *I picked Jerry out.*

pick someone or something up (from something) **1.** to lift up or raise someone or something from a lower place. (*Someone* includes *oneself.*) □ *Please help me pick this guy up from the pavement. He passed out and fell down.* 🅃 *Help me pick up this guy from the ground, will you?* □ *Please pick the papers up.* □ *Slowly, she picked herself up from the ground.* **2.** to fetch someone or something from something or some place. □ *I picked her up from the train station.* 🅃 *Please pick up my cousin from the airport.* □ *I have to pick my dog up from the vet.* □ *The police picked Max up for questioning.* **3.** to acquire someone or something. □ *They* *picked some valuable antiques up at an auction.* 🅃 *She picked up a cold last week.* 🅃 *I picked up a little German while I was in Austria.*

pick up to increase, as with business, wind, activity, etc. □ *Business is beginning to pick up as we near the holiday season.* □ *The wind picked up about midnight.*

pick up (after someone or something) to tidy up after someone or a group. (*Someone* includes *oneself.*) □ *I refuse to pick up after you all the time.* □ *I refuse to pick up after your rowdy friends.* □ *Why do I always have to pick up?* □ *You have to learn to pick up after yourself.*

piece something together to fit something together; to assemble the pieces of something, such as a puzzle or something puzzling, and make sense of it. □ *The police were unable to piece the story together.* 🅃 *The detective tried to piece together the events leading up to the crime.*

pile in(to something) to climb into something in a disorderly fashion. □ *Everyone piled into the car, and we left.* □ *Come on. Pile in!*

pile off (something) to get down off something; to clamber down off something. □ *All the kids piled off the wagon and ran into the barn.* □ *She stopped the wagon, and they piled off.*

pile on((to) someone or something) to make a heap of people on someone or something. □ *The football players piled onto the poor guy holding the ball.* □ *They ran up to the ballcarrier and piled on.*

pile out (of something) to climb out of something, such as a car. □ *All the kids piled out of the van and ran into the school.* □ *The van pulled up, and the kids piled out.*

pile someone in(to something) to bunch people into something in a disorderly fashion. (*Someone* includes *oneself.*) □ *She piled the kids into the van and headed off for school.* 🅃 *She piled in the kids and closed the doors.* □ *Pile them in and let's go.* □ *They piled themselves into the car and sped off.*

pile something up to make something into a heap. □ *Carl piled all the leaves up and set them afire.* 🅃 *Please pile up the leaves.*

pile up **1.** to gather or accumulate. ☐ *The newspapers began to pile up after a few days.* ☐ *Work is really piling up around here.* **2.** [for a number of vehicles] to crash together. ☐ *Nearly twenty cars piled up on the tollway this morning.*

pilot someone or something through (something) to guide or steer someone or something through something, especially through a waterway. (Literal or figurative with people or things.) ☐ *We hired someone to pilot us through the harbor entrance.* ☐ *The channel was treacherous, and we hired someone to pilot the ship through.* ☐ *John offered to pilot us through the bureaucracy when we went to the courthouse.*

pilot something in(to something) to steer or guide something into something. (Usually refers to steering a ship.) ☐ *We need to signal for a pilot to pilot our ship into the harbor.* 🅃 *Fred piloted in the freighter.* ☐ *Mary piloted the ship in.*

pilot something out (of something) to steer or guide something out of something. (Usually refers to steering a ship.) ☐ *The chubby little man with a pipe piloted the huge ship out of the harbor.* ☐ *The storm made it very difficult to pilot the ship out.*

pin someone down (on something) AND **nail someone down (on something)** to demand and receive a firm answer from someone to some question. ☐ *I tried to pin him down on a time and place, but he was very evasive.* 🅃 *Don't try to pin down the mayor on anything!* ☐ *I want to nail her down on a meeting time.* ☐ *It's hard to pin her down. She is so busy.*

pin something up to raise something and hold it up with pins. ☐ *I will pin this hem up and then sew it later.* 🅃 *Please pin up the hem so I can see where to sew it.*

pinch something back to pinch off a bit of the top of a plant so it will branch and grow more strongly. ☐ *You should pinch this back so it will branch.* 🅃 *Pinch back the new leaves at the top.*

pipe up (with something) to interject a comment; to interrupt with a comment. ☐ *Nick piped up with an interesting thought.* ☐ *You can always count on Alice to pipe up.*

pitch in (and help) (with something) to join in and help someone with something. ☐ *Would you please pitch in and help with the* *party?* ☐ *Come on! Pitch in!* ☐ *Please pitch in with the dishes!* ☐ *Can't you pitch in and help?*

pitch someone or something out ((of) something) to throw someone or something out of something or some place. ☐ *The usher pitched the drunk out of the theater.* 🅃 *The usher pitched out the annoying person.* ☐ *The officer arrested the driver because he pitched a can out the car window.*

plan something out to make thorough plans for something. ☐ *Let us sit down and plan our strategy out.* 🅃 *We sat down and planned out our strategy.*

plane something down to smooth something down with a plane. ☐ *I will have to plane the door down before I hang it again.* 🅃 *I planed down the edge of the door for you.*

play along (with someone or something) **1.** to play a musical instrument with someone or a group. ☐ *The trombonist sat down and began to play along with the others.* ☐ *Do you mind if I play along?* **2.** to pretend to cooperate with someone or something in a joke, scam, etc. ☐ *I decided that I would play along with Larry for a while and see what would happen.* ☐ *I don't think I want to play along.*

play out to run out; to finish. ☐ *The whole incident is about to play out. Then it all will be forgotten.* ☐ *When the event plays out, everything will return to normal.*

play someone or something up to emphasize someone or something; to support or boost someone or something. ☐ *Her mother kept playing Jill up, hoping she would get chosen.* 🅃 *She played up her daughter to anyone who would listen.* ☐ *Don't play our weak points up so much.*

play something back (to someone) to play a recording to someone. ☐ *Can you play the speech back to me?* 🅃 *Please play back the speech to me, so I can hear how I sound.* ☐ *Let me play it back.*

play something through to play something, such as a piece of music or a record, all the way through. ☐ *I played the album through, hoping to find even one song I liked.* 🅃 *As I played through the album, I didn't hear anything I liked.*

play up to someone to flatter someone; to try to gain influence with someone. □ *It won't do any good to play up to me. I refuse to agree to your proposal.* □ *I played up to my dad, but he still wouldn't let me go to the concert.*

play (up)on something **1.** to make music on a musical instrument. (*Upon* is formal and less commonly used than *on.*) □ *Can you play upon this instrument, or only the one you are holding?* □ *I can't play on this! It's broken.* **2.** to exploit something, such a word, for some purpose; to develop something for some purpose. (*Upon* is formal and less commonly used than *on.*) □ *You are just playing on words!* □ *You are playing on a misunderstanding.* **3.** [for light] to sparkle on something. □ *The reflections of the candles played on the surface of the soup.* □ *The lights played on the crystal goblets.*

plot something out to map something out; to outline a plan for something. □ *I have an idea about how to remodel this room. Let me plot it out for you.* [T] *I plotted out my ideas for the room.*

plow something back into something to put something, such as a profit, back into an investment. □ *We plowed all the profits back into the expansion of the business.* [T] *Bill and Ted plowed back everything they earned into the company.*

plow something in to work something into the soil by plowing. □ *Lay the fertilizer down and plow it in.* [T] *Plow in the fertilizer as soon as you can.*

plow something under (something) to push something under the surface of the soil or of water. □ *The farmer plowed the wheat stubble under the surface of the soil.* □ *The farmer plowed the stubble under.*

plow through something to work through something laboriously. □ *I have to plow through all the paperwork this weekend.* □ *Will you help me plow through all these contracts?*

pluck something off ((of) someone or something) to pick something off someone or something. (The *of* is colloquial.) □ *She plucked the mosquito off his back before it could bite him.* [T] *She plucked off the bud.* □ *There is an unnecessary branch on the plant. Please pluck it off.*

pluck something out (of something) to snatch something out of something. □ *She plucked the coin out of his hand and put it in her shoe.* 🅃 *Reaching into the fountain, Jane plucked out the coin.* □ *Mary plucked it out.*

pluck up someone's courage to bolster someone's, including one's own, courage. □ *I hope you are able to pluck up your courage so that you can do what has to be done.* □ *Some good advice from a friend helped pluck up my courage.*

plug away (at someone or something) to keep working at someone or something. □ *I will just keep plugging away at Fred. I will convince him yet.* □ *I won't leave him alone. I'll keep plugging away.*

plug something in(to something) to connect something to something else, usually by connecting wires together with a plug and socket. □ *Plug this end of the wire into the wall.* 🅃 *Plug in the lamp and turn it on.* □ *Please plug this in.* □ *Is the vacuum cleaner plugged in?*

plug something up to fill up a hole; to block a hole or opening. □ *Please plug this hole up so the cold air doesn't get in.* 🅃 *Can you plug up the hole?*

plump something up to pat or shake something like a pillow into a fuller shape. □ *Todd plumped his pillow up and finished making the bed.* 🅃 *He plumped up his pillow.*

plunge in(to something) to dive or rush into something; to immerse oneself in something. □ *Ned took off his shoes and plunged into the river, hoping to rescue Frank.* □ *He plunged into his work and lost track of time.* □ *Barry strode to the side of the pool and plunged in.*

plunge something in(to someone or something) to drive or stab something into someone or something. □ *The murderer plunged the knife into his victim.* 🅃 *She plunged in the dagger.* □ *Ken plunged the cooked pasta into cold* water.

point someone or something out to identify someone or something in a group; to select someone or something from a group. □ *I don't know what June looks like, so you will have to point her out.* 🅃 *Will you point out June, please?* □ *I pointed the door out to her.*

poke out (of something) to stick out of something; to extend out of something. □ *The bean sprouts were beginning to poke out of the soil of the garden.* □ *I knew there were little birds in the birdhouse, because a little head poked out now and then.*

poke something in(to something) to stick or cram something into something. □ *He poked his finger into the jam, pulled it out again, and licked it.* 🅃 *Jeff poked his finger into the pie crust.* □ *Don't poke your finger in!*

polish something off to eat, consume, exhaust, or complete all of something. □ *Who polished the cake off?* 🅃 *Who polished off the cake?* 🅃 *She polished off her chores in record time.*

polish something up to rub something until it shines. □ *Polish the silver up and make it look nice and shiny.* 🅃 *If you will polish up the silver, I will put it away.*

ponder (up)on something to think on something; to consider something. (*Upon* is formal and less commonly used than *on*.) □ *Ponder upon this awhile. See what you come up with.* □ *I need to ponder on this.*

pop out (of something) to jump out of something; to burst out of something. □ *Suddenly, a little mouse popped out of the drawer.* □ *I opened the drawer and a mouse popped out.*

pop something in(to something) to fit, snap, or press something into place in something. □ *Lee popped the lever into place, and the machine began to function.* 🅃 *Lee popped in the plastic part, and the toy ran beautifully.* □ *He popped the part in.*

pop something on((to) something) to snap something onto something. □ *Denise took one more sip of the medicine and popped the lid onto the bottle.* 🅃 *She popped on the lid when she was finished.* □ *Mary popped the top on and put the box away.*

pop something out (of something) to release something from something so that it jumps or bursts out, possibly with a popping sound. □ *Sue popped the cork out of the champagne bottle.* □ *It took a little effort to pop the cork out.*

pop up (some place) to appear suddenly and unexpectedly some place. □ *I never know where Henry is going to pop up next.* □ *A* *new problem has popped up.* ☐ *Guess who popped up at the office today?*

pounce (up)on someone or something to spring or swoop upon someone or something; to seize someone or something. (*Upon* is formal and less commonly used than *on*.) ☐ *As Gerald came into the room, his friend Daniel pounced on him and frightened him to death.* ☐ *The cat pounced upon a mouse.* ☐ *The preacher pounced on me after church and talked my ear off.* ☐ *The teacher pounced on all my spelling errors immediately.*

pound away (at someone or something) to hammer or batter constantly on someone or something. ☐ *The cops pounded away at the poor guy, and then they put him in handcuffs.* ☐ *The jackhammer kept pounding away at the pavement.* ☐ *Two jackhammers pounded away all morning.*

pound something down to hammer, flatten, or batter something. ☐ *Please pound that nail down so that no one gets hurt on it.* 🅃 *Yes, please pound down that nail!* ☐ *The butcher pounded the chicken breasts down.*

pound something in(to someone) See *hammer something in(to someone).*

pound something in(to something) See *hammer something in(to something).*

pour out (of something) [for someone or something] to stream or gush out of something or some place. ☐ *The water poured out of the broken pipe and flooded the basement.* ☐ *The pipe split and the water just poured out.*

pour something off ((of) something) to spill liquid off the top of something. (The *of* is colloquial.) ☐ *Valerie poured the cream off the milk.* 🅃 *Valerie poured off the cream.* ☐ *She poured the water off.*

power something up to start something, such as an engine. ☐ *You should power the engine up and let it run awhile before you drive away.* 🅃 *Power up the engine and mow the grass.*

power up to start an engine. □ *Well, let's power up so we will be ready to leave with the others.* □ *It's time to power up and get going.*

press against someone or something to push or bear upon someone or something. □ *I pressed against Henry, trying gently to get him to move out of the way.* □ *Don't press against the glass door!*

press down on someone or something to push down on someone or something. □ *The weight of all the covers was pressing down on me, and I couldn't sleep.* □ *Press down on this lever and the recorder will start.*

press on something to push or depress something, such as a button, catch, snap, etc. □ *Press on this button if you require room service.* □ *Don't press on this because it rings a loud bell.*

press something against someone or something to push or force something against someone or something. □ *The person in line behind Betty kept pressing his elbow against her.* □ *I pressed my hand against the door and it opened.*

press something in(to something) **1.** to force something into something, such as a mold. □ *Now, you need to press the clay into the mold carefully.* 🅃 *Now, hold the mold with one hand and press in the clay.* □ *Press it in.* **2.** to force or drive something into the surface of something. □ *You are standing on my chewing gum, and you have pressed it into the carpet!* 🅃 *Don't press in the gum by standing on it.* □ *You pressed the gum in!*

press something on(to something) to put pressure on something and cause it to stick to the surface of something. □ *I pressed the label onto the envelope and took it to the post office.* 🅃 *I pressed on the label.* □ *With much effort, I pressed the label on so it would stick.*

press something out (of something) to squeeze something out of something by applying pressure. □ *The Indians press the acid out of the manioc before they use it as food.* □ *Gene used an iron to press the wrinkles out of his suit coat.* 🅃 *They pressed out the acid.* □ *Gerald pressed the wrinkles out.*

press (up)on someone or something to put pressure on someone or something. (*Upon* is formal and less commonly used than *on*.) □

The crowd pressed upon the child, squeezing out all his breath. □ *The load presses on your car's springs very heavily.*

presume (up)on someone or something to take unwelcome advantage of someone or something. (*Upon* is formal and less commonly used than *on.*) □ *I didn't mean to seem to presume upon you. I apologize.* □ *I did not feel that you presumed on me.*

prevail (up)on someone or something (to do something) to appeal to someone or a group to do something. (*Upon* is formal and less commonly used than *on.*) □ *I will prevail upon her to attend the meeting.* □ *I prevailed on the committee to no avail.*

prey (up)on someone or something to take advantage of someone or something. (*Upon* is formal and less commonly used than *on.*) □ *The people of that island prey on tourists and do not give them good treatment.* □ *I really don't want to seem to prey on your kindness.*

print something out **1.** to write something out by drawing letters. □ *Please print it out. I can't read your handwriting.* [T] *Print out your name, please.* **2.** to use a computer printer to print something. □ *I will print a copy out and send it to you.* [T] *Please print out another copy.*

print something up to set something in type and print it; to print something by any process. □ *This looks okay to me. Let's print it up now.* [T] *Print up the final version.*

prune something off ((of) something) to cut something off something. (The *of* is colloquial.) □ *Claire pruned the dead branch off the apple tree.* [T] *She pruned off the dead branch.*

pry into something to snoop into something; to get into someone else's business. □ *Why are you prying into my affairs all the time?* □ *I wish you wouldn't pry into things.*

pry something off ((of) something) to use a lever to get something off something. (The *of* is colloquial.) □ *Tom pried the top off the jelly jar.* [T] *He pried off the jar top.* □ *Tom pried it off.*

pry something up to raise something, as with a lever. □ *See if you can pry that trapdoor up.* [T] *Pry up that lid.*

puff out to swell out. ☐ *The frog's throat puffed out, and we expected to hear a croak.* ☐ *The sail puffed out, and the boat began to move.*

puff someone or something up to boost or promote someone or something. (*Someone* includes *oneself.*) ☐ *Judy puffed Nell up so much that Nell could not begin to live up to her own reputation.* 🅃 *Don't puff up your own interests so much.* ☐ *Wally puffed himself up so much that he couldn't live up to his own image.*

puff something out to cause something to swell out or expand outward. ☐ *The frog puffed its throat out and croaked.* 🅃 *The frog puffed out its throat and croaked a mighty croak.*

puff up (into something) to assume a larger shape by filling up with air or water; to swell up into something. ☐ *The strange-looking fish puffed up into a round ball.* ☐ *The fish puffed up and stuck out its spines.*

pull in(to some place) to drive into some place. ☐ *A strange car just pulled into our driveway.* ☐ *Some stranger just pulled in.*

pull off (something) to steer or turn a vehicle off the road. ☐ *I pulled off the road and rested for a while.* ☐ *I had to pull off and rest.*

pull out (of something) **1.** to withdraw from something. ☐ *For some reason, he pulled out of the coalition and went his own way.* ☐ *The other side got impatient with the negotiations and pulled out.* **2.** to drive out of something, such as a driveway, parking space, garage, etc. ☐ *The car pulled out of the driveway and nearly hit a truck.* ☐ *Look out! A car is about to pull out!*

pull someone in(to something) to get someone involved in something. ☐ *Please don't pull me into this argument.* 🅃 *Don't pull in anyone else.* ☐ *It's not my affair. Don't pull me in!*

pull someone or something up to drag or haul someone or something upward or to an upright position. (*Someone* includes *oneself.*) ☐ *Bob had slipped down into the creek, so I reached down and pulled him up.* 🅃 *I pulled up Bob and nearly fell in myself.* ☐ *Nick pulled the cushion up and propped it against the back of the sofa.*

☐ *The injured soldier pulled himself up with the greatest of difficulty.*

pull something down to tear something down; to raze something, such as a building. ☐ *The developers decided not to pull the historic house down.* 🅃 *They tried to pull down the old house.*

pull something down over someone or something to draw something down over someone or something. ☐ *Lucy's mother pulled the dress down over Lucy and buttoned it up in back.* ☐ *Sarah pulled the cover down over the birdcage and turned out the lights.*

pull something off ((of) something) to tug or drag something off something else. (The *of* is colloquial.) ☐ *Sam pulled the covers off the bed and fell into it, dead tired.* 🅃 *He pulled off the covers.* ☐ *Sam pulled them off.*

pull something out to withdraw something. ☐ *Arthur pulled his sword out and saluted the knight.* 🅃 *He pulled out his sword.*

pull something up (out of something) to draw something upward out of something. ☐ *The worker pulled a cold wet dog up out of the well.* 🅃 *He pulled up the dog out of the well.* ☐ *Sam reached down and pulled the dog up.*

pull through (something) to survive something. ☐ *I am sure that your uncle will pull through the illness.* ☐ *I'm glad he pulled through.*

pull up (some place) to arrive at a place in a vehicle; [for a vehicle] to arrive some place. ☐ *She pulled up at the front door exactly on time.* ☐ *Alice pulled up exactly on time.*

pump something in(to someone or something) to try to force something, such as a gas, liquid, information, or money into someone or something. ☐ *First you have to pump some air into the ball to make it hard.* 🅃 *I pumped in the air.* ☐ *The hospital oxygen system pumped life-giving oxygen into Karen's lungs.* ☐ *The small pump near the aquarium pumped air in.* ☐ *I helped pump anatomical terms into Fred for the big test he was having the next day.* 🅃 *I pumped in the knowledge.* ☐ *Congress tried to pump* *money into the economy, but only created inflation.* □ *The young teacher worked hard to pump new life into the classroom.*

pump something out to empty something by pumping. □ *I need to buy a large pump to pump my basement out.* 🅃 *I have to pump out my basement.*

pump something out (of someone or something) to remove something from someone or something by force or suction. □ *The doctors pumped the poison out of her.* 🅃 *They pumped out the poison.* □ *They used electric pumps to pump the water out.*

punch in to record one's arrival at one's workplace at a certain time. □ *What time did you punch in?* □ *I punched in at the regular time.*

punch out to record that one has left one's workplace at a certain time. □ *Why didn't you punch out when you left last night?* □ *I punched out at the regular time.*

punch something out (of something) to press on something and make it pop out of something. □ *She punched the stickers out of the page and stuck them onto her schoolbooks.* 🅃 *Jane punched out the stickers.* □ *Punch another one out for me.*

punch something up to register a figure on a cash register. □ *Jake punched the total up, and the register drawer opened.* 🅃 *He punched up the total too carelessly.*

push (oneself) away (from something) to move oneself back and away from something. □ *The skater pushed herself away from the wall.* □ *Tom pushed himself away from the table when he had eaten enough.*

push out to spread out; to expand outward. □ *The sides of the box pushed out, and I was afraid it would break.* □ *His little tummy pushed out when he was full.*

push someone or something out (of something) to force someone or something out of something. (*Someone* includes *oneself*.) □ *Nick pushed the intruder out of the house.* 🅃 *Nick pushed out the intruder.* □ *Elaine opened the door and pushed the dog out.* □ *He* *pushed himself out of the door of the plane and parachuted to the ground.*

push someone or something up to raise or lift someone or something. ☐ *Jake is sliding down again. Push him up.* 🅃 *Push up the window, please.*

push something off on(to) someone to place one's task onto another person; to make someone else do an unwanted job. ☐ *Don't push the dirty work off onto me.* ☐ *Kelly pushed her job off on me.* ☐ *I will try to push the cleaning off onto Sally and Todd.*

put on to pretend; to deceive. ☐ *She is not really that way. She is just putting on.* ☐ *Stop putting on. Act yourself.*

put oneself out to inconvenience oneself. ☐ *I just don't know why I put myself out for you!* ☐ *No, I did not put myself out at all. It was no trouble, in fact.* ☐ *She refused to put herself out even one little bit.*

put out to generate lots of something. (Colloquial.) ☐ *What a great machine. It really puts out!* ☐ *The outlet of the dam really puts out!*

put someone off **1.** to delay action with someone. ☐ *I hate to keep putting you off, but we are not ready to deal with you yet.* 🅃 *I had to put off the plumber again. He really wants his money.* **2.** to repel someone. ☐ *You really put people off with your scowling face.* 🅃 *You put off people with your frown.*

put someone on to tease or deceive someone. ☐ *You can't be serious! You're just putting me on!* ☐ *Stop putting me on!*

put someone or something over to succeed in making someone or something be accepted. (*Someone* includes *oneself.*) ☐ *The public relations expert helped put John over to the public.* ☐ *Do you think we can put this over?* ☐ *Do you think I put myself over all right?*

put someone out to annoy or irritate someone. ☐ *He really put me out when he used a saucer for an ashtray.* ☐ *I didn't mean to put you out. I had no idea you were so touchy.*

put someone up (for something) to nominate or offer someone for some office or task. □ *I put Henry up for dogcatcher.* [T] *We put up Shannon for treasurer.*

put something across (to someone) to make something clear to someone. □ *I don't know how to put this point across to my class. Can you help?* □ *Can you help me put this across?*

put something down to take the life of a creature mercifully. □ *It's kind to put fatally ill animals down.* [T] *We put down our old dog last year.*

put something off (until something) to postpone or delay something until something else happens or until some future time. □ *I can't put this off until tomorrow.* [T] *I will put off the review until next week.* □ *I can put it off forever if you want.*

put something on to dress in an article of clothing. □ *Put your coat on, and let's go.* [T] *Put on your coat, and let's go.*

put something up (for sale) to offer something for sale. □ *We had to put the farm up for sale because the crops failed once too often.* [T] *They put up their house for sale.* □ *They are going to sell the house themselves. They put it up last Saturday.*

puzzle something out to figure something out. □ *It took me a while to puzzle it out.* [T] *I puzzled out the answer to the question.*

Q

quarrel (with someone) (about someone or something) to have an argument with someone about the subject of someone or something. ☐ *Please don't quarrel with me about money.* ☐ *You are always quarreling with Claire.* ☐ *They are quarreling about Donna.*

quarrel (with someone) (over someone or something) to have an argument with someone about who is going to have someone or something. ☐ *Todd quarreled with Carl over who was going to get the new secretary.* ☐ *They are quarreling over Sally.* ☐ *Don't quarrel over money.*

queue up (for something) to line up for something. (Typically British.) ☐ *We had to queue up for tickets to the play.* ☐ *You must queue up.*

quiet down to become quiet; to become less noisy. ☐ *Please quiet down.* ☐ *Ask them to quiet down.*

quiet someone or something down to make someone or some creature more quiet. (*Someone* includes *oneself.*) ☐ *Please go and quiet the children down.* 🅃 *Try to quiet down the children.* ☐ *Please quiet that dog down.* ☐ *He was able to quiet himself down by taking a tranquilizer.*

quit on someone **1.** [for something] to quit while someone is using it. ☐ *This stupid car quit on me.* ☐ *I hope this thing doesn't quit on me.* **2.** [for one] to leave one's job, usually suddenly or unannounced. ☐ *Wally, the mayor, quit on us at the last minute.* ☐ *My boss quit on me.* ☐ *I don't know what to do. Both of my waitresses quit on me over the weekend.*

R

race with someone or something to enter a speed contest with someone or something. □ *I refuse to race with Carla. She is much too fast for me.* □ *I can't race with a horse!*

rack something up **1.** to place something onto or into its rack. □ *You had better rack the billiard balls up when you finish this time.* [T] *Please rack up the balls.* **2.** to accumulate a number of things, particularly a score, a win, etc. □ *The Bears racked their fourth victory up.* [T] *They hope to rack up a few more points before the end of the game.*

raffle something off to dispose of something by a drawing or raffle. □ *They will raffle a television set off.* [T] *They are going to raffle off a television set this weekend at the school.*

rage through something **1.** [for a fire] to burn rapidly through an area or a building. □ *The fire raged through the unoccupied building.* □ *When the fire began to rage through the forest, we knew we had better head for the river.* **2.** [for someone] to move rapidly through some sequence or process, as if in a rage. □ *Harry raged through the contract, looking for more errors.* □ *She raged through the book, angry with everything she read.*

railroad someone into something to force someone into doing something in great haste. □ *The committee tried to railroad me into signing the contract.* □ *You can't railroad me into doing anything!*

railroad something through (something) to force something through some organization or legislative body without due consideration. □ *The committee railroaded the new constitution through the ratification process.* □ *Mary felt she could railroad the legislation through.*

rain down on someone or something to fall or drop down on someone or something like rain. ☐ *The ashes from the incinerator rained down on us, getting our clothes dirty.* ☐ *The hail rained down on us, some of it quite large.*

rain in on someone or something [for rain] to enter a window or other opening and get someone or something wet. ☐ *Carol left the window open, and it rained in on her in the night.* ☐ *The storm rained in on my carpet!*

rain something down (on someone or something) to pour something, such as criticism or praise, onto someone or something. ☐ *The employees rained criticism down on the manager for the new policy on sick leave.* 🅃 *The audience rained down compliments on the performers.*

rain something out [for rain] to force the cancellation of an outdoor event. ☐ *It looked as if the storm would rain the picnic out, but it blew over before causing any trouble.* 🅃 *The storm rained out the game.*

raise someone or something up to lift someone or something up. (*Someone* includes *oneself.*) ☐ *The aides raised the dying man up while the nurse spread clean linen beneath him.* 🅃 *Jane raised up the lid.* ☐ *He raised himself up with the greatest of difficulty.*

raise up to lift oneself up; to get up or begin to get up. ☐ *She raised up and then fell back onto her bed. She was too weak to get up.* ☐ *I could not raise up enough to see out the window.*

rake something off ((of) something) to remove something from something by raking. (The *of* is colloquial.) ☐ *Please rake the leaves off the lawn.* 🅃 *Rake off the leaves.* ☐ *Please rake them off.*

rake something out to clean something by raking. ☐ *Please rake the gutter out.* 🅃 *You ought to rake out the flower beds. They are a mess.*

rake something out (of something) to clean something out of something by raking. ☐ *You ought to rake the leaves out of the gutter so the water will flow.* 🅃 *Please rake out the leaves.*

rake something up **1.** to gather and clean up something with a rake. ☐ *Would you please rake these leaves up before it rains?* 🅃 *Please* *rake up the leaves.* **2.** to clean something up by raking. ☐ *Would you rake the yard up?* 🅃 *I will rake up the yard.* **3.** to find some unpleasant information. ☐ *His opposition raked an old scandal up and made it public.* 🅃 *That is ancient history. Why did you have to rake up that old story?*

rally around someone or something to unite or assemble in support of someone or something. ☐ *All the other workers rallied around Fred in his fight with management.* ☐ *They rallied around the principle that Fred stood for.*

ram something through (something) **1.** to force something through something. ☐ *He rammed his fist through the window, cutting himself in the process.* ☐ *Harry put the brick up to the window glass and rammed it through. Next time he would remember his key.* 🅃 *The brick rammed through the glass.* **2.** to force something through a deliberative body, usually not allowing due consideration. ☐ *They rammed the bill through the city council.* ☐ *The President was unable to ram the measure through Congress.* 🅃 *They rammed through the bill.*

ram through something to crash or pound through something. ☐ *The car rammed through the back of the garage.* ☐ *I was afraid that the truck would ram through the fence.*

ramble on to go on and on aimlessly; to wander about aimlessly. (Usually figurative. As with a road, a speaker, a speech, etc.) ☐ *The road rambled on through mile after mile of wilderness.* ☐ *The speaker rambled on for almost an hour without really saying anything.*

ramble on (about someone or something) [for someone] to talk endlessly and aimlessly about someone or something. ☐ *I wish you wouldn't ramble on about your first husband all the time.* ☐ *Must you ramble on so?*

range from something to something to vary from one thing to another. ☐ *The weather ranges from bad to terrible in this part of the north.* ☐ *The appraisals of the property ranged from high to low.*

rap something out (on something) to tap out the rhythm of something on something. ☐ *Try to rap the rhythm out on the table.* 🅃 *He* *rapped out the rhythm on the table.* □ *Rap it out and hum the song as you do.*

rattle around in something **1.** to make a rattling noise inside something. □ *What is rattling around in this package?* □ *There is something rattling around in my glove compartment.* **2.** to ride about in a rattly vehicle. □ *I am perfectly happy to rattle around in my ten-year-old car.* □ *Todd rattles around in his grandfather's old car.* **3.** to live in a place that is much too big. (Figurative.) □ *We have been rattling around in this big old house for long enough. Let's move to a smaller place.* □ *I can't afford to rattle around in a three-story house any longer.*

rattle something off to recite something with ease; to recite a list quickly and easily. □ *He rattled the long list of names off without even taking a breath.* 🅃 *He rattled off the long list of names without even taking a breath.*

reach back (in)to something to extend back into a particular period in time. □ *This policy reaches back into the last century.* □ *Our way of making fine candies reaches back to the recipes used by the founder of the company.*

reach down to extend downward. □ *The stems of the plant reached down almost to the floor.* □ *The drapes don't quite reach down to the floor.*

reach in(to something) to stick one's hand into something to grasp something. □ *Bob reached into the cookie jar and found it empty.* □ *Bob went to the cookie jar and reached in.*

reach out **1.** to extend one's grasp outward. □ *He reached out, but there was no one to take hold of.* □ *I reached out and grabbed onto the first thing I could get hold of.* **2.** to enlarge one's circle of friends and experiences. □ *If you are that lonely, you ought to reach out. Get to know some new friends.* □ *I need to reach out more and meet people.*

reach out (after someone or something) to extend one's grasp to someone or something. □ *Don reached out after Doris, but she slipped away before he could get a good hold on her.* □ *Doris reached out after the door, but it slammed closed.* □ *As she reached out, the door closed.*

reach out into something to extend one's grasp out into something, such as the darkness. □ *Laura reached out into the darkness, looking for the light switch.* □ *Jane reached out into the night, hoping to find a lamp or even a candle.*

reach out to someone **1.** to offer someone a helping hand. □ *You reached out to me just when I needed help the most.* □ *I reach out to other people in trouble because I would want someone to do that for me.* **2.** to seek someone's help and support. □ *When I reached out to Don for help, he turned me down.* □ *Jane reached out to her friends for the help and support that she needed.*

reach something down to hand something down. (Colloquial.) □ *Please reach the hammer down to me.* 🆃 *Would you reach down the hammer to Jane?*

read someone out (for something) to chastise someone verbally for doing something wrong. □ *The coach read the player out for making a silly error.* □ *She really read the players out.* 🆃 *The coach read out the whole team.*

read someone out of something to make a case for the removal of someone from something. □ *The chairman read the absent members out of the organization.* □ *Dave was read out of the club.*

read something back (to someone) to read back some information to the person who has just given it. □ *Yes, I have written the telephone number down. Let me read it back to you to make sure I have it right.* 🆃 *Please read back the letter to me.* □ *Did you copy the number correctly? Please read it back.*

read something in((to) something) to presume inferences as one reads something; to imagine that additional messages, ideas, or biases are present in something that one is reading. □ *Just accept the words for what they mean. Don't read something else into it.* □ *Don't read anything in.*

read something off to read aloud a list. □ *Nick read the list of the names off, and I wasn't on the list.* 🆃 *Jane read off the names.*

read something over to read something, concentrating on form as well as content. □ *Please read this over and report back to me when you are finished.* 🆃 *I will read over the report and talk to you later.*

read through something to look through some reading material. ☐ *I read through your proposal and find that it has merits.* ☐ *Please read through this at your convenience.*

read up (on someone or something) to study about someone or something by reading. ☐ *I have to read up on Milton Berle for a report I have to write.* ☐ *I can't write a word about him until I read up.*

rear back 1. [for a horse] to pull back onto its hind legs in an effort to move backwards rapidly. ☐ *The animal reared back in terror.* ☐ *The horse reared back and almost threw its rider.* **2.** [for a person] to pull back and stand up or sit up straighter. ☐ *He reared back in his chair and looked perturbed.* ☐ *Tom reared back in his chair, waiting for something else to happen.*

rear up 1. [for a horse] to lean back on its hind legs and raise its front part up, assuming a threatening posture or avoiding something on the ground such as a snake. ☐ *The horse reared up suddenly, throwing the rider onto the ground.* ☐ *When the horse reared up, I almost fell off.* **2.** [for something, especially a problem] to raise up suddenly. (Figurative.) ☐ *A new problem reared up and cost us a lot of time.* ☐ *A lot of new costs reared up toward the end of the month.*

reason something out to figure something out; to plan a reasonable course of action. ☐ *Now let's be calm and try to reason this out.* T *Let us reason out our difficulties.*

record something on something to make a record of something on the surface of something. ☐ *Nancy recorded the appointment on the calendar that served as a blotter on the top of her desk.* ☐ *Please record this on your calendar.*

recount something to someone to tell something to someone; to narrate a series of events, in order. ☐ *Carl recounted the events of the day to his wife.* ☐ *The strange events were recounted by a number of people.*

recruit someone into something to seek out and induct someone into something. ☐ *The colonel tried to recruit ten people a week into the army.* ☐ *The army recruited almost no one during the month of December.*

recuperate from something to recover from something; to be cured or to heal after something. □ *I hope that you recuperate from your illness soon.* □ *Has she recuperated from her surgery yet?*

reel something in to bring in something, such as a fish, by winding up the line on a reel. □ *With great effort, she reeled the huge fish in.* 🅃 *Hurry and reel in the fish!*

reel something off to recite a list or sequence of words, rapidly, from memory. □ *Jane reeled her speech off flawlessly.* 🅃 *Tony reeled off his speech as fast as he could.*

reel under something **1.** to stagger under the weight of something. □ *Tony reeled under the weight of the books.* □ *She knew she would reel under the heavy load.* **2.** to stagger because of a blow. □ *The boxer reeled under the blow to his chin.* □ *Max reeled under the beating that Lefty gave him.* **3.** to suffer because of a burden. (Figurative.) □ *Gary reeled under the responsibilities he had been given.* □ *I was just reeling under the burdens of my new job.*

refer someone back to someone or something to suggest that someone go back to someone or something, such as the source. □ *I referred the client back to the lawyer she had originally consulted.* □ *Tom referred the customer back to the manufacturer who had made the shoddy product.*

refer someone to someone or something to direct someone to someone or something; to send someone to someone or something. □ *The front office referred me to you, and you are now referring me to someone else!* □ *They should have referred you to the personnel department.*

refer something back (to someone or something) to send something back to someone or a group for action. □ *The Senate referred the bill back to committee.* □ *John had not seen it, so I referred it back to him.* 🅃 *They referred back all the bills.*

refrain from something to hold back from doing something; to choose not to do something as planned. □ *I wish you would refrain from shouting.* □ *Please refrain from hollering.*

regain something from someone or something to take possession of one's property or right from someone or something. □ *I* *intend to regain my money from Herb.* ☐ *The used car agency regained the car from the delinquent buyer.*

rely (up)on someone or something to depend on someone or something; to trust in someone or something. (*Upon* is formal and less commonly used than *on.*) ☐ *I know I can rely upon you to do a good job.* ☐ *Can we rely on this old car to get us there?*

remain up to stay awake and out of bed. ☐ *I remained up throughout most of the night.* ☐ *I cannot remain up much longer.*

remain within (something) to stay inside something or some place. ☐ *Please try to remain within the boundaries of the campus.* ☐ *Everyone else went out, but I decided to remain within.*

remark (up)on someone or something to comment on someone or something. (*Upon* is formal and less commonly used than *on.*) ☐ *She remarked upon his tardiness and then continued the lesson.* ☐ *There is no need to remark on me or anything I do or don't do.*

rend something from someone or something to tear something from someone or something. ☐ *Harry rent the burning clothing from the man who had just fled from the burning building.* ☐ *God rent the veil from the temple.*

report back to someone (on someone or something) to return to someone with information or an explanation of someone or something. ☐ *I need you to report back to me on Walter by noon.* ☐ *I'll report back to you as soon as I can.*

report back (to someone or something) **1.** to go back to someone or something and present oneself. ☐ *Report back to me at once!* ☐ *I'll report back immediately.* **2.** to present information or an explanation to someone. ☐ *Please report back to me when you have the proper information.* ☐ *I'll report back as soon as I have all the information.*

report for something to present oneself for something. ☐ *Please report for duty on Monday morning at eight sharp.* ☐ *I can't report for my examination at the time we agreed upon.*

rest up (for something) to take it easy in advance of something tiring. ☐ *Excuse me, but I have to go rest up for the concert tonight.* ☐ *I really need to rest up a while.*

rest up (from something) to recover or recuperate from something tiring. □ *I need about a week to rest up from my vacation.* □ *I'll need a few days to rest up.*

rest (up)on something to lie on something; to take it easy on something. (*Upon* is formal and less commonly used than *on*.) □ *Here, rest upon this mat.* □ *I'll just rest on this chair, thanks.* □ *She rested upon the couch for a while and then went out to weed the garden.*

retaliate against someone or something to take revenge against someone or something. □ *The administration will retaliate against the students by closing down the cafeteria.* □ *The students retaliated against the administration.*

retire from something to withdraw from something. (Usually to terminate a working career permanently.) □ *I retired from the company early.* □ *When do you intend to retire from your job?*

retire someone or something from something to take someone or something out of service permanently. □ *The company retired the vice president from the job and gave it to someone else.* □ *It is time to retire my automobile from service.*

rev something up to race an engine in one or more short bursts. □ *George revved the engine up and took off.* 🅃 *He revved up the engine.*

rev up to increase in amount or activity. □ *Production revved up after the strike.* □ *We're hoping business will rev up soon.*

revenge oneself (up)on someone or something to retaliate against someone or something. (*Upon* is formal and less commonly used than *on*.) □ *There is no need for you to revenge yourself upon Walter. It was an accident.* □ *I will revenge myself on the whole world!* □ *She did not know how she would revenge herself on Joe, but she knew she would.*

reverberate through something [for sound] to roll through or pass through a space. □ *The thunder reverberated through the valley.* □ *The sound of the organ reverberated through the church.*

reverberate with something to echo or resound with something. ☐ *The hall reverberated with the rich basso voice of Walter Rogers.* ☐ *The church reverberated with the roar of the pipe organ.*

ricochet off something [for some rapidly moving object, such as a bullet] to bounce off something at an oblique angle. ☐ *The bullet ricocheted off the wall and struck the gunman.* ☐ *Bullets were ricocheting off the walls from all angles.*

ride away to depart, riding a bike or a horse or similar animal. ☐ *She got on her horse and rode away.* ☐ *They rode away without even saying good-bye.*

ride off to depart, riding something such as a horse or a bicycle. ☐ *Betty said good-bye and rode off.* ☐ *We rode off, each one in a different direction.*

ride on to continue to ride, traveling onward. ☐ *We rode on for at least an hour before a rest stop.* ☐ *They rode on for a while.*

ride someone or something down to chase down someone or some creature while riding on horseback. ☐ *The mounted policeman rode the mugger down and captured him.* 🆃 *The rider rode down the thief.* 🆃 *We had to ride down the runaway horse.*

ride something down to ride on something that is going down, such as an elevator. ☐ *You take the stairs, and I will ride the elevator down.* ☐ *I don't want to ride the cable car down. I will walk.*

ride something out to endure something; to remain with something to the termination of something. ☐ *Things are rough in my department at the office, but I think I can ride it out.* 🆃 *I can ride out the storm if I can remember to be patient.*

ride up (on someone) **1.** [for someone on a horse] to approach someone, riding. ☐ *I rode up on him and frightened him.* ☐ *I guess I was in the house when you rode up.* **2.** [for clothing, especially underpants] to keep moving higher on one's body. ☐ *I don't like it when my pants ride up on me.* ☐ *I hate it when my underpants ride up.*

ride (up)on someone or something to use someone or something as a beast of burden. (*Upon* is formal and less commonly used than *on.)* ☐ *As a game, the children used to ride on their father.* ☐ *We rode upon burros along the narrow mountain trails.*

rifle through something to ransack something; to search through something looking for something to steal. ☐ *The teenager quickly rifled through the cabinets, looking for something worth eating.* ☐ *The soldiers rifled through every house they could break into.*

rig someone or something out (in something) to outfit someone or something in something; to decorate or dress someone or something in something. (*Someone* includes *oneself.*) ☐ *Joan rigged her daughter out in a witch's costume for the Halloween party.* 🅃 *He rigged out his car with lights for the parade.* ☐ *Alice rigged her bicycle out in festive colors.* ☐ *She rigged herself out in a clown suit and joined the circus for a day.*

rig something up to prepare something, perhaps on short notice or without the proper materials. ☐ *We don't have what's needed to make the kind of circuit you have described, but I think we can rig something up anyway.* 🅃 *We will rig up whatever you need.*

ring someone back to call someone back on the telephone. ☐ *I will have to ring you back later.* ☐ *Please ring me back when you have a moment.* 🅃 *I will ring back the caller when I have time.*

ring someone up to call someone on the telephone. (Chiefly British.) ☐ *I will ring her up when I get a chance.* 🅃 *I have to ring up a whole list of people.*

ring something up (on something) to record the amount of a sale on a cash register. ☐ *Jane rang the purchases up one by one on the cash register.* 🅃 *She rang up the purchases on the register as quick as lightning.* ☐ *She rang them up and collected the money.*

rinse someone or something down to wash or clean someone or something with water or other fluid. ☐ *I rinsed him down for an hour and still didn't get the smell of skunk off him.* 🅃 *I had to rinse down the driveway.*

rinse someone or something off to wash or clean someone or something by flushing with water or other fluid. (*Someone* includes *oneself.*) ☐ *Mother rinsed the baby off and dried him with a soft* *towel.* T *She rinsed off the baby.* □ *Coming out of the sea, she rinsed herself off with fresh water.*

rinse something out **1.** to clean cloth or clothing partially by immersing it in water and squeezing it out. □ *Can you please rinse this rag out? It's all dirty.* T *Please rinse out your clothes to make sure there is no soap left in them.* **2.** to launder something delicate, such as feminine underwear, using a mild soap. □ *I have to go rinse a few things out.* T *After I rinse out some things, I will be right with you.* **3.** to clean the inside of a container partially by flushing it out with water. □ *Rinse the bottle out and throw it away.* T *Rinse out the bottle and throw it away.*

rinse something out (of something) to remove something from something by flushing it with water. □ *See if you can rinse the dirt out of this jacket.* T *I can't rinse out the dirt.* □ *Then I'll rinse it out.*

rip into someone or something **1.** to attack someone or something. □ *The raccoons ripped into the trash bags, scattering papers and stuff all over the street.* □ *The horrid murderer ripped into the helpless victim.* **2.** to criticize or censure someone or something severely. □ *The drama critic ripped into Larry.* □ *The critics really ripped into Larry's poor performance.*

rip off [for something] to tear or peel off. □ *My pocket ripped off and my money is gone now!* □ *A piece of the bumper ripped off my car.*

rip someone or something up to tear someone or something into bits; to mutilate someone or something. (*Someone* includes *oneself.*) □ *Careful! That machine will rip you up if you fall in.* T *I ripped up the contract and threw the pieces in the air.* □ *I got mad and ripped the contract up.* □ *The dog fell into the lawn mower and ripped itself up badly.*

rip something down to tear something down. (Refers to something that has been posted or mounted.) □ *The custodian ripped all the posters down at the end of the day.* T *He ripped down the posters.*

rip something off ((of) someone or something) to tear something away from someone or something. (The *of* is colloquial.) □ *I ripped the cover off of the book accidentally.* T *I ripped off the* *book cover.* ☐ *He ripped the shirt off the injured man and began to treat the wound.* ☐ *Alice ripped the cover off.*

rip something out (of someone or something) to tear something out of someone or something. ☐ *The high priest ripped the beating heart out of the sacrificial victim.* 🅃 *The priest ripped out the victim's heart.* ☐ *He ripped the heart out and kicked the victim down the steep side of the pyramid.*

rip something up to take something up by force and remove it. (Usually refers to something on the floor or ground, such as carpeting or pavement.) ☐ *They are going to rip all the broken sidewalk up.* 🅃 *The workers ripped up the pavement and loaded the pieces into a truck.*

rise up **1.** to come up; to ascend. (Also without *up*, but not eligible as an entry.) ☐ *The water is rising up fast. You had better get to higher ground.* ☐ *As the water rose up, it covered the houses and streets.* **2.** to get up from lying down. ☐ *The deer rose up and darted off into the woods.* ☐ *I rose up and brushed off my clothing.*

rise (up) against someone or something to challenge someone or something; to rebel against someone or something. ☐ *The citizens rose up against their elected officials.* ☐ *They rose against the abusive power of the government.*

rivet something on(to) something to attach something to something with rivets. ☐ *The pockets of these jeans are riveted onto the body of the pants.* 🅃 *You should rivet on this part of the frame to the wall.* ☐ *Okay. I'll rivet it on the wall.*

roar something out to bellow something out loudly. ☐ *Walter roared his protest out so everyone knew how he felt.* 🅃 *Jane roared out her criticism.*

roll about to move about, turning or rotating, as a wheel or a ball. ☐ *The ball rolled about awhile and then came to rest.* ☐ *His eyes rolled about in amazement before he spoke.*

roll away to move away, rotating, turning over, turning, or moving on wheels. ☐ *The ball rolled away and fell down a storm sewer.* ☐ *The cart rolled away, and we had to chase it down the hill.*

roll back [for something] to return, rotating or turning or moving on wheels. ☐ *I rolled the ball away, thinking it would roll back. It didn't.* ☐ *I struck the golf ball away from the sand trap, but it rolled back.*

roll by **1.** to pass by, rotating, as a wheel or a ball; to move past, rolling on wheels. ☐ *The wheel of a car rolled by, all by itself. It must have come off a car somewhere down the road.* ☐ *The traffic rolled by relentlessly.* **2.** to move past, as if rolling. ☐ *The years rolled by, and soon the two people were old and gray.* ☐ *The clouds were rolling by, spreading patterns of light and dark across the land.*

roll down to move downward, rotating, as a wheel or a ball, or to move downward on wheels. ☐ *I pushed the wagon up the driveway, and it rolled down again.* ☐ *Don't place the cart at the top of the hill. It will roll down.*

roll down something to move downward, along something, rotating, as a wheel or a ball, or moving downward on wheels. ☐ *The ball rolled down the hall to the end.* ☐ *The cart went rolling down the hill all by itself.*

roll off (someone or something) to flow or fall off someone or something. (Both literal and figurative.) ☐ *The ball rolled off the shelf and bounced across the room.* ☐ *The ball rolled off and struck the lampshade.* ☐ *The insults rolled off Walter like water off a duck's back.*

roll on **1.** [for something] to continue rolling. ☐ *The ball rolled on and on.* ☐ *The cart came rolling down the hill and rolled on for a few yards at the bottom.* **2.** [for something] to be applied by rolling. ☐ *This kind of deodorant just rolls on.* ☐ *She rolled on too much paint and it dripped from the ceiling.* **3.** to move on slowly and evenly. (Figurative.) ☐ *The years rolled on, one by one.* ☐ *As the hours rolled on, I learned just how bored I could get without going to sleep.*

roll over to turn over; to rotate once. ☐ *The old man rolled over and started snoring again.* ☐ *Please roll over and give me some more space in the bed.*

roll something away to cause something to move away, rotating, turning over, turning, or moving on wheels. ☐ *Jane rolled the ball* *away and it was lost.* 🅃 *Jane rolled away the ball.* ☐ *Please roll the cart away.*

roll something back **1.** to return something to someone by rotating it, as with a wheel or a ball, or moving it back on wheels. ☐ *I intercepted the ball and rolled it back.* 🅃 *Jane rolled back the ball.* **2.** to reduce prices. ☐ *The store rolled all its prices back for the sale.* 🅃 *The protesters demanded that they roll back their prices.*

roll something down **1.** to move something down, making it rotate like a wheel or a ball, or moving it on wheels. ☐ *Don't carry the ball down; roll it down!* 🅃 *I rolled down the ball as you asked.* **2.** to crank down something, such as a car window. ☐ *Please roll the window down and get some air in this car.* 🅃 *Please roll down the car window.*

roll something off ((of) someone or something) to cause something to roll away, off someone or something. (The *of* is colloquial.) ☐ *The other workers quickly rolled the wheel off of the injured man.* 🅃 *Please roll off the wheel quickly!* ☐ *We had to roll the heavy stone off the neighbor's lawn.*

roll something on(to something) to apply something or a coat of a substance by rolling something saturated with the substance on the thing to be coated. ☐ *You should roll another coat of paint onto this wall over here.* 🅃 *Roll on another coat.* ☐ *Okay, I'll roll it on.*

roll something out **1.** to bring or take something out by rolling it; to push something out on wheels. ☐ *Jane rolled her bike out to show it off.* 🅃 *Alice rolled out her bicycle for us to see.* **2.** to flatten something by rolling it. ☐ *You should roll the pastry out first.* 🅃 *They rolled out the steel in a huge mill.*

roll something up to coil or rotate something into a coil or roll of something. ☐ *I rolled the poster up and put it back in its mailing tube.* 🅃 *I have to roll up this paper.*

romp through something to run through something fast and playfully. ☐ *The conductor romped through the slow movement of the symphony as if it were a march.* ☐ *The cast romped through the last act, knowing that the play would be closed that very night.*

room together [for two or more people] to share a room, as in a college dormitory. □ *Sarah and I roomed together in college.* □ *We don't want to room together anymore.*

root around (for something) to dig or shuffle in or through something, looking for something. □ *Alice rooted around in her desk drawer for a pen.* □ *I'll root around here and see if I can find it.* □ *The pigs rooted around, looking for something to eat.* □ *I opened the drawer and began to root around to see if I could find a screwdriver.*

root someone or something out (of something) to seek and remove someone or something from something or some place; to seek to discover and bring someone or something to light. □ *The committee wanted to root all the lazy people out of the club.* 🅃 *The manager rooted out all the deadwood.* 🅃 *We rooted out all the problem files and gave them to Walter to fix.*

root something up [for a pig] to find something in the ground by digging with its nose. □ *The pigs will root your plants up if they get out of their pen.* 🅃 *The pigs will root up your plants if they get out of their pen.*

rope someone in(to something) to persuade or trick someone into doing something. □ *You can't rope me into doing it. I'm wise to your tricks.* 🅃 *The con artists roped in the unsuspecting tourist.* □ *They tried to rope me in.*

rope someone or something up to tie someone or some creature up with a rope. □ *Rope this guy up tight so he won't get away.* 🅃 *The sheriff roped up the bandit.* 🅃 *The cowboy roped up the calf in a few seconds.*

rope something off to isolate something with a rope barrier. □ *The police roped the scene of the accident off.* 🅃 *The police roped off the scene of the accident.*

rot off to decompose and fall off. □ *If you don't clean your smelly feet, they'll rot off!* □ *A few old branches finally rotted off, but the ancient tree looked as if it would survive the wet spell.*

rot out to decompose and fall out. □ *If you don't brush your teeth, they'll rot out!* □ *Some of the rafters in the shed rotted out, but we replaced them easily.*

rough someone up to treat someone roughly. □ *Max wanted to rough Lefty up a bit, but the boss said no.* 🆃 *Lefty roughed up Max.*

rough something in to construct or draw something initially, temporarily, or crudely. □ *The carpenter roughed the doorways in without consulting the plans.* 🆃 *The carpenter roughed in the doorways without consulting the plans.*

rough something out to make a rough sketch of something. □ *I will rough it out and have one of the staff artists attend to the details.* 🆃 *Jane roughed out a picture of the proposed building.*

rough something up to scrape or rub something in a way that makes it rough. □ *All you have to do is rough the ground up, sow the seeds, and then water them.* 🆃 *Rough up the surface a little before you paint it.*

round down to something to discard a fractional part of a number. □ *You should round down to whole numbers.* □ *Round down to the next number if the fraction is less than half.*

round someone or something up to locate and gather someone or something. □ *Please round the suspects up for questioning.* 🆃 *The police rounded up the usual suspects.* □ *They failed to round Max and Lefty up, however.* 🆃 *The cowboys rounded up all the cattle for market.* □ *It takes many reporters to round the news up for television.*

round something down to reduce a fractional part of a number to the next lowest whole number. □ *You can round this figure down if you want. It won't affect the total all that much.* 🆃 *Please round down all figures having fractions less than one-half.*

round something off to change a fractional part of a number to the closest whole number. □ *Please round all your figures off.* 🆃 *Round off everything.*

round something off (with something) to finish something with something; to complement something with something. □ *We rounded the meal off with a sinful dessert.* 🆃 *We rounded off the meal with a sinful dessert.*

round something out to complete or enhance something. □ *We will round the evening out with dessert and brandy at a nice* *restaurant.* T *They rounded out the meal with dessert.* T *That's a fine way to round out a meal.*

rub (away) at something to chafe or scrape something, repeatedly. □ *The side of his shoe rubbed away at the side of his desk until the paint wore off.* □ *Don't rub at your sore. It will get worse.*

rub off ((of) something) [for something] to become detached from something because of incidental rubbing or scraping. (The *of* is colloquial.) □ *The label rubbed off this can. What do you think it is?* □ *I can't tell what it is. The label rubbed off.*

rub off on(to) someone [for a trait] to transfer from one person to another. □ *I hope that your good humor rubs off on our children.* □ *I wish it would rub off on Mary.*

rub off on(to) someone or something [for something, such as a coating] to become transferred to someone or something through the contact of rubbing. □ *Look what rubbed off on me!* □ *The wet paint rubbed off onto my pants leg.*

rub someone or something down to stroke or smooth someone or some creature, for muscular well-being. □ *Sam rubbed his horse down after his ride.* T *He rubbed down his horse.* □ *The trainer rubbed Sam down.*

rub something away to remove something by chafing or rubbing. □ *See if you can rub some of the dirt away.* T *Rub away the dirt if you can.*

rub something in(to something) to cause something to penetrate a surface by rubbing it against the surface. □ *Rub this lotion into your muscles. It will stop the aching.* T *Try rubbing in this lotion.* □ *Please rub it in.*

rub something off ((of) something) to remove something from something by rubbing. (The *of* is colloquial.) □ *The butler rubbed the tarnish off the pitcher.* T *The butler rubbed off the dark tarnish.* □ *Yes, please rub that stuff off.*

rub something out to obliterate something by rubbing. □ *See if you can rub those stains out.* T *Rub out the graffiti on the side of the car if you can.*

rub (up) against someone or something to bump or scrape against someone or something. ☐ *The cat rubbed up against me and seemed friendly.* ☐ *The side of the car rubbed against the fence.*

rule against someone or something to give a judgment against someone or something. ☐ *The judge ruled against the prosecutor.* ☐ *The judge ruled against my motion.* ☐ *I hope the board doesn't rule against my proposal.*

rule for someone or something See the following entry.

rule in favor of someone or something AND **rule for someone or something** [for a judge or deliberating body] to award a decision to someone or something or to render a decision favoring someone or something. ☐ *The judge ruled for the defendant.* ☐ *The examining board ruled in favor of dismissing George.*

rule on something to give a decision or judgment about something. ☐ *How long will it be before the court rules on your petition?* ☐ *The boss will rule on your request tomorrow.*

rule someone or something out to eliminate someone or something from consideration. (*Someone* includes *oneself.*) ☐ *I can rule Tom out as a suspect. He was in Denver.* 🅃 *Don't rule out Tom.* ☐ *You can rule this one out.* ☐ *I'll have to rule myself out. I can't run for office.*

rummage through something to toss things about while searching through something. ☐ *I rummaged through my top drawer, looking for any two socks that matched.* ☐ *Mary spent some time rummaging through the toolbox before she found what she was looking for.*

rumple someone or something up to bring disorder to someone['s clothing] or something. (*Someone* includes *oneself.*) ☐ *One of the little boys knocked another boy down and rumpled him up.* 🅃 *He rumpled up Dan's shirt.* ☐ *I have to keep from rumpling myself up before the party.*

run around with someone to go places with someone; to socialize with someone. ☐ *I used to run around with Alice and Jill before we all graduated.* ☐ *Carl and Jane used to run around with each other after school.*

run away (from someone or something) to flee someone or something. □ *Please don't run away from me. I mean you no harm.* □ *Our dog ran away from the lawn mower.*

run down **1.** to come down, running; to go down, running. □ *I need to talk to you down here. Can you run down?* □ *I will run down and talk to you.* **2.** [for something] to lose power and stop working. □ *The clock ran down because no one was there to wind it.* □ *The toy ran down and wouldn't go again until it had been wound.* **3.** to become worn or dilapidated. □ *The property was allowed to run down, and it took a lot of money to fix it up.* □ *The old neighborhood has certainly run down since we moved away.*

run down to someone or something to come or go down to someone or something, rapidly. □ *Sally ran down the slope to Bob, who stood waiting for her with outstretched arms.* □ *I ran down to the well to get some water for Ed, who had the hiccups.*

run in(to something) **1.** [for a liquid] to flow into something or a place. □ *The water is running into the basement!* □ *It's running in very fast.* **2.** to enter something or a place on foot, running. □ *The boys ran into the room and out again.* □ *They ran in and knocked over a lamp.* **3.** to stop by a place for a quick visit or to make a purchase quickly. □ *I have to run in the drugstore for a minute.* □ *I ran into the store for some bread.* □ *I want to visit Mrs. Potter. I can't stay long. I can only run in for a minute.* □ *All right. If you just run in.*

run off **1.** to flee. □ *The children rang our doorbell and then ran off.* □ *They ran off as fast as they could.* **2.** to have diarrhea. □ *He said he was running off all night.* □ *One of the children was running off and had to stay home from school.* **3.** [for a fluid] to drain away from a flat area. □ *By noon, all the rainwater had run off the playground.*

run off with someone or something **1.** to take someone or something away, possibly running. □ *Fred ran off with Ken. They'll be back in a minute.* □ *Who ran off with my dictionary?* **2.** to capture and take away someone or something; to steal someone or something. □ *The kidnappers ran off with little Valerie.* □ *The kids ran off with a whole box of candy, and the storekeeper is going to press charges.*

run on **1.** to continue running. □ *I wanted to stop her and ask her something, but she just ran on.* □ *The joggers had a chance to stop and rest, but they just ran on.* **2.** to continue on for a long time. □ *The lecture ran on and bored everyone to tears.* □ *How long is this symphony likely to run on?*

run out (of something) **1.** to leave something or a place, running. □ *Everyone ran out of the theater when they smelled smoke.* □ *They ran out screaming.* **2.** to use all of something and have none left. □ *I am afraid that we have run out of eggs.* □ *Check again. I don't think we have run out.*

run out of time to have used up most of the allotted time; to have no time left. □ *You have just about run out of time.* □ *I ran out of time before I could finish the test.*

run out on someone to depart and leave someone behind. □ *My date ran out on me at the restaurant, and I had to pay the bill.* □ *Her boyfriend ran out on her when she needed him the most.*

run over **1.** to come by for a quick visit. □ *Can you run over for a minute after work?* □ *I will run over for a minute as soon as I can.* **2.** to overflow. □ *The bathtub ran over and there was water all over the floor.* □ *She poured the coffee until the cup ran over.*

run over someone or something to drive, steer, or travel so as to pass over someone or something. □ *The bus ran over the fallen man.* □ *That car almost ran over my toe.*

run over (something) to exceed a limit. □ *The lecture ran over the allotted time.* □ *The students ran over the time allotted for the exam.* □ *I thought I had our order for food exactly right, but when the people showed up, we ran over.*

run over something with someone to review something with someone. □ *I would like to run over this with you one more time.* □ *I want to run over the proposal with Carl again.*

run someone or something down **1.** to criticize or deride someone or something. (*Someone* includes *oneself*.) □ *Please stop running me down all the time. I can't be that bad!* 🅃 *You run down everybody!* □ *All the critics ran the play down.* □ *Poor Sally is always running herself down.* **2.** to collide with and knock down someone or something. ☐ *The driver ran three pedestrians down.* 🅃 *Mary ran down a stop sign.* **3.** to hunt for and locate someone or something. ☐ *Could you run some information down for me?* 🅃 *I was finally able to run down my old friend.*

run someone or something in(to something) to take or drive someone or something into something or some place. (*Someone* includes *oneself.*) ☐ *Let me run you into the city this morning. I need the car today.* 🅃 *Do you want to go to town? I have to run in George and you can come along.* ☐ *As soon as I run George in, I'll talk to you.* ☐ *Bill ran himself into town to get the medicine.*

run someone or something off to drive someone or something away from something. ☐ *The defenders ran the attackers off time after time.* 🅃 *We had to run off the attackers.* 🅃 *The police came and ran off the raccoons.*

run someone or something out (of something) to chase someone or something out of something or some place. ☐ *The old man ran the kids out of his orchard.* 🅃 *He ran out the kids.*

run something down to use something having batteries, a motor, or an engine until it has no more power and stops. ☐ *Who ran my electric toothbrush down?* 🅃 *Someone ran down my batteries.*

run something in(to something) to guide or route something, such as a wire or a pipe, into something or a place. ☐ *The worker ran the circuit into each room.* ☐ *He ran the circuit in as instructed.* 🅃 *He ran in the circuit as specified.*

run something off **1.** to duplicate something using a mechanical duplicating machine. ☐ *If the master copy is ready, I will run some other copies off.* 🅃 *I'll run off some more copies.* **2.** to get rid of something, such as fat or energy, by running. ☐ *The little boys are very excited. Send them outside to run it off.* 🅃 *They need to run off their energy.*

run something out (of something) to drive or steer something out of something or some place. ☐ *The cowboys ran the cattle out of the corral.* 🅃 *They ran out the cattle.* ☐ *They ran the horses out too.*

run something up **1.** to raise or hoist something, such as a flag. ☐ *Harry ran the flag up the flagpole each morning.* 🅃 *Will you* *please run up the flag today?* **2.** to cause something to go higher, such as the price of stocks or commodities. □ *A rumor about higher earnings ran the price of the computer stocks up early in the afternoon.* 🅃 *They ran up the price too high.* 🅃 **3.** to stitch something together quickly. 🅃 *She's very clever. I'm sure she can run up a costume for you.* □ *The seamstress ran a party dress up in one afternoon.* **4.** to accumulate indebtedness. □ *I ran a huge phone bill up last month.* 🅃 *Walter ran up a hotel bar bill that made his boss angry.*

rush in(to something) **1.** to run or hurry into a thing or a place. □ *Everyone rushed into the shelter when the rain started.* □ *They all rushed in at once.* **2.** to begin doing something without the proper preparation. □ *Don't rush into this job without thinking it through.* □ *Mary rushed in without thinking.*

rush off (from some place) to hurry away from some place. □ *I'm sorry, but I will have to rush off from this meeting before it's over.* □ *Mary had to rush off before the party was over.*

rush out (of something) to exit in a hurry. □ *Everyone rushed out of the room at the same time.* □ *They rushed out because they smelled smoke.*

rush someone or something in(to something) to lead or carry someone or something into something or some place hurriedly. □ *I rushed her into the hospital emergency room, and everything was soon all right.* 🅃 *The nurse rushed in the emergency medical equipment.*

rush someone or something out (of something) to lead or guide someone or something out of something or some place hurriedly. □ *The ushers rushed everyone out of the church so they could clean the place before the next wedding.* 🅃 *They rushed out another edition of the newspaper that afternoon.* □ *We will have to rush another edition out.*

rush something off (to someone or something) to send something quickly to someone or something. □ *I will rush your order off to you immediately.* 🅃 *I need to rush off this package to Walter.*

rush something through (something) to move something through some process or office in a hurry. □ *He was in a hurry so we* *rushed his order through the order department.* ☐ *He asked us to rush it through.*

rush through something to hurry to get something finished; to race through something. ☐ *Please don't rush through this business. Get it right.* ☐ *Timmy rushed through dinner so he could go out and play.*

rustle something up to manage to prepare a meal, perhaps on short notice. (Folksy.) ☐ *I think I can rustle something up for dinner.* [T] *I'll rustle up some ham and eggs.*

S

.sail into someone or something **1.** to crash into someone or something with a boat or ship. □ *The boat sailed into the dock, causing considerable damage.* □ *I was in my skiff when a larger boat sailed into me.* **2.** to crash into someone or something. □ *The missile sailed into the soldiers, injuring a few.* □ *The car sailed into the lamppost.*

sail (right) through something **1.** to travel through something in a boat or ship. □ *The line of boats sailed right through the Grenadines in the daylight hours.* □ *We sailed through the narrows without a pilot.* **2.** to go through something very quickly and easily. (Figurative.) □ *The kids just sailed right through the ice cream and cake. There was not a bit left.* □ *You have sailed through your allowance already.*

salt something away **1.** to store and preserve a foodstuff by salting it. □ *The farmer salted a lot of fish and hams away for the winter.* 🅃 *She salted away a lot of food.* **2.** to store something; to place something in reserve. (Figurative.) □ *I need to salt some money away for my retirement.* 🅃 *I will salt away some money for emergencies.*

save something up (for something) to accumulate an amount of money for the purchase of something. □ *I'm saving my money up for a car.* 🅃 *Save up your money.* □ *You should save it up.*

save up (for something) to accumulate something for some purpose. □ *I can't buy a car because I am saving up for college.* □ *I don't have the money now, but I am saving up.*

scale something down to reduce the size or cost of something. □ *The bad economy forced us to scale the project down.* 🅃 *Liz scaled down the project.*

scare someone or something off to frighten someone or some creature away. □ *The dog's barking scared the burglar off.* 🅃 *The barking scared off the prowler.* □ *My dog scared the skunk off.*

scheme against someone or something to plot or conspire against someone or something. □ *A group of generals was plotting against the government.* □ *They schemed against Roger until he caught them and put an end to it.*

scour something off ((of) something) to clean something off something by scouring. (The *of* is colloquial.) □ *See if you can scour the rust off the cookie sheet.* 🅃 *I will scour off the rust.* □ *Please help me scour it off.*

scour something out to clean something out by scouring. □ *Would you scour the pans out?* 🅃 *Please scour out the pans—don't just wash them.*

scout around (for someone or something) to look around for someone or something. □ *I don't know who would do a good job for you, but I'll scout around for a likely candidate.* □ *You stay here. I'll scout around.*

scout someone or something up to search for and find someone or something. □ *I'll scout a costume up for the Halloween party.* 🅃 *Can you scout up a date for Friday night?*

scrape by (on something) AND **scrape by (with something)** to manage just to get by with something. □ *There is not really enough money to live on, and we just have to scrape by on what we get.* □ *We can't scrape by with only that amount of money.* □ *I think we can just scrape by again this month.*

scrape by (something) to manage just to get by something. □ *I scraped by the man standing at the gate and got into the theater without a ticket.* □ *Mary scraped by the cart that was blocking the crowded hallway.*

scrape by (with something) See *scrape by (on something).*

scrape something away (from something) to scratch or rasp something off something. □ *Ted scraped the rough places away from the fender he was repairing.* 🅃 *Ted scraped away the rough* *places.* ☐ *Mary couldn't polish her shoes until she scraped the mud away.*

scrape something off ((of) someone or something) to rub or stroke something off someone or something. (The *of* is colloquial.) ☐ *I sat down and scraped the caked mud off of me. It was everywhere!* 🅃 *Jake scraped off the caked mud.* ☐ *Mary scraped the frosting off her piece of cake.*

scrape something out to empty something by scraping. ☐ *Scrape the pan out. Don't leave any of that good sauce inside.* 🅃 *Please scrape out the pan.*

scrape something out (of something) to remove something by scraping. ☐ *Scrape all the peanut butter out of the jar before you discard it.* 🅃 *Scrape out the peanut butter.* ☐ *Please scrape it out.*

scrape through (something) **1.** to move through something, scraping or rubbing the sides. ☐ *The car, going at a very high speed, scraped through the tunnel.* ☐ *It just managed to scrape through.* **2.** to get by something just barely; to pass a test just barely. ☐ *Alice passed the test, but she just scraped through it.* ☐ *I just scraped through my calculus test.*

scratch someone or something out to mark out the name of someone or something. ☐ *I scratched John out and wrote in George instead.* 🅃 *I scratched out John and forgot about him.* ☐ *Donna scratched the name of the defunct company out.*

scratch someone or something up to damage or mar someone or something by scratching. ☐ *Being thrown clear of the car in the accident didn't break any bones, but it scratched her up a lot.* 🅃 *Who scratched up my coffee table?* ☐ *I didn't scratch it up.*

screen someone or something out (of something) to filter someone or something out of something. ☐ *The test screened all the unqualified candidates out of the group.* 🅃 *We screened out the suppliers who were not financially sound.* ☐ *We screened some of the applicants out.* 🅃 *Walter screened out the rocks from the soil.*

screw something down to secure something to the floor or a base by the use of screws. ☐ *You had better screw these seats down or someone will knock them over.* 🅃 *Please screw down the threshold.*

scrub someone or something down to clean someone or something thoroughly by rubbing. (*Someone* includes *oneself.*) □ *The mother scrubbed the baby down gently and put lotion on her.* 🅃 *Please scrub down this floor.* □ *He scrubbed himself down and put on clean clothes.*

scrub someone or something off to clean someone or something by rubbing. (*Someone* includes *oneself.*) □ *Mother scrubbed Timmy off.* 🅃 *Liz scrubbed off the countertop.* □ *He scrubbed himself off and went to work.*

scrub something off ((of) something) to clean something off something by scrubbing. (The *of* is colloquial.) □ *I have to scrub the mud off the porch steps.* □ *Did you scrub all the grease off?* 🅃 *Tina scrubbed off the grease.*

scrub something out to clean out the inside of something by rubbing or brushing. □ *Please scrub these pots out and put them away.* 🅃 *Jim will scrub out the pots.*

scrub something out (of something) to clean something out of something by scrubbing. □ *Please scrub the gravy out of the pot.* 🅃 *Are you going to scrub out the burned material?*

scrub up **1.** to clean oneself up. □ *You have to scrub up before dinner.* □ *Please go scrub up before you come to the table.* **2.** to clean oneself, especially one's hands and arms, as a preparation for performing a surgical procedure. (A special use of sense 1.) □ *The surgeon scrubbed up thoroughly before the operation.* □ *When you finish scrubbing up, someone will help you on with sterile clothing.*

seal something off (from someone or something) to make something inaccessible to someone or something. □ *The police sealed the building off from everyone.* 🅃 *They sealed off the building from all the reporters.* □ *We sealed the room off from the outside air.*

see someone off to accompany someone to the point of departure for a trip and say good-bye upon departure. □ *We went to the train station to see Andy off.* 🅃 *We saw off all the scouts going to camp.*

see something through to stay with a project all the way to its completion. □ *They will see the job through.* □ *I will see this whole thing through, don't worry.*

see through someone or something to recognize the deception involved with someone or something. ☐ *I know what you're up to! I see through you!* ☐ *I see through this proposal.*

see to someone or something to tend to or care for someone or something. ☐ *Please go see to the baby. She's crying again.* ☐ *Ted went to see to whoever was at the door.*

seep in(to something) [for a fluid] to trickle or leak into something. ☐ *Water is seeping into the basement.* ☐ *Water is seeping in very slowly.*

seep out (of something) [for a fluid] to trickle or leak out of something. ☐ *A lot of oil has seeped out of the car onto the driveway.* ☐ *There is oil seeping out. There must be a leak.*

seep through something [for a fluid] to permeate something and escape. ☐ *The oil seeped through the gasket onto the ground.* ☐ *Some water seeped through the ceiling, ruining our carpet as well as the ceiling.*

seize onto someone or something to grab onto someone or something. ☐ *The beggar seized onto the well-dressed gentleman and demanded money.* ☐ *Tony seized onto the doorknob and gave it a hard jerk.*

seize up to freeze or halt; to grind suddenly to a stop. ☐ *The engine seized up, and we were almost thrown out of the car.* ☐ *My knee seized up in the middle of a football game.*

seize (up)on something **1.** to grasp something tightly. (*Upon* is formal and less commonly used than *on*.) ☐ *Dave seized upon the knob of the door and yanked hard.* ☐ *I seized on the railing and held on tight.* **2.** to take hold of something, such as a plan, an idea, etc. (Figurative.) ☐ *I heard her ideas and seized upon them immediately.* ☐ *The committee seized on the idea at once.* ☐ *The plan was seized upon at once.*

sell out (to someone) **1.** to sell everything to someone. ☐ *The farmer finally gave up and sold out to a large corporation.* ☐ *I refuse to sell out no matter what they offer me.* **2.** to betray someone or something to someone. ☐ *I think that you have sold out to the enemy!*

sell someone or something out to betray someone or something. (*Someone* includes *oneself.*) ☐ *The small country didn't know how to conduct espionage. They sold their own agent out.* 🅃 *They sold out their own agent.* ☐ *The agent sold her country out.* ☐ *You're asking me to sell myself out!*

sell something off to sell all of something. ☐ *We ended up with a large stock of out-of-style coats, and we had to sell them all off at a loss.* 🅃 *We sold off all the excess stock.*

send away (for something) to order something to be brought or sent from some distance. ☐ *I sent away for a new part to replace the one that was broken.* ☐ *I couldn't find the part locally. I had to send away for it.*

send for someone or something to make a request that someone or something be brought. ☐ *Mr. Franklin sent for his secretary.* ☐ *I think we should send for an ambulance.*

send off for something to dispatch an order for something to a distant place. ☐ *I sent off for the proper contest entry forms.* ☐ *Did you send off for a new license?*

send out (for someone or something) to send an order by messenger, telephone, cable, or fax that someone or something is to come or be delivered. ☐ *We sent out for a public stenographer to record the will as Uncle Herman dictated it.* ☐ *There was no one there who could take dictation, so we had to send out.* ☐ *We sent out for sandwiches.*

send someone in for someone to send someone into a game as a replacement for someone else. ☐ *The coach sent Jill in for Alice, who was beginning to tire.* ☐ *Ted sent Bill in for Wally.*

send someone in(to something) to make someone go into something or some place. ☐ *George sent me into the house for a hammer.* 🅃 *The boys know where it is. He should have sent in the boys.* ☐ *George sent me in.*

send someone off (to something) to send someone away to something or some place, especially away on a journey; to be present when someone sets out on a journey to something or some place. ☐ *We sent both kids off to camp this summer and had peace in the* *house for the first time in years.* 🅃 *Liz sent off Karen to the store.* □ *I had to send them off. They were getting to be annoying.*

send someone out (for someone or something) to send someone out to search for someone or something. □ *We sent Gerald out for Walter, who was supposed to have been there already.* 🅃 *Karen sent out Liz for some medicine.*

send someone over ((to) some place) to order someone to go to some place. □ *I sent Dave over to the main office.* □ *I will send someone else over.* 🅃 *Please send over someone else.*

send something by something **1.** to dispatch something by a particular carrier. □ *I will send it to you by special messenger.* □ *We sent the package by air freight.* **2.** to deliver something to something or some place. (Informal.) □ *I will send the parcel by your office this afternoon.* □ *We sent your order by your house, but no one was there to receive it.*

send something off (to someone or something) to dispatch something to someone, something, or some place. □ *I will send the package off to you in tomorrow's mail.* 🅃 *Karen sent off a letter to her aunt.* □ *She sent it off only yesterday.*

separate something out (of something) to remove something out from something. □ *She used a filter to separate the dirt particles out of the water.* 🅃 *A filter separated out the impurities.* □ *It separated the sand out.*

serve something up to distribute or deliver food for people to eat. □ *The cook served the stew up and then passed around the bread.* 🅃 *Can you serve up the food now?*

serve under someone or something to carry out one's responsibility under the direction or in the employment of someone or something. □ *I served under the president of the company as special assistant.* □ *Jane served under the court as an investigator.*

set in to begin; to become fixed for a period of time. □ *A severe cold spell set in early in November.* □ *When high temperatures set in, the use of electricity went up considerably.*

set off (for something) to leave for something or some place. ☐ *We set off for Springfield three hours late.* ☐ *It was after noon before we could set off.*

set off on something to begin on a journey or expedition. ☐ *When do you plan to set off on your journey?* ☐ *We will set off on our adventure tomorrow morning.*

set one (back) on one's feet AND **set one on one's feet again** to reestablish someone; to help someone become active and productive again. ☐ *Gary's uncle helped set him back on his feet.* ☐ *We will all help set you on your feet again.*

set one on one's feet again See the previous entry.

set out (on something) to begin a journey; to begin a project. ☐ *We set out on our trip exactly as planned.* ☐ *We set out as planned.*

set out to do something to begin to do something; to intend to do something. ☐ *Jill set out to weed the garden, but pulled up a few valuable plants in the process.* ☐ *I set out to repair the door, not rebuild the whole house.*

set someone down (on(to) something) to place a person one is carrying or lifting onto something. ☐ *I set the small boy down onto the desk and gave him a piece of candy.* [T] *I set down the child on the chair.* ☐ *Jane set her down.*

set someone off **1.** to cause someone to become very angry; to ignite someone's anger. ☐ *That kind of thing really sets me off!* [T] *Your behavior set off Mrs. Franklin.* ☐ *When I mentioned high taxes it really set Walter off. He went into a rage.* **2.** to cause someone to start talking or lecturing about a particular subject. ☐ *When I mentioned high taxes it really set Walter off. He talked and talked.* ☐ *The subject set Karen off, and she talked on endlessly.*

set someone or something up to place someone or something in an upright position. ☐ *He was asleep, but we tried to set him up anyway.* [T] *I set up the lamp, which had fallen over again.*

set someone up (for something) **1.** to prepare someone for a deception. (*Someone* includes *oneself.*) ☐ *The crooks set the old lady up for their standard scam.* [T] *They set up their victim for* *the scam.* ☐ *It didn't take much to set Max up.* ☐ *They set themselves up to be cheated.* **2.** to make someone become part of a joke. (*Someone* includes *oneself.*) ☐ *The comedian was highly skilled at setting members of the audience up for a gag.* 🅃 *The joker set up a friend for the butt of the joke.* ☐ *So, you thought you could set me up!* ☐ *You really set yourself up for that one!*

set something down (on something) **1.** to place something on the surface of something. ☐ *Andy set the hot skillet down on the countertop and burned a hole in it.* 🅃 *He set down the skillet on the counter.* ☐ *Please set it down carefully.* **2.** to write something on paper. ☐ *Let me set this down on paper so we will have a record of what was said.* 🅃 *I will set down this note on paper.* ☐ *She set it down in a very neat hand.* **3.** to land an airplane on something. ☐ *The pilot set the plane down on the runway.* ☐ *I can't set the plane down on this field!*

set something down to something to blame something on something; to regard something as the cause of something. ☐ *She set his rude behavior down to indigestion.* ☐ *I just set her crankiness down to lack of sleep.*

set something in(to something) to install something into its place. ☐ *The movers set the stove into its proper place, and the plumber hooked it up two weeks later.* 🅃 *They set in the stove.* ☐ *It was difficult, but they set it in properly.*

set something off **1.** to ignite something, such as fireworks. ☐ *The boys were setting firecrackers off all afternoon.* 🅃 *They set off bomb after bomb.* **2.** to cause something to begin. ☐ *The coach set the race off with a shot from the starting pistol.* 🅃 *She set off the race with a gunshot.* **3.** to make something distinct or outstanding. ☐ *The lovely stonework sets the fireplace off quite nicely.* 🅃 *The white hat really sets off Betsy's eyes.*

set something up (for something) to arrange something for a particular time or event. ☐ *I will set a meeting up for tomorrow.* 🅃 *Can you set up a meeting for tomorrow?* ☐ *Yes, I'll set it up.*

set something (up)on something to place something on the surface of something. ☐ *Mrs. Franklin set a bowl of fruit upon the table.* ☐ *I set my empty glass on the counter.*

settle down **1.** to become calm. □ *Please settle down. Relax.* □ *I will try to settle down so I can think straight.* **2.** to get quiet. □ *Will you all please settle down so we can begin?* □ *Settle down! Let's get this meeting over with!* **3.** to abandon a free life-style and take up a more stable and disciplined one. (Often with thoughts of marriage, home ownership, and childbearing.) □ *I wish Charles would settle down.* □ *Haven't you ever thought of settling down and raising a family?*

settle down somewhere to establish a residence somewhere. (Also without *down*, but not eligible as an entry.) □ *After retiring, they settled down in a little cabin near a lake.* □ *We really wanted to settle down in a small town in the South.*

settle in(to something) **1.** to become accustomed to something, such as a new home, job, status, etc. □ *By the end of the first week he had settled into his new job.* □ *He settled in with no problems.* **2.** to get comfortable in something. □ *I love to settle into my new reclining chair.* □ *Jan sat down in the chair and settled in.*

settle someone down to make someone become quiet. (*Someone* includes *oneself.*) □ *The principal had to go into the classroom and settle the students down.* □ *At last the little boys settled themselves down and went to sleep.*

shake something down See *shake something out.*

shake something out **1.** to clean something of dirt or crumbs by shaking. □ *Please shake the tablecloth out.* [T] *Can you shake out your coat? It's really dusty.* **2.** AND **shake something down** to test something to find out what the problems are. (Figurative.) □ *I need to spend some time driving my new car to shake it out.* [T] *We need to shake out this car before I make the final payment.* □ *The ship ran well when I shook it down.*

shake something up **1.** to mix something by shaking. □ *I am going to shake the salad dressing up before I serve it.* [T] *Please shake up the salad dressing.* **2.** to upset an organization or group of people by some administrative action. □ *The board of directors shook middle management up by firing a few of the old-timers.* [T] *They shook up the firm by taking the company public.*

shape someone up **1.** to cause someone to get into good physical condition. □ *The jogging shaped him up, but it harmed his joints.*

🅃 *The jogging shaped up Karen in about three weeks.* **2.** to cause someone to become productive, efficient, competent, etc. ☐ *The manager decided she had to shape everyone in the office up.* 🅃 *The new director shaped up the salespeople virtually overnight.*

shape up **1.** to get into good physical condition. ☐ *I really need to shape up. I get out of breath too easily.* ☐ *If you don't shape up, you might develop heart trouble.* **2.** to become productive, efficient, competent, etc. ☐ *You are going to have to shape up if you want to keep your job.* ☐ *The boss told her to shape up or find another job.*

shift out of something to change out of a particular mode, time, gear, attitude, etc. ☐ *She quickly shifted out of second gear into third.* ☐ *I hope you can shift out of that bad attitude into a more pleasant state before the guests arrive.*

shine out **1.** to shine or radiate light; to shine forth. ☐ *She snapped on the flashlight and a reassuring light shone out.* ☐ *The hallway was cheery and a bright light shone out, inviting us in.* **2.** [for a characteristic] to make itself very evident. ☐ *His good humor shone out, especially when he was surrounded by grouches.* ☐ *Sarah's basically good character shone out almost all the time.*

shine something up to polish something. (Also without *up*, but not eligible as an entry.) ☐ *Tom shined his shoes up.* 🅃 *Fred shined up the furniture.*

shine something (up)on someone or something to cast a beam of light onto someone or something. (*Upon* is formal and less commonly used than *on*.) ☐ *Please shine your flashlight on Sam so we can see him.* ☐ *The sun shone its rays on the fields.*

shine through (something) **1.** [for rays of light] to penetrate something. ☐ *The bright light of day shone through the windows.* ☐ *The light shone through and lit up the room.* **2.** [for something that was obscured or hidden] to become visible or evident. ☐ *Her basic intelligence shone through in spite of her country ways.* ☐ *Her intelligence shone through in most instances.*

shine up to someone to flatter someone; to try to get into someone's favor. ☐ *The cat shined up to the man every day, but it still got thrown out of the house every night.* ☐ *Are you trying to shine up to me? What will that accomplish?*

shoot in(to something) to run or dart into something or some place. ☐ *A mouse shot into the crack in the wall of the barn.* ☐ *A little mouse shot in.*

shoot out to pop or dart out. ☐ *A car shot out right in front of me.* ☐ *The frog's tongue shot out.*

shoot up to grow rapidly. ☐ *The seeds germinated and sprouts shot up almost overnight.* ☐ *Tim shot up just after he turned twelve.*

short out [for an electrical circuit] to go out because of a short circuit. ☐ *All the lights in the house shorted out when lightning struck.* ☐ *This radio has shorted out, I think.*

shout someone down to stop someone from speaking by shouting, yelling, or jeering. ☐ *The audience shouted the politician down.* 🅃 *They shouted down the speaker.*

shove off (for something) **1.** to begin a journey to something or some place by pushing a boat or ship out onto the water. ☐ *We will shove off at about noon, headed for Barbados.* ☐ *Go up to the bow of the boat and shove off when I tell you.* **2.** to depart for something or some place, using any form of transportation. ☐ *The car is all warmed up and ready to go. Let's shove off.* ☐ *Let's shove off pretty soon.*

show off (to someone) to make an exhibition of oneself to someone. ☐ *Ed was making a nuisance of himself, showing off to the girls.* ☐ *Stop showing off, Ed.*

show someone around (something) to give someone a tour of something or some place; to lead someone in an examination of something or some place. (*Someone* includes *oneself*.) ☐ *I would be happy to show you around the factory.* ☐ *Can I show you around?* ☐ *I'll show myself around. Don't worry. I can find the way.*

show someone or something off (to someone) to show someone or something to someone proudly. ☐ *She was very pleased to show her daughter off to everyone.* 🅃 *Liz showed off her daughter to Karen.* 🅃 *Richard showed off his new shoes to everyone in the office.*

show someone out (of something) to usher or escort someone out of something or some place. □ *The butler showed Roger out of the main hall into the orangery.* □ *May I show you out, sir?*

show someone through (something) to give someone a tour of something or some place. □ *I would be happy to show you through the office complex.* □ *This is our office area. Let me show you through.*

shrink up to shrivel; to recede. □ *My shirt shrank up when you washed it!* □ *The bruise on Tom's arm shrank up when he put ice on it.*

shrivel up to contract; to shrink. □ *The goldfish must have jumped out of its bowl during the night. Anyway, it's on the floor all shriveled up this morning.* □ *The new plants shriveled up in the burning sun.*

shrug something off to ignore something; to dismiss something. □ *No, you didn't hurt my feelings. I just shrugged your comment off.* Ⓣ *Liz couldn't shrug off the remark.*

shut off to stop operating; to turn off. □ *The machine shuts off automatically.* □ *What time do the lights shut off?*

shut someone or something down to close a business; to force someone who runs a business to close. □ *Sam's business was failing, and finally the bank shut him down.* Ⓣ *The bank shut down Tom's shop.*

shut someone up to cause someone to stop talking or making other noise. □ *I don't know how to shut him up. He just talks on and on.* Ⓣ *Shut up that loudmouth!*

shut something down to turn something off. □ *They shut the machine down so they could repair it.* Ⓣ *They had to shut down the machine.*

shut up to be quiet. (Slang. Rude.) □ *Shut up! You talk too much!* □ *Please shut up when I am on the phone.*

shy away (from someone or something) to draw away from someone or something that is frightening or startling; to avoid dealing with someone or something. □ *The child shied away from the doctor.* □ *I won't hurt you. Don't shy away.*

sift something out (of something) to get rid of something in something else by sifting. □ *Dan sifted the impurities out of the flour.* 🅃 *Walter sifted out the foreign matter.*

sign in to indicate that one has arrived somewhere and at what time by signing a piece of paper or a list. □ *Please sign in so we will know you are here.* □ *Did you remember to sign in this time?*

sign off 1. [for a broadcaster] to announce the end of programming for the day; [for an amateur radio operator] to announce the end of a transmission. □ *Wally signed off and turned the transmitter off.* □ *Wally failed to sign off at the scheduled time last night.* **2.** to quit doing what one has been doing and leave, go to bed, quit trying to do something, etc. (Figurative.) □ *I have to sign off and get to bed. See you all.* □ *When you finally sign off tonight, please turn out all the lights.*

sign off on something to sign a paper, indicating that one has finished with something or agrees with the state of something. □ *Michael signed off on the book and sent it to be printed.* □ *I refuse to sign off on this project until it is done correctly.*

sign on to announce the beginning of a broadcast transmission. □ *The announcer signed on and then played "The Star-Spangled Banner."* □ *We usually sign on at six in the morning.*

sign out to indicate in writing that one is leaving or going out temporarily. □ *I forgot to sign out when I left.* □ *Please sign out every time you leave.*

sign someone in to record that someone has arrived somewhere and at what time by recording the information on a paper or a list. (*Someone* includes *oneself.*) □ *I will sign you in. What is your name?* 🅃 *Do I have to sign in everyone?* □ *I'll sign myself in. You don't need to.*

sign someone out (of some place) to make a record of someone's departure from some place. (*Someone* includes *oneself.*) □ *Did someone sign you out of the factory, or did you just open the door and leave?* 🅃 *I signed out those two who just left.* □ *Please sign me out. I have to leave in a hurry.* □ *Do I have to sign myself out?*

sign someone up (for something) to record the agreement of someone to participate in something. (*Someone* includes *oneself.*) □ *Has anyone signed you up for the party?* Ⓣ *Can you sign up Liz for the party?* □ *I would be happy to sign her up.* □ *I signed myself up for the class.*

sign someone up (with someone or something) to record the agreement of someone to join a group of people or an organization. (*Someone* includes *oneself.*) □ *I found Tom in the hall, and we went to sign him up with Alice.* Ⓣ *Tom signed up his friends with the agency.* □ *Tom signed all his friends up with the new bicycle club.* □ *I signed myself up with the crew of the* Felicity Ann.

sign something away to sign a paper in which one gives away one's rights to something. □ *Valerie signed her rights away.* Ⓣ *She signed away her claim to the money.*

sign something in to record that something has been received at a particular time by recording the information on a paper or a list. □ *I have to sign this tape recorder in, then I will be right with you.* Ⓣ *Should I sign in this tape recorder now?*

sign something out (of some place) to make a record of the borrowing of something from some place. □ *Dave signed the tape recorder out of the library.* Ⓣ *Dave signed out the tape recorder.* □ *Mary signed a projector out.*

sign something over (to someone) to sign a paper granting the rights to or ownership of something to a specific person. □ *Larry signed all the rights to his book over to the publisher.* Ⓣ *He signed over all the rights to the publisher.* □ *Steve signed all rights over.*

sign up (for something) to record one's agreement to participate in something. □ *I want to sign up for guitar lessons.* □ *We will sign up as soon as possible.*

sing out to sing more loudly. □ *Sing out, please. This is a very large hall.* □ *The sopranos will have to sing out more.*

sing something out to sing or announce something loudly. □ *He sang the names out loud and clear.* Ⓣ *She sang out "The Star-Spangled Banner" in a loud voice.*

single someone or something out (for something) to choose or pick someone or something for something; to select an eligible person or thing for something. □ *The committee singled her out for a special award.* 🅃 *We singled out Liz for special honors.* 🅃 *They singled out my entry for special mention.*

sink back (into something) to lean back and relax in something, such as a soft chair. □ *I can't wait to get home and sink back into my easy chair.* □ *He sank back and went to sleep almost immediately.*

sink down to sink or submerge. □ *The sun sank down and darkness spread across the land.* □ *She sat in the chair and sank down, enjoying her moment of relaxation.*

sink in(to someone or something) to penetrate someone or something. (Used figuratively in reference to someone's brain or thinking.) □ *It finally began to sink into me that we were really, totally lost.* □ *When what she said finally sank in, I was shocked and amazed.*

sink something in((to) someone or something) **1.** to drive or push something into someone or something. □ *The brave hero sank the wooden stake into the vampire.* 🅃 *The hero sank in the stake.* □ *Jamie sank it in, and the movie ended.* **2.** to invest time or money in someone or something. (Sometimes implying that it was wasted.) □ *You would not believe how much money I've sunk into that guy!* □ *She sank a lot of money in the stock market.*

siphon something off (from something) to suck or draw a liquid off from something. □ *Harry siphoned the cream off the milk.* 🅃 *He siphoned off the cream.* □ *He siphoned it off.* □ *Frank siphoned all the water off from the fish tank.*

sit around to relax sitting; to waste time sitting. □ *Don't just sit around! Get moving!* □ *I need to sit around every now and then and reorganize my thoughts.*

sit back to push oneself back in one's seat; to lean against the back of one's seat. □ *Please sit back. I can't see around you.* □ *I sat back and made myself comfortable, assuming that the movie would bore me to sleep.*

sit down to be seated; to sit on something, such as a chair. □ *Please sit down and make yourself comfortable.* □ *Can I sit down here?*

sit in (for someone) to act as a substitute for someone. □ *I am not a regular member of this committee. I am sitting in for Larry Smith.* □ *Do you mind if I sit in? My representative can't be here.*

sit in (on something) to attend something as a visitor; to act as a temporary participant in something. □ *Do you mind if I sit in on your discussion?* □ *Please do sit in.*

sit (something) out to elect not to participate in something. □ *I think I will not join in this game. I'll sit it out.* 🅃 *I'll sit out this round.* □ *I'm not playing, thanks. I'll just sit out.*

sit through something to remain seated and in attendance for all of something. □ *I can't stand to sit through that class one more time!* □ *Do I have to sit through the whole lecture?*

sit up **1.** to rise from a lying to a sitting position. □ *When the alarm went off, he sat up and put his feet on the floor.* □ *She couldn't sleep, so she sat up and read a book.* **2.** to sit straighter in one's seat; to hold one's posture more upright while seated. □ *Please sit up. Don't slouch!* □ *You wouldn't get such terrible backaches if you would sit up properly.*

sit up with someone to remain awake and attend someone throughout the night. □ *I sat up with a sick friend all night.* □ *I had to sit up with Timmy because he had a tummyache.*

size someone or something up to scrutinize someone or something and form a judgment. 🅃 *The boxer had sized up his opponent by watching videotapes of previous fights.* 🅃 *He came into the house and sized up the kitchen and dining room.*

skim through something to go through something hastily; to read through something hastily. □ *She skimmed through the catalogs, looking for a nice gift for Gary.* □ *I will skim through your manuscript and see if it looks promising.*

skip over someone or something not to choose someone or something next in line. □ *She skipped over me and chose the next one in line.* □ *I skipped over the red ones and took a blue one.*

slack off to wane or decline; to decrease in intensity. ☐ *Finally the rains slacked off, and we could go outside and walk around.* ☐ *When business slacks off a bit, we have a sale.*

slap something on to dress in something hastily. ☐ *Henry slapped a shirt on and went out to say something to the garbage hauler.* 🆃 *He slapped on a shirt and ran to the bus stop.*

slap something on(to someone or something) to place something onto someone or something by slapping. ☐ *Tim slapped a sign onto Gary that said "kick me."* 🆃 *Tim came up to Gary's back and slapped on a sign.* ☐ *Tim slapped a sign on.*

slap something together to make up something very quickly. ☐ *This is very carelessly done. Someone has just slapped it together.* ☐ *This house was just slapped together. It is really poorly constructed.*

sleep in to remain in bed, sleeping past one's normal time of arising. ☐ *I really want to sleep in this morning.* ☐ *I slept in both Saturday and Sunday.*

sleep something off to sleep away the effect of alcohol or drugs. ☐ *Jeff is in his room, sleeping it off.* 🆃 *Jeff is sleeping off the effects of the night before.*

sleep through something to remain sleeping through some event. ☐ *I didn't hear the storm. I guess I slept through it.* ☐ *Wally slept through the entire opera—even the loud part.*

slice in(to something) to cut into something, usually with a knife or something similar. ☐ *Betty sliced into the cake and discovered it was chocolate all the way through.* ☐ *It wasn't until she sliced in that she found out what kind of cake it was.*

slice something off to cut something off with slicing motions. ☐ *Sue sliced the dead branches off with a rusty machete.* 🆃 *Karen sliced off a nice piece of turkey.*

slice through something to cut through something with slicing motions. ☐ *The chef sliced through the ham as if it were butter.* ☐ *The knife was too dull to slice through the tomato.*

slide out of something to slip or glide out of something without much effort. □ *Mary slid out of the car and ran to the front door.* □ *The floppy disk slid out of the computer.*

slide something in(to something) to insert something into something effortlessly. □ *Henry slid the end of the seat-belt buckle into its holder and started the car.* 🅃 *Slide in the buckle and make sure it's tight.* □ *Slide it in quickly so we can start up.*

slide something out (of something) to cause something to slip or glide out of something without much effort. □ *The hunter slid his knife out of its sheath and got ready to skin the deer.* 🅃 *He slid out the heavy box.* □ *Tony slid the box out.*

slim down to become thinner; to become narrower. □ *You have really slimmed down a lot since I last saw you.* □ *I need to eat less so I can slim down.* □ *He slimmed down quite a bit after he had his health problem.*

slim someone down to cause someone to lose weight. □ *They started to slim her down in the hospital, but she gained the weight back as soon as she got out.* 🅃 *The dietician slimmed down all the patients under his care.*

slip in(to something) to slide or glide into something, such as clothing, a sleeping bag, a tight place, etc. □ *I don't want to slip into a cold sleeping bag. How can I warm it up?* □ *I opened the bag and slipped in.*

slip off ((of) someone or something) to fall away from or off someone or something. (The *of* is colloquial.) □ *The jacket slipped off of Sally, but she grabbed it before it hit the floor.* □ *She hung the jacket on the back of the chair, but it slipped off.*

slip off (to some place) to sneak away to some place. □ *Judy and Jeff slipped off to the movies unnoticed.* □ *They slipped off and no one cared.*

slip out (of something) **1.** to sneak out of a place unnoticed. □ *Gloria slipped out of the theater at intermission.* □ *She slipped out and went home.* **2.** to slide out of an article of clothing. □ *She slipped out of her dress and hung it neatly in the closet.* □ *Ted slipped out of his T-shirt and left it on the floor where it fell.*

slip something off to let an item of clothing slide off one's body; to remove an item of clothing. □ *He slipped his coat off and put it on a chair.* 🆃 *She slipped off her shoes and relaxed.*

slip something on to put on an article of clothing, possibly in haste or casually. □ *I will go in and slip my bathing suit on and join you in a minute.* 🆃 *She slipped on her shoes and we left.*

slip up to make an error. □ *I hope you don't slip up again. Try to be more careful.* □ *I will try not to slip up.*

slip up on something to make an error in something. □ *I guess I slipped up on that last job.* □ *Fred slipped up on that list—there are a lot of names missing.*

slouch down to slump or droop down. □ *Don't always slouch down, Timmy! Stand up straight.* □ *I slouch down because I am tired.*

slouch over to lean or crumple and fall to one side; [for someone] to collapse in a sitting position. □ *He slouched over and went to sleep in his chair.* □ *When he slouched over, I thought something was wrong.*

slow down to decrease speed; to go slower. □ *Please slow down. You are going too fast.* □ *Slow down or you will skid.*

slow someone or something down to cause someone or something to decrease speed or go slower. (*Someone* includes *oneself*.) □ *Slow him down if you can. He is going too fast.* 🆃 *Slow down that car!* □ *Please slow your car down!* □ *Slow yourself down a little. You are working too hard and too fast.*

slow up to go slower; to go more slowly in order for someone or something to catch up. □ *Slow up a little! I can't keep up with you!* □ *Please slow up. I can't follow your lecture when you talk so fast.*

slump over **1.** [for someone] to collapse and fall over in a sitting position. □ *Just after the gunshot, Bruno slumped over and slid from his chair.* **2.** to fall over heavily; to collapse and droop from an upright position. □ *How can you work when you slump over your desk that way?* □ *He slumped over suddenly, and we were afraid that he was ill.*

smash into something to crash into something; to bump or crash into something. □ *Judy smashed into the coffee table and hurt her leg.* □ *The car smashed into the side of a bus and caused a lot of damage.*

smash out of something to break [one's way] out of something. □ *The prisoner smashed out of his cell.* □ *The horse smashed out of its stable.*

smash something in to crush something inward; to make something collapse inward by striking it. □ *Andy gave one good kick and smashed the drum in.* 🅃 *Liz smashed in the window.*

smash something up to break something up; to destroy something. □ *I hope the children don't smash the good china up if we use it tonight.* 🅃 *The angry worker smashed up the bucket.*

smash through something to break [one's way] through some sort of barrier. □ *The fleeing car smashed through the police barrier.* □ *Max got angry and smashed through the office door.*

smooth something down to make something flat or smooth by pressing. □ *She smoothed her skirt down, fluffed her hair, and went into the boardroom.* 🅃 *Karen smoothed down the bedclothes.*

smooth something out **1.** to flatten or even something by smoothing or pressing. □ *Wally smoothed the bedspread out.* 🅃 *Wally finished making the bed by smoothing out the spread.* **2.** to polish and refine something. (Figurative.) □ *The editor smoothed John's style out.* 🅃 *You need to smooth out your delivery when you speak.*

snap back (after something) to return to normal after an accident or similar event. □ *He is upset now, but he will snap back after things settle down.* □ *Things will snap back in no time at all.*

snap back (at someone) to give a sharp or angry response to someone. □ *The telephone operator, unlike in the good old days, snapped back at the caller.* □ *Please don't snap back. I've had a bad day.*

sneak in(to some place) to enter a place quietly and in secret, perhaps without a ticket or permission. □ *The kids tried to sneak into the rock concert, but they were stopped by the guards.* □ *Never try to sneak in. Sometimes they arrest you for trespassing.*

sneak out (of some place) to go out of a place quietly and in secret. ☐ *I sneaked out of the meeting, hoping no one would notice.* ☐ *Jamie saw me and sneaked out with me.*

sneak up on someone or something to approach someone or something quietly and in secret. ☐ *Please don't sneak up on me like that.* ☐ *I sneaked up on the cake, hoping no one would see me. Someone did.*

snoop around (something) to look around in a place, trying to find out something secret or learn about someone else's affairs. ☐ *Why are you snooping around my house?* ☐ *I am not snooping around.*

snow someone or something in [for heavy snowfall] to block someone or something in a place. ☐ *The sudden storm snowed us in.* 🅃 *The storm snowed in most of the people in town.* 🅃 *We hoped it hadn't snowed in the fire engines.*

soak in(to something) [for moisture] to penetrate something. ☐ *The rain soaked into the parched ground as fast as it fell.* ☐ *I'm glad it soaked in. I was afraid it would run off.*

soak something off ((of) something) to remove something, such as a label or surface soil, from something by soaking it in a liquid. (The *of* is colloquial.) ☐ *She soaked the labels off the bottles and jars.* 🅃 *Please soak off the label.* ☐ *Soak the labels off, don't scrape them off.*

soak something out (of something) to remove something, such as a stain, from something by soaking in a liquid. ☐ *Dan soaked the stain out of his shirt and then washed it.* 🅃 *Dan soaked out the stain.* ☐ *I couldn't soak the stain out.*

soak through something [for liquid] to work its way through something, such as cloth or paper. ☐ *Please wipe up that mess before it soaks through the tablecloth.* ☐ *It's too late. The grape juice has soaked through the carpet into the mat.*

soap someone or something down to cover someone or something thoroughly with soap or suds. (*Someone* includes *oneself*.) ☐ *Mother soaped Tim down and rinsed him in warm water.* 🅃 *She soaped down the floor.* ☐ *He soaped himself down and then rinsed off.*

sober someone up **1.** to take actions that will cause a drunken person to become sober. (*Someone* includes *oneself.*) □ *Some coffee ought to sober him up.* □ *He tried to sober himself up because he had to drive home.* 🅃 *They tried to sober up the guys who had been out all night.* **2.** to cause someone to face reality. □ *The harsh reality of what had happened sobered him up immediately.* 🅃 *The lecture sobered up all the revelers.*

sober up to return to sobriety from a drunken state. □ *Jeff sobered up in an hour and could function again.* □ *I don't think that Tex has sobered up since the early 1960s.*

sort something out **1.** to sort something; to arrange according to class or category. □ *Let's sort these cards out.* 🅃 *Would you please sort out your socks?* **2.** to study a problem and figure it out. □ *I can't sort this out without some more time.* 🅃 *Let's sort out this mess and settle it once and for all.*

sound off to speak something loudly; to call out one's name or one's place in a numerical sequence. □ *All right, sound off, you guys!* □ *Each one sounded off.*

sound off (about something) to complain loudly about something; to make a fuss over something. □ *She is always sounding off about something.* □ *Betty sounds off all the time.*

speak out to speak loudly; to speak to be heard. □ *Please speak out. We need to hear you.* □ *They won't hear you in the back row if you don't speak out.*

speak out (about someone or something) to express oneself about someone or something; to tell what one knows about someone or something. □ *I could keep silent no longer. I had to speak out about the alleged accident.* □ *I had to speak out!*

speak out (against someone or something) to speak negatively and publicly about someone or something; to reveal something negative, in speech, about someone or something. □ *I don't want to speak out against my friends, but I am afraid I have to.* □ *The citizens spoke out against corruption in government.* □ *They felt that they had to speak out.*

speak up to speak loudly. □ *Please speak up. I can't hear you.* □ *No one will be able to hear you if you do not speak up.*

speak up for someone or something to speak in favor of someone or something; to come forward and express favorable things about someone or something. ☐ *I hope you will speak up for me when the time comes.* ☐ *I will speak up for the proposed legislation.*

speed someone or something up to cause someone or something to move faster. ☐ *We tried to speed him up, but he is just a very slow person.* 🅃 *We sped up the process, but it still took too long.*

speed up to go faster. ☐ *Please speed up. We are late.* ☐ *All the cars sped up.*

spice something up **1.** to make some food more spicy. ☐ *Judy spiced the cider up by adding cinnamon and nutmeg.* 🅃 *She spiced up the chili too much.* **2.** to make something more interesting, lively, or sexy. (Figurative.) ☐ *I'm afraid that they spiced the musical up too much. Some people walked out.* ☐ *Judy liked to spice her lectures up by telling jokes.* 🅃 *She spiced up each lecture with a joke.* 🅃 *They spiced up the play too much.*

spin off [for something] to part and fly away from something that is spinning; [for something] to detach or break loose from something. ☐ *The blade of the lawn mower spun off, but fortunately no one was injured.* ☐ *The lid to the pickle jar spun off easily after I got it loosened.*

splash down [for a space capsule] to land in the water. ☐ *The capsule splashed down very close to the pickup ship.* ☐ *It splashed down at noon.*

split off (from something) to separate away from something; to sever connection with and separate from something. ☐ *A large iceberg split off from the glacier and made an enormous splash.* ☐ *A giant ice cube split off and floated away.*

split people up to separate two or more people. ☐ *I am going to have to split you two up if you don't stop talking to each other.* 🅃 *I will have to split up those two.*

split someone or something up (into something) to divide people or things up into something, such as groups. (*Someone* includes *oneself.*) ☐ *I had to split the group up into two sections—there were so many who showed up.* 🅃 *I split up the class into two dis-*

cussion sections. □ *I split them up.* □ *They split themselves up into smaller groups.*

split something off ((of) something) to sever connection with something and separate. (The *of* is colloquial.) □ *Dave split a piece of wood off the log to use for kindling.* 🅃 *He split off a stick of wood.* □ *Jamie took a log and split a stave of wood off.*

sponge someone or something down to remove the [excess] moisture from someone or something. □ *The fight manager sponged his boxer down.* 🅃 *I will sponge down the countertop.*

sponge something away to absorb, wipe up, or wipe away something. □ *Try sponging the stain away with some soda water.* 🅃 *I will sponge away the mess.*

spread out to separate and distribute over a wide area. □ *The sheriff told the members of the posse to spread out and continue their search.* □ *The grease spread out and stained a large area of the carpet.*

spread something on(to something) to distribute a coating of something onto something. □ *Spread the butter onto the bread evenly.* 🅃 *Spread on the butter evenly.* □ *Donna spread the paint on with a roller.*

spread something out to open, unfold, or lay something over a wider area. □ *Spread the wet papers out so they will dry.* 🅃 *She spread out the papers to dry them.*

spring up to appear or develop suddenly; to sprout, as with a seedling. □ *We knew it was really spring when all the flowers sprang up.* □ *It seems as if the tulips sprang up overnight.* □ *The dog's ears sprang up when the refrigerator opened.* □ *A little breeze sprang up and cooled things off.*

spruce someone or something up **1.** to tidy up and groom someone or something. (*Someone* includes *oneself.*) □ *Laura's mother took a few minutes to spruce her daughter up for the party.* 🅃 *She spruced up her daughter.* □ *Let's spruce the house up this spring.* □ *He spruced himself up a bit and then rang the doorbell.* **2.** to refurbish or renew someone or something. (*Someone* includes *oneself.*) □ *Do you think we should try to spruce this room up a little?*

T *Yes, let's spruce up this room.* T *We spruced up the house for the holidays.* □ *She bought all new clothes so she could spruce herself up for her new job.*

squash something down to crush something down; to pack something down. □ *Squash the ice cream down so the air will be pushed out.* T *Who squashed down my hat?*

squeak by (someone or something) **1.** to manage just to squeeze past someone or something. □ *I squeaked by the fat man in the hallway only to find myself blocked by another.* □ *I just barely squeaked by.* **2.** to manage just to get past a barrier represented by a person or thing, such as a teacher or an examination. □ *Judy just squeaked by Professor Smith, who has a reputation for flunking just about everyone.* □ *I took the test and just squeaked by.*

squeak something through to manage just to get something accepted or approved. □ *I just managed to squeak the proposal through.* □ *Tom squeaked the application through at the last minute.*

squeak through (something) **1.** to manage just to squeeze through an opening. □ *The child squeaked through the opening and escaped.* □ *Sally squeaked through and got away.* **2.** to manage just to get past a barrier, such as an examination or interview. □ *Sally just barely squeaked through the interview, but she got the job.* □ *I wasn't too alert, and I just squeaked through.*

squeeze someone or something up to press people or things close together. □ *The usher tried to squeeze us up so she could seat more people.* T *Don't squeeze up the cars too tight in the parking area.*

squeeze (themselves) up [for people] to press themselves closely together. (Also in other persons.) □ *Everyone squeezed themselves up in the tiny car so there would be room for one more.* □ *Let's squeeze up so Jamie can sit down.* □ *They squeezed themselves up so they would take less space.* □ *Let's squeeze ourselves up to make more room.*

squirm out (of something) **1.** to crawl or wiggle out of something. □ *The worm squirmed out of its hole and was gobbled up by a bird.* □ *The worm squirmed out.* **2.** to escape doing something; to escape the responsibility for having done something. □ *You can't* *squirm out of it. You have to do it.* ☐ *He agreed to go but squirmed out at the last minute.* ☐ *You did it and you can't squirm out of it by denying it!*

stack something up to make a stack of some things. ☐ *Please stack these books up.* 🅃 *Liz stacked up the papers and took them to the garage.*

stack up [for something] to accumulate, as in stacks. (Often used in reference to vehicular traffic.) ☐ *Your work is stacking up. You will have to work late to finish it.* ☐ *I hate to let my work stack up. I have to do it sooner or later.* ☐ *Traffic is stacking up on the expressway.*

stake someone out (on someone) to assign someone to watch someone or to spy on someone. ☐ *The police staked a detective out on Fred.* 🅃 *They staked out a detective on Fred.* ☐ *Fred needed watching, so the police staked someone out.*

stake something off to mark out the boundaries of an area of land with stakes. ☐ *The prospectors staked an area off for themselves.* 🅃 *The prospectors staked off an area in which they would look for gold.*

stalk in(to some place) to stride into a place, perhaps indignantly. ☐ *Carl stalked into the manager's office and began his tirade.* ☐ *He stalked in and began to complain.*

stalk out of some place to stride out of a place indignantly. ☐ *Jeff stalked out of the store and went straight to the police.* ☐ *Mary got angry and stalked out of the meeting.*

stall someone or something off to hold someone or something off; to postpone the action of someone or something. ☐ *Please stall them off while I try to get out the back door.* 🅃 *I will stall off the bill collector for a while.*

stammer something out to manage to say something, but only haltingly. ☐ *Fred stammered the words out haltingly.* 🅃 *He stammered out the name of the winner.*

stampede out of some place [for a crowd of people or other creatures] to move rapidly out of a place, as if in panic. ☐ *The patrons* *stampeded out of the smoky theater.* ☐ *The cattle stampeded out of the corral.*

stand around to wait around, standing; to loiter. ☐ *Please don't stand around. Get busy!* ☐ *Why are all these people standing around doing nothing?*

stand aside **1.** to step aside; to get out of the way. ☐ *Please stand aside while the bridal party passes by.* ☐ *The guests stood aside while the bride and groom left.* **2.** to withdraw and ignore something; to remain passive while something happens. ☐ *He just stood aside and let his kids get away with murder.* ☐ *She stood aside and did not try to come between them.*

stand back (from someone or something) to stand or move well away and to the rear of someone or something. ☐ *Stand back from Sam. He is really angry.* ☐ *Would you please stand back from the edge?* ☐ *Stand back!*

stand by to wait in a state of readiness. ☐ *I may need your help in a minute. Please stand by.* ☐ *Stand by while I find your records in this computer.*

stand down to step down, particularly from the witness stand in a courtroom. ☐ *The bailiff told the witness to stand down.* ☐ *Please stand down and take your seat.*

stand in (for someone) to represent someone; to substitute for someone. ☐ *I will stand in for Roger in tonight's performance of the play. He is sick.* ☐ *He is sick, so I will stand in.*

stand out (from someone or something) to be prominent when compared to someone or something. ☐ *As a programmer, she stands out from all the others.* ☐ *This one stands out from all the rest.* ☐ *It really stands out.*

stand out (from something) to protrude from something. ☐ *One very straight branch in particular stood out from the tree and looked suitable for a post.* ☐ *The branch stood out and made a perfect place to hang my shirt while I worked.*

stand up **1.** to arise from a sitting or reclining position. ☐ *He stood up and looked across the valley.* ☐ *She had been sitting for so long* *that it was a pleasure to stand up.* **2.** to be in a standing position. □ *I've been standing up all day, and I'm exhausted.* □ *I stood up throughout the whole trip because there were no more seats on the train.* **3.** to wear well; to remain sound and intact. □ *This material just doesn't stand up well when it's washed.* □ *Her work doesn't stand up under close scrutiny.* **4.** [for an assertion] to remain believable. (Figurative.) □ *His testimony will not stand up in court.* □ *When the police checked the story, it did not stand up.*

stand up against someone or something to challenge or hold one's own against someone or something. □ *He's good, but he can't stand up against Jill.* □ *Can this tent stand up against the wind?*

stare someone down to pressure someone to capitulate, back down, or yield by staring. □ *Don't try to stare me down, I have nerves of steel.* 🅃 *I tried to stare down my opponent, but it didn't work.*

start off to begin; to set out on a journey. □ *When do you want to start off?* □ *We will start off as soon as we can get ready.*

start off (by doing something) to begin a process by doing a particular thing first. □ *Can I start off by singing the school song?* □ *That's a good way to start off.*

start off (on something) **1.** to begin a series or sequence. □ Today *I start off on the first volume of my trilogy.* □ *I am ready to start off now.* **2.** to begin a journey. □ *When do we start off on our trip?* □ *I'm ready to start off. What about you?*

start out to begin. □ *Whenever you are ready, we will start out.* □ *We can't start out until Tom is here.*

start out as something to begin one's career as something. □ *I started out as a clerk and I'm still a clerk!* □ *I wanted to start out as an assistant manager.*

start over to begin again. □ *I have messed this up so much that there is nothing to do now but start over.* □ *When you start over, try to do it right this time.*

start someone off (on something) to cause someone to begin on a task or job. □ *I have to start Jeff off on this task, then I will talk* *to you.* T *I will start off my workers on the job tomorrow.* □ *Let me know what time to start them off.*

start something up to start something, such as an engine or a motor. □ *Start your lawn mower up and get that grass cut!* T *Start up your car and let's go.*

start up to begin; to begin running, as with an engine. □ *The car started up without a problem.* □ *The engines of the plane started up one by one.*

stay away (from someone or something) to avoid someone or something. □ *Stay away from me!* □ *Please stay away!*

stay back (from something) to keep one's distance from someone or something. □ *Stay back from the lawn mower!* □ *This is dangerous. Stay back!*

stay on (after someone or something) See *linger on (after someone or something).*

stay out (of something) **1.** to keep out of something or some place. □ *Stay out of here!* □ *Please stay out until we are ready.* **2.** to remain uninvolved in some piece of business. □ *I decided to stay out of it and let someone else handle it.* □ *My help wasn't needed there, so I just stayed out.*

stay up (for something) to remain awake and out of bed for some nighttime event. □ *I will stay up for her arrival.* □ *I can't stay up that late.*

steal away to sneak away quietly. □ *She stole away in the still of the night.* □ *I plan to steal away during the second act because I have to get to bed early.*

steam something off ((of) something) to loosen and remove something by an application of steam. (The *of* is colloquial.) □ *Toby steamed the old paper off the wall.* T *Toby steamed off the old paper.* □ *It is hard to steam the paper off.*

steam something out (of something) to remove something embedded, through an application of steam. □ *The cleaner was not able to steam the wrinkles out of my jacket.* T *I tried to steam out the gum.* □ *I will try to steam them out.*

steam something up to cause something to be covered with water vapor due to the presence of steam. □ *Our breaths steamed the windows up.* 🅃 *Our breaths steamed up the windows.*

steam up to become covered with a film of steam or water vapor. □ *The windows steamed up, and we had to wipe them so we could see out.* □ *The window has steamed up, and I can't see.*

step aside to step out of the way. □ *Please step aside. You are in the way.* □ *I stepped aside just in time.*

step back (from someone or something) to move back from someone or something; to move back so as to provide space around someone or something. □ *Please step back from the injured woman. Give her some air.* □ *Step back and give her some air.*

step out into something to go out from a place into a different set of conditions. □ *Julie stepped out of her previous job into a whole new world.* □ *Wally stepped out into the bright sunlight.*

step out (of something) **1.** to go out of a place. □ *She stepped out of the house without a coat and nearly froze to death.* □ *Jamie stepped out and nearly froze her nose.* **2.** to take one step to get out of pants of some type that have been dropped. □ *He stepped out of his pants and pulled off his shirt.* □ *He dropped his pants and stepped out.*

step out (on someone) to be unfaithful to a spouse or lover. □ *Jeff has been stepping out on Judy.* □ *I was not stepping out!*

step outside **1.** to go outside, as to get some fresh air. □ *I need to step outside for a minute to get a breath of air.* □ *Tom and Harry stepped outside for a moment.* **2.** to go outside to fight or settle an argument. □ *I find that insulting. Would you care to step outside?* □ *Max invited Lefty to step outside.*

step over (to) some place to move to a place a few steps away. □ *Please step over here and I'll show you some other merchandise.* □ *If you will step over to the display case, I will show you some earrings.*

step right up to come right to where the speaker is; to come forward to the person speaking. (Typically used by people selling things.) □ *Please step right up and buy a ticket to see the show.* □ *Don't be shy! Step right up and buy one of these.*

step something up **1.** to make something more active. □ *I hope we can step the pace of business up in the next few days.* 🅃 *We can step up business considerably by putting out a larger sign.* **2.** to make something go or run faster. □ *The engineer stepped the motors up and the production line moved even faster.* 🅃 *Please step up the speed of your activity.* □ *The new manager stepped production up considerably.*

step up to increase. □ *Industrial production stepped up a large amount this last quarter.* □ *Traffic has stepped up since the road was paved.*

step up to something to walk to something, especially a counter or a bar. □ *Jake stepped up to the ticket counter and bought a single ticket for the balcony.* □ *When Wally stepped up to the ticket window, he learned that the show was sold out.*

stick around to remain in the general vicinity. (Colloquial.) □ *Please stick around. I need to talk to you after the meeting.* □ *I will stick around for a while, but I have another appointment.*

stick out to project outward. □ *You can't lock your suitcase because there is a bit of cloth sticking out.* □ *Some cloth stuck out of the top of the drawer.*

stick out (from someone or something) to project outward from someone or something. □ *His right arm, which was in a cast, stuck out from him like a crane.* □ *His arm stuck out.*

stick out (of someone or something) to protrude from someone or something. □ *The arrow stuck out of him, wobbling as he staggered.* □ *A dollar bill stuck out of the book. What a strange bookmark.*

stick someone or something up to rob someone or a business establishment. (Presumably with the aid of a gun.) □ *Max tried to stick the drugstore up.* 🅃 *Max stuck up the store.* □ *He stuck the store up.*

stick something down to fasten something down, as with glue or paste. □ *Get some glue and stick this wallpaper down, please.* [T] *Stick down this wallpaper, would you?*

stick something in(to someone or something) to insert something into someone or something. □ *The lab technician stuck a needle into my arm and took some blood out.* [T] *She stuck in the needle.* □ *Harry stuck the needle in with great care.*

stick something out **1.** to cause something to project outward. □ *Don't stick your tongue out at me!* [T] *She stuck out her tongue at me!* **2.** to endure something; to stay with something. (The *something* is usually *it.*) □ *I will stick it out as long as I can.* □ *She stuck it out as long as she could; then she started looking for another job.*

stick together **1.** to adhere to one another. □ *The noodles are sticking together. What shall I do?* □ *You need to keep the pieces separate while you fry them or else they will stick together.* **2.** to remain in one another's company. (Figurative.) □ *Let us stick together so we don't get lost.* □ *They stuck together through thick and thin.*

stir someone up to get someone excited; to get someone angry. □ *The march music really stirred the audience up.* [T] *The accusing letter stirred up Martha.*

stir something up **1.** to mix something by stirring. □ *Please stir the pancake batter up before you use it.* [T] *Please stir up the batter.* **2.** to foment trouble. □ *Why are you always trying to stir trouble up?* [T] *Are you stirring up trouble again?*

stitch something up to sew something together; to mend a tear or ripped seam. □ *I tore my shirt. Would you stitch it up, please?* [T] *Please stitch up my shirt.*

stock up (on something) to build up a supply of something in particular. □ *I need to stock up on food for the party.* □ *We need fresh vegetables. We will have to stock up before the weekend.*

stoop down to dip, duck, or squat down. □ *I had to stoop down to enter the tiny door.* □ *Stoop down so you don't bump your head.*

stoop over to bend over. ☐ *Carl stooped over to pick up his napkin and lost his balance.* ☐ *As he stooped over, he lost his balance and fell.*

stop by (some place) to go to a place and stop and then continue. (The *some place* may be any expression of a location.) ☐ *Stop by my place for dinner sometime.* ☐ *Please stop by before the end of the day.*

stop in (some place) to pay a brief visit to a place. ☐ *Do you want to stop in Adamsville or just drive on through?* ☐ *Let's stop in for a few minutes.*

stop over (some place) to stay one or more nights at a place. ☐ *We stopped over in Miami for one night.* ☐ *We had to stop over, but we stayed in a very nice hotel.*

stop something up (with something) to plug something with something. ☐ *Gary stopped the sink up with bacon grease.* 🅃 *He stopped up the sink with grease.* ☐ *Try not to stop the sink up.*

stop up [for something] to become clogged. ☐ *The sink stopped up again!*

storm in(to some place) to burst into something or some place angrily. ☐ *The army stormed into the town and took many of the citizens as prisoners.* ☐ *Leonard stormed in, shouting at everyone.*

storm out (of some place) to burst out of some place angrily. ☐ *Carol stormed out of the office in a rage.* ☐ *She got mad and stormed out.*

straighten out **1.** to become straight. ☐ *The road finally straightened out.* ☐ *The train tracks straightened out on the plain.* **2.** to improve one's behavior or attitude. ☐ *I hope he straightens out before he gets himself into real trouble.* ☐ *Fred had better straighten out soon if he wants to get a job.*

straighten someone or something out to make someone's body or something straight or orderly. (*Someone* includes *oneself.*) ☐ *The undertaker straightened Sam out in his coffin.* 🅃 *The undertaker straightened out the corpse in the coffin.* ☐ *Can you straighten this spoon out?* ☐ *Straighten yourself out and see if your bed is going to be long enough.*

straighten something out **1.** to make something straighter. □ *I can't straighten this row of books out.* 🅃 *Please straighten out this line of people.* **2.** to bring order to something that is disorderly. □ *See if you can straighten this mess out.* 🅃 *Will you straighten out this mess?*

straighten something up to make something less messy. □ *This room is a mess. Please straighten it up.* 🅃 *Can you straighten up this room?*

straighten up **1.** to sit or stand more vertically. □ *Please straighten up. Don't slouch.* □ *I have to remind Timmy constantly to straighten up.* **2.** to behave better. □ *Come on! Straighten up or I will send you home!* □ *I wish you would straighten up. Your behavior is very bad.*

stream down (on someone or something) [for a liquid or light] to flow downward onto someone or something. □ *The water streamed down on all of them.* □ *The light broke through the clouds and streamed down on all of them.* □ *It streamed down and soaked them all.*

stream in(to something) to flow or rush into something. □ *The people streamed into the hall, each seeking the best possible seat.* □ *Water streamed into the room from the broken pipe.* □ *Complaints about the performance streamed in.*

stretch out [for one] to extend and stretch one's body to its full length. □ *She lay down, stretched out, and relaxed for the first time in days.* □ *I need a bigger bed. I can't stretch out in this one.*

stretch someone or something out to extend or draw out someone or something. (*Someone* includes *oneself.*) □ *Molly stretched the baby out to change his clothes.* 🅃 *She stretched out the baby, who had rolled into a ball.* □ *Stretch the chicken out and skin it.*

stretch something out (to someone or something) to reach something out to someone or something. □ *Jeff stretched his hand out to Tiffany.* 🅃 *He stretched out his hand to the visitor.* □ *The visitor approached and stretched her hand out.*

strike back (at someone or something) to return the blows of someone or something; to return the attack of someone or something. □ *The victim struck back at the mugger and scared him away.* □ *The victim struck back in the courts.*

strike for something to conduct a work stoppage in order to gain something. □ *The workers were striking for longer vacations.* □ *We are striking for fundamental human rights.*

strike out **1.** [for a baseball player] to accumulate three strikes. □ *Jeff struck out for the fourth time this season.* □ *I knew I would strike out this inning.* **2.** to have a series of failures. (Figurative.) □ *It was a hard job. Finally I struck out and had to go into another line of work.* □ *I keep striking out when it comes to the opposite sex.*

strike out (at someone or something) to hit at someone or something with the intention of threatening or harming. □ *Dave would strike out at anyone who came near him, but it was all bluff.* □ *He was mad, and when anyone came close, he struck out.*

strike something down [for a court] to invalidate a law. □ *The higher court struck the ruling of the lower court down.* [T] *The court struck down the ruling.*

string someone along to maintain someone's attention or interest, probably insincerely. □ *You are just stringing me along because you like to borrow my car. You are not a real friend.* □ *Rachel strung her along for the sake of old times.*

strip down to remove one's clothing. □ *The doctor told Joe to strip down for his examination.* □ *Joe stripped down for the examination.*

struggle through (something) to get through something in the best way possible. □ *I am going to struggle through this dull book to the very end.* □ *The book was dull, but I struggled through.*

stumble through something to get through a sequence of something awkwardly and falteringly. □ *The cast stumbled through the first act and barely finished the second.* □ *Mary stumbled through her speech and fled from the stage.*

subsist on something to exist on something; to stay alive on something. □ *We can only subsist on this amount of money. We need* *more!* ☐ *They are able to do no more than subsist on what Mrs. Harris is paid.*

succumb to something to yield to something, especially a temptation, fatal disease, a human weakness, etc. ☐ *He finally succumbed to his pneumonia.* ☐ *She did not succumb to the disease until the last.*

suck something up to pick something up by suction, as with a vacuum cleaner, or through a straw. ☐ *Will this vacuum suck all this dirt up?* 🅃 *The vacuum cleaner sucked up all the dirt.*

sum (something) up to give a summary of something. ☐ *I would like to sum this lecture up by listing the main points I have covered.* ☐ *It is time for me to sum up.* 🅃 *She summed up the president's speech in three sentences.*

surge in(to something) to burst or gush into something or some place. ☐ *The water surged into the valley after the dam broke.* ☐ *The doors opened, and the people surged in.*

surge out (of something) to burst forth or gush out of something or some place. ☐ *The water surged out of the huge crack in the dam.* ☐ *We saw the crack where the water surged out.*

surge up to rush or gush upwards. ☐ *A spring of fresh water surged up under the stone and flowed out on the ground.* ☐ *The oil surged up and blew out into the open air in a tall column of living blackness.*

swallow someone or something up **1.** to eat or gobble up someone or something. ☐ *The fairy-tale wolf threatened to swallow Gwen up in one bite.* 🅃 *The wolf swallowed up the meat in one bite.* **2.** to engulf or contain something. (Figurative.) ☐ *The garage seemed to swallow the cars up.* 🅃 *The huge sweater swallowed up the tiny child.*

swallow something down to swallow something. ☐ *Here, take this pill and swallow it down.* 🅃 *Liz swallowed down the pill.*

swear at someone or something to curse someone or something. ☐ *Please don't swear at the children.* ☐ *Scott swore at the police station as he drove by.*

swear by someone or something **1.** to utter an oath on someone or something. ☐ *I swear by Jupiter that I will be there on time.* ☐ *She swore by her sainted mother that she would never do it again.* ☐ *The sheriff swore by his badge that he would lock her up if she ever did it again.* **2.** to announce one's full faith and trust in someone or something. ☐ *I would swear by Roger any time. He is a great guy, and anything he does is super.* ☐ *I swear by this computer. It has always served me well.*

swear someone in (as something) to administer an oath to someone who then becomes something. ☐ *The judge swore Alice in as street commissioner.* 🅃 *The judge swore in Alice as the new director.* ☐ *She swore Alice in.*

sweep something off ((of) something) to clean something by sweeping. (The *of* is colloquial.) ☐ *The waiter swept the crumbs off the tablecloth.* ☐ *Jake swept the counter off and wiped it clean.* 🅃 *He swept off the back porch.* 🅃 *He swept off the crumbs from the tablecloth.*

sweep something out to clean something out by sweeping. ☐ *Someone has to sweep the garage out.* 🅃 *Don't sweep out this room. I'll do it.*

sweep something up **1.** to clean up and remove something, such as dirt, by sweeping. ☐ *Please sweep these crumbs up.* 🅃 *Can you sweep up these crumbs?* **2.** to clean up some place by sweeping. ☐ *Please sweep this room up.* 🅃 *Can you sweep up this room, please?* **3.** to arrange something, such as hair, into a curve or wave. ☐ *The hairstylist swept her hair up over the top. No one liked it.* 🅃 *Sweep up my hair the way it looks in this picture.*

sweep up to clean up by sweeping. ☐ *Would you sweep up this time?* ☐ *Please give me a few minutes to sweep up before you come to visit.*

swell up to enlarge; to inflate; to bulge out. ☐ *I struck my thumb with a hammer, and it swelled up something awful.*

swish something off ((of) someone or something) to brush something off someone or something. (The *of* is colloquial.) ☐ *The barber swished the loose hairs off of Paul's collar.* 🅃 *The barber swished off the loose hairs.* ☐ *Jamie swished the hairs off.*

switch back (to something) **1.** to return to using or doing something. □ *I decided to switch back to my old shampoo.* □ *I switched back and was glad I did.* **2.** [for a road] to reverse upon itself. □ *The road switched back twenty times in three miles.* □ *It switched back every now and then.*

switch off **1.** [for something] to turn itself off. □ *At midnight, all the lights switched off automatically.* □ *The television switched off after I went to sleep.* **2.** [for someone] to stop paying attention. (Figurative.) □ *I got tired of listening and switched off.* □ *You could see that the audience was switching off.*

switch someone or something off to cause someone or something to be quiet or stop doing something. □ I *got tired of listening to her, so I punched the button and switched her off.* 🅃 *I switched off the television set.*

switch something back (to something) to return something to the way it was. □ *I switched the television back to the previous channel.* 🅃 *I switched back the channel to what I was watching before.* □ *I switched it back and then went to sleep.*

switch something on to close an electrical circuit that causes something to start functioning or operating. □ *Please switch the fan on.* 🅃 *I switched on the fan.*

swoop down (up)on someone or something to dive or plunge downward on someone or something. (Both literal and figurative uses.) □ *The eagle swooped down upon the lamb.* □ *The children swooped down on the ice cream and cake.*

T

take off **1.** to take flight. ☐ *When does this plane take off?* ☐ *We took off on time.* **2.** [for someone] to leave. (Colloquial.) ☐ *It's late. I've got to take off now.* ☐ *We will have to take off about midnight, since we have to get up early in the morning.* **3.** to become active and exciting. (Colloquial.) ☐ *Did the party ever take off, or was it dull all night?* ☐ *Things began to take off about midnight.*

take off from something to take flight from something or some place. ☐ *The plane took off from the busy airport right on schedule.* ☐ *We will take off from the airport on one side of town, fly across the city, and land at our destination within three hours.*

take out after someone or something to set out chasing or running after someone or something. ☐ *Mary took out after Claire but couldn't catch her.* ☐ *The dog took out after the rabbit.*

take over (from someone) to assume the role or job of someone. ☐ *I take over for the manager next month.* ☐ *Liz takes over and will be in charge.*

take someone in **1.** to give someone shelter. ☐ *Do you think you could take me in for the night?* 🅃 *I don't take in strangers.* **2.** to deceive someone. ☐ *Those crooks really took me in. I was a fool.* 🅃 *The con artists took in a lot of innocent people.*

take someone or something away to remove someone or something. ☐ *The police came and took her away.* 🅃 *He took away the extra food.*

take someone or something off (something) to remove someone or something from the surface of something. ☐ *Bob helped take his* *children off the merry-go-round.* ☐ *Please take your books off the table.* ☐ *I'll take them off.*

take someone or something on to agree to deal with someone or something; to begin to handle someone or something. ☐ *I did not agree to take him on.* 🅃 *I wouldn't have taken on this project if I had thought there would be no help.*

take someone or something out (of something) to carry, lead, or guide someone or something out of something or some place. ☐ *He was becoming quite ill from the smoke, and I had to take him out of the room.* 🅃 *They took out the people.* ☐ *Let's take them out as soon as we can.*

take something apart to break something to pieces; to disassemble something. ☐ *Tim took his watch apart, and that was the end of it.* 🅃 *Don't take apart every mechanical device you own!*

take something down (in something) to write something down in something, such as writing, a notebook, etc. ☐ *Please take these figures down in your notebook.* 🅃 *Take down these figures in your record of this meeting.* ☐ *I will ask my secretary to take some notes down about what happens at this meeting.* 🅃 *Please take down some notes on this.* ☐ *I will take them down and type them later.*

take something in **1.** to reduce the size of a garment. ☐ *This is too big. I'll have to take it in around the waist.* 🅃 *I'll have to take in these pants.* **2.** to bring something or a creature into shelter. ☐ *I didn't want Joan to take the stray cat in, but she did it anyway.* 🅃 *Joan always takes in stray animals.* **3.** to view and study something; to attend something involving viewing. ☐ *The mountains are so beautiful! I need an hour or so to take it all in.* 🅃 *I want to sit here a minute and take in the view.* 🅃 *Would you like to take in a movie?* **4.** to receive money as payment or proceeds. ☐ *How much did we take in today?* 🅃 *The box office took in nearly a thousand dollars in just the last hour.* **5.** to receive something into the mind, usually visually. ☐ *Could you take those explanations in? I couldn't.* 🅃 *I could hardly take in everything she said.*

take something off to remove something, such as an article of clothing. ☐ *Please take your coat off and stay awhile.* 🅃 *Please take off your coat.*

take something over **1.** to assume responsibility for a task. □ *It looks as if I'm going to have to take the project over.* 🅃 *I will take over the project.* **2.** to acquire all of an asset. □ *Carl set out to take the failing airline over.* 🅃 *He took over the failing company.*

take something up **1.** [for someone or a group] to deliberate something. □ *When will the board of directors take this issue up?* 🅃 *Let's take up that matter now.* **2.** to raise something, such as the height of a hem. □ *The skirt is too long. I'll have to take it up.* 🅃 *Can you take up this skirt for me?* **3.** to continue with something after an interruption. □ *They took it up where they left off.* 🅃 *Let's take up this matter at the point we were at when we were interrupted.* 🅃 *We must take up our work again.* **4.** to begin something; to start to acquire a skill in something. □ *When did you take this hobby up?* 🅃 *I took up skiing last fall.*

take too much on to accept too many tasks; to accept a task that is too big a burden for one. □ *Nancy has a tendency to take too much on and then get exhausted.* 🅃 *I always take on too much and then I have no time of my own.*

talk around something to talk, but avoid talking directly about the subject. □ *You are just talking around the matter! I want a straight answer!* □ *He never really said anything. He just talked around the issue.*

talk back (to someone) to challenge verbally a parent, an older person, or one's superior. □ *Please don't talk back to me!* □ *I've told you before not to talk back!*

talk down to someone to speak to someone condescendingly. □ *You would be more convincing if you didn't talk down to your audience.* □ *Please don't talk down to me. I can understand anything that you are likely to say.*

talk oneself out to talk until one can talk no more. □ *She talked herself out and was silent for the rest of the day.* □ *I talked until I talked myself out.*

talk someone into something to convince someone to do something through discussion. (*Someone* includes *oneself.*) □ *I think I can talk June into it.* □ *She finally talked herself into making the dive from the highest board.*

talk something out to settle something by discussion. ☐ *Let's not get mad. Let's just talk it out.* 🅃 *Please, let's talk out this matter.*

talk something up to promote or advertise something by saying good things about it to as many people as possible. ☐ *Let's talk the play up around campus so we can get a good audience* 🅃 *I will talk up the play all I can.*

tally something up to add something up. ☐ *Please tally everything up and tell me the total.* 🅃 *Let's tally up everything and ask for donations.*

taper off to slacken off gradually; to cease something gradually; to reduce gradually. ☐ *Activity finally tapered off in the middle of the afternoon.* ☐ *I hope that business doesn't taper off in the summer this year.*

team up against someone or something to join with someone else against someone or something. ☐ *Let's team up against Paul and Tony in the footrace.* ☐ *We teamed up against the group from the other school.*

team up (with someone) to join with one or more persons; to collaborate with two or more persons. ☐ *I intend to team up with a friend and go into the painting business.* ☐ *I do better by myself. I don't want to team up.*

tear away (from someone or something) to leave someone or something, running. ☐ *Dave tore away from Jill, leaving her to find her own way home.* ☐ *Roger tore away from the meeting, trying to make his train.*

tear down something to race down something very fast. ☐ *The girls tore down the hallway as fast as they could run.* ☐ *They tore down the stairs and ran out the door.*

tear off (from someone or something) to leave someone or something in a great hurry. ☐ *I hate to tear off from you guys, but I'm late for dinner.* ☐ *It's time for me to go. I have to tear off.*

tear (oneself) away (from someone or something) to force oneself to leave someone or something. ☐ *Do you think you can tear yourself away from your friends for dinner?* ☐ *I could hardly tear myself away from the concert.*

tear out (of some place) to leave a place in a great hurry. □ *The kids tore out of the house after they broke the window.* □ *They saw what they had done and tore out.*

tear someone or something down to criticize someone or something mercilessly. (*Someone* includes *oneself.*) □ *What is the point in tearing Frank down? He is doing his best and it's as good as anyone else can do, too.* 🅃 *Don't tear down Frank or the others!* □ *Ann tore our efforts down mercilessly.* □ *You are always tearing yourself down!*

tear someone or something up to rip someone or something into many pieces. □ *Don't get close to that machine. It can tear you up.* 🅃 *The lawn mower tore up the paper left in the yard.*

tear someone up to cause someone to grieve seriously. □ *The news of the accident really tore her up.* 🅃 *The news tore up the whole family.*

tear something away (from someone or something) **1.** to peel something from someone or something. □ *The paramedic tore the clothing away from the burn victim and began to treat the wounds immediately.* 🅃 *She tore away the clothing from the victim.* □ *She tore the clothing away.* **2.** to snatch something away from someone or something. □ *I tore the grenade away from the child and threw it in the lake.* 🅃 *Liz tore away the cover from the book.* □ *She tore it away.*

tear something down to raze something. □ *The workers tore the building down and carried the debris away.* 🅃 *They tore down the building.*

tear something off ((of) someone or something) to peel or rip something off someone or something. (The *of* is colloquial.) □ *Max tore the tie off his victim and ran away with it.* 🅃 *He tore off the tie.* □ *Max tore the label off the can.*

tear something out (of something) to remove something from something by ripping or tearing. □ *Tear the coupons out of the magazine and save them.* 🅃 *Please tear out the coupons.* □ *I tore them all out.*

tell someone where to get off to rebuke someone; to put one in one's place. (Idiomatic. Also literal uses, as with a train conductor indicating a debarkation point to a passenger.) □ *You really told him where to get off!* □ *If she keeps acting like that to me, I will tell her where to get off.*

tense up (for something) to become rigid or firm; to become anxious and ready for something. (Both literal and figurative uses.) □ *Liz tensed up for the game and was very nervous.* □ *He tensed up and that made it hard to give him the injection he needed.*

test out (of something) to score high enough on a placement test that one does not need to take a particular course. □ *I tested out of calculus.* □ *I don't know enough to test out.*

test something out to try something out; to test something to see if it works. □ *I can't wait to test my new stereo out.* [T] *I will test out the stereo.*

thaw out to warm up from being frozen. □ *How long will it take for the chicken to thaw out?* □ *I can't wait for the cake to thaw out. I want some now!*

thaw someone or something out to raise the temperature of someone or something above freezing. □ *We need to get inside so I can thaw my brother out. His toes are almost frozen.* [T] *Did you thaw out the chicken?*

thin down to become thinner or slimmer. □ *He stopped eating altogether so he could thin down.* □ *I have to thin down so I can get into my new suit.*

thin out to spread out; to become less dense. □ *The trees began to thin out as we got higher up the mountain.* □ *The crowd began to thin out as we got a little farther from the theater.*

thin something out to make something less dense; to scatter something. □ *You will have to thin the young plants out, because there is not room for all of them.* [T] *Can you thin out these young plants?*

think back (on someone or something) to contemplate someone or something in the past. □ *I like to think back on my family and the way we used to do things together.* □ *It makes me feel* *good to think back on those things.* □ *I like to think back and relive those days.*

think back (to something) to remember back to something in the past. □ *Now, try and think back to the night of January 16.* □ *I can't think back. My mind is preoccupied with other things.*

think something out to go through something in one's mind; to think through something. □ *I have to take some time and think this out before I can respond to you.* 🅃 *I thought out this proposal very carefully before I presented it to you.*

think something over to think about something and whether one will choose to do it. □ *I need a few minutes to think it over.* 🅃 *Let me think over your request for a day or so.*

think something through to consider carefully and try to settle something in one's mind. □ *Let me think this through and call you in the morning.* 🅃 *I will think through this matter and get back to you.*

think something up to invent something. □ *I don't have a good answer, but I'll think something up.* 🅃 *I'll think up a good answer.*

thrash something out to argue something through to a settlement. □ *We will have to get together and thrash this out.* 🅃 *We will thrash out this disagreement together.*

throng in(to something) [for a crowd] to swarm into some place. □ *The eager crowd thronged into the department store to partake in the advertised sale.* □ *The doors opened, and they thronged in.*

throng out (of something) [for a crowd] to swarm out of something or some place. □ *The people thronged out of the concert hall at the end of the program.* □ *At half past ten, the crowd thronged out.*

throw someone over (for someone else) to break up with a lover in favor of someone else. □ *Sarah threw Jason over for Larry.* 🅃 *She threw over Jason for Walter.* □ *I knew that eventually she would throw him over.*

throw something off to cast something, such as a coat, off one's body. ☐ *He threw his jacket off and dived into the icy water.* Ⓣ *He threw off his jacket.*

throw something together to assemble or create something in a hurry. ☐ *I think I can throw something acceptable together for dinner.* Ⓣ *I can throw together something that is quite edible.*

throw something up **1.** to build or erect something in a hurry. ☐ *They sure threw that building up in a hurry.* Ⓣ *They threw up the building in only a few weeks.* **2.** to vomit something. ☐ *Poor Wally threw his dinner up.* Ⓣ *He threw up his dinner.*

throw up to vomit. ☐ *I was afraid I would throw up, the food was so horrible.* ☐ *This food is bad enough to make you throw up.*

thrust out to stick out; to stab outward; to protrude outward. ☐ *A deck thrust out from the back of the house, offering a lovely view of the stream far below.* ☐ *As he grew angrier, his chin thrust out farther and farther.*

thrust someone or something back to push someone or something backward and away. ☐ *Tom moved forward, but the guard thrust him back.* Ⓣ *He thrust back the door, which had closed on his foot.*

tide someone over (until something) to supply someone until a certain time or until something happens. ☐ *Will this amount tide us over until next week?* Ⓣ *There is enough food here to tide over the entire camp until next month.* ☐ *Yes, this will tide us over.*

tidy something up to clean something up; to make something more orderly. ☐ *Please tidy this room up.* ☐ *This room needs to be tidied up immediately.*

tidy up to clean up [oneself or a place]. ☐ *Please tidy up. This place is a mess.* ☐ *Please tidy up. You are a mess.*

tie in (with someone or something) to join with someone or something; to connect with someone or something. ☐ *I would like to tie in with you and see if we can solve this together.* ☐ *We would like for you to tie in and share your expertise.* ☐ *I tied in with a manufacturer who will produce the toy I invented.* ☐ *His answer to the committee ties in with what his secretary told us.*

tie in(to something) to fasten or connect to something. □ *Can you fix it so my computer can tie into Rachel's?* □ *This one will not tie into her computer.* □ *It just won't tie in.*

tie someone down (to someone or something) to encumber someone with someone or something; to make someone responsible to or for someone or something. (*Someone* includes *oneself.*) □ *Please don't tie me down to your uncle. Let your sister help out.* □ *Yes, don't tie me down all week.* □ *I'll be tied down until I'm fifty!* □ *I don't want to tie myself down to a dog.*

tie someone or something down to fasten someone or something down by tying or binding. (*Someone* includes *oneself.*) □ *The robbers tied Gary down so he couldn't get up and get away.* T *They tied down Gary.* □ *Please tie the chairs down so they don't fall off the boat in the storm.* □ *It was so windy, I almost had to tie myself down to stay on deck.*

tie someone or something in(to something) to seek to establish a connection between someone or something and something else. □ *The police tried to tie Sarah into the crime.* T *They tried to tie in Liz, too.* □ *Can we tie your computer into the system?* □ *Yes, you can tie it in.*

tie someone or something up to keep someone or something busy or occupied. T *Sally tied up the photocopy machine all afternoon.* □ *The well-wishers tied my telephone up all day long.* □ *The meeting tied me up all afternoon.*

tie something back to bind or fasten something back out of the way. □ *George tied the curtains back to let a little more light in.* □ *Let me tie the vines back out of the way.*

tie something off to tie the ends of blood vessels closed to prevent bleeding. □ *The surgeons tied all the blood vessels off—one by one—as they were exposed.* T *They tied off all the vessels very quickly.*

tie something up to block or impede something, such as traffic or progress. □ *The stalled bus tied traffic up for over an hour.* T *The stalled bus tied up traffic.*

tighten something up to make something tighter. □ *Tighten your seat belt up. It looks loose.* T *Can you tighten up all the bolts?*

tighten up **1.** [for something] to get tighter. □ *The door hinges began to tighten up, making the door hard to open and close.* □ *His grip around the handle tightened up and he refused to let go.* **2.** [for someone or a group] to become miserly. □ *The government tightened up, and our budget was slashed.* □ *We almost went out of business when we couldn't get credit because the bank tightened up.* **3.** [for someone or something] to become more restrictive or better enforced. □ *The boss is tightening up on matters of this type.* □ *There are more rules, and the people who enforce them are tightening up.*

time in to record one's arrival time. □ *Did you remember to time in this morning?* □ *When did she time in?*

time out to record one's departure time. □ *Did you remember to time out when you left work?* □ *I timed out at the regular time.*

time someone in to record someone's arrival time. □ *I timed you in at noon. Where were you?* 🅃 *My job is to time in people.*

time someone out to record someone's departure time. □ *Harry had to time everyone out because the time clock was broken.* 🅃 *I had to time out everyone.*

tinker (around) (with something) to meddle with something; to play with something, trying to get it to work or work better. □ *Let me tinker around with it for a while and see if I can get it to work.* □ *Please don't tinker with the controls.* □ *I have the stereo set just the way I want it. Don't tinker around.*

tip someone off (about someone or something) AND **tip someone off (on someone or something)** to give someone a valuable piece of news about someone or something. □ *I tipped the cops off about Max and where he was going to be that night.* 🅃 *I tipped off the mayor about the financial crisis.* □ *Yes, I am the one who did it. What tipped you off?*

tip someone off (on someone or something) See the previous entry.

tip something over to cause something to fall over. □ *Did you tip this chair over?* 🅃 *Who tipped over the chair?*

tire out to become exhausted. ☐ *I tire out easily.* ☐ *When I had the flu, I found that I tired out easily.*

tire someone out to exhaust someone. ☐ *The extra work tired him out a lot.* 🅃 *Too much work will tire out the horses.*

tone something down to cause something to have less of an impact on the senses of sight or sound; to lessen the impact of something prepared for public performance or consumption. ☐ *This is rather shocking. You had better tone it down a bit.* 🅃 *Tone down this paragraph.* 🅃 *Tone down the color of the walls. They're very red.*

tool something up to equip a factory or production line with tools and machines. ☐ *The manager closed down the factory so she could tool it up for the new models.* 🅃 *She tooled up the factory in record time.*

tool up to become equipped with tools. ☐ *I need some money so I can tool up to do the job.* ☐ *The factory tooled up to make the new cars in only two weeks.*

top something off (with something) to celebrate an end to something with something; to complete the top of something, such as a building. ☐ *They topped the evening off with a bottle of champagne.* 🅃 *They topped off the evening with a bottle of champagne.* ☐ *The workers topped the building off with a flag.*

topple over [for something very tall] to fall over. ☐ *I was afraid that Jimmy's stack of blocks would topple over.* ☐ *The stack of books toppled over and ended up as a jumbled mess on the floor.*

toss something together to assemble something hastily. ☐ *This report is useless. You just tossed it together!* ☐ *This meal was just tossed together, but it was delicious.*

total something up to add up the total of something. ☐ *Please total the bill up and let me see the cost.* 🅃 *Total up the bill and give it to me.*

touch down [for an airplane] to come in contact with the ground. ☐ *Flight twelve is due to touch down at midnight.* ☐ *When will this plane touch down?*

touch someone or something off to ignite or excite someone or something. ☐ *She is very excitable. The slightest thing will touch her off.* 🅃 *The appearance of the fox touched off a furor in the henhouse.*

touch something up to fix up the minor flaws in something. ☐ *It's only a little scratch in the finish. We can touch it up easily.* 🅃 *I can touch up the scratch easily.*

touch (up)on something to mention something; to discuss something briefly. (*Upon* is formal and less commonly used than *on*.) ☐ *The lecturer only touched upon the question of new technology.* ☐ *She only touched on the main issue.*

tough something out to endure something; to endure the rigors of something to the very end. ☐ *I will tough this out to the very end.* 🅃 *I can tough out anything for a few days.*

toughen someone or something up to cause someone or something to be stronger, more uncompromising, or more severe. (*Someone* includes *oneself*.) ☐ *A few days behind the counter at the discount store will toughen her up quickly.* 🅃 *Having to deal with people toughened up the clerk quickly.* ☐ *She tried to toughen the skin on her palms up.* ☐ *I need to toughen myself up if I am going to deal with the public.*

toughen up to become tougher, stronger, or more severe. ☐ *She will toughen up after a while. You have to be tough around here to survive.* ☐ *You are going to have to toughen up if you want to play on the team.*

tow someone or something away to pull something, such as a car or a boat, away with another car, boat, etc. (The *someone* refers to the property of someone, not the person.) ☐ *If I don't get back to my car, they will tow me away.* 🅃 *The truck towed away my car.* ☐ *A big truck came and towed the illegally parked car away.*

tow someone or something in(to something) to pull something, such as a car or a truck, into something, such as a garage. (The *someone* refers to the property of someone, not the person.) ☐ *They had to tow my car into the garage to be repaired.* 🅃 *They towed in my car.* ☐ *They towed me in!*

tow someone or something out (of some place) to pull something, such as a car, out of something, such as a ditch. (The *someone* refers to the property of someone, not the person.) □ *The farmer used his tractor to tow Andrew out of the ditch.* □ *He towed the car out of the ditch.* 🅃 *He towed out the car.*

track someone or something down to search out where someone or something is. □ *I don't know where Anne is. I'll try to track her down.* 🅃 *I'll track down Anne for you.* □ *I will try to track the book down for you.*

track something in(to some place) to bring something, such as mud, into a place on the bottom of one's feet. □ *Please don't track mud into the office.* 🅃 *Don't track in any mud!* □ *You tracked it in!*

track something up to mess something up by spreading around something dirty or messy with one's feet. □ *Please don't track the floor up!* 🅃 *Claire tracked up the floor.*

trade something in (for something) AND **trade something in (on something)** to return something, such as a car, to a place where cars are sold as partial payment on a new car. □ *I traded my old car in on a new one.* 🅃 *I traded in my old jalopy for a newer car.* □ *This car is old. It's time to trade it in.*

trade something in (on something) See the previous entry.

trade something off **1.** to get rid of something in an exchange. □ *I traded my car off.* 🅃 *I traded off my old car for a new one.* **2.** to sacrifice something in an exchange. □ *You end up trading security off for more money.* 🅃 *Don't trade off your job security.*

trick someone into something to deceive someone into doing something. □ *She tried to trick him into doing it her way.* □ *I didn't want to do it, but I was tricked into it.*

trick someone out of something AND **trick something out of someone** to get something from someone by trickery. □ *You can't trick me out of my money. I'm not that dumb!* □ *Stay alert so that no one tricks you out of your money.* □ *They tricked the information out of Bob.*

trick something out of someone See the previous entry.

trigger someone or something off to cause someone or something to go into action. ☐ *Your rude comments triggered her off.* 🅃 *Your comments triggered off quite an uproar.*

trigger something off to set something off, such as an explosion. ☐ *We were afraid that the sparks from the engine would trigger an explosion off.* 🅃 *The sparks triggered off an explosion.*

trim something away (from something) to cut something away from something. ☐ *The butcher trimmed the fat away from the steak.* 🅃 *Please trim away the fat from the meat.* ☐ *Oh, yes. Trim it away.*

trim something off ((of) someone or something) to cut something off someone or something. ☐ *I asked the barber to trim the beard off of Ralph.* 🅃 *The barber trimmed off Ralph's beard.* ☐ *Please trim it off.*

trip someone up **1.** to cause someone to trip; to entangle someone's feet. (*Someone* includes *oneself.*) ☐ *The rope strewn about the deck tripped him up.* 🅃 *The lines tripped up the crew.* ☐ *He tripped himself up in the lines.* **2.** to cause someone to falter. (Figurative. *Someone* includes *oneself.*) ☐ *Mary came in while the speaker was talking, and the distraction tripped him up.* 🅃 *The noise in the audience tripped up the speaker.* ☐ *Take care and do not trip yourself up.*

trot someone or something out to bring out and display someone or something. (Figurative.) ☐ *The boss trotted the new vice president out for us to meet.* 🅃 *The boss trotted out his daughter and introduced her as a new vice president.* 🅃 *Fred trotted out his favorite project for everyone to see.*

try out (for something) to audition for a part in some performance or other activity requiring skill. ☐ *I intend to try out for the play.* ☐ *I'm going to try out too.*

try something out on someone to see how someone responds to something or some idea. ☐ *Let me try this idea out on you and see what you think.* 🅃 *Let me try out this new medicine on her.*

tuck something in((to) something) to fold or stuff something into something. ☐ *Please tuck your shirttail into your pants at* *once!* 🅃 *Tuck in your shirttail.* □ *When you make the bed, you have to tuck the sheets in.* □ *I tucked a handkerchief into the breast pocket of my jacket.* □ *She tucked a note into the box.*

tumble out of something to fall, topple, or drop out of something. □ *Don't let the baby tumble out of the chair!* □ *The children tumbled out of the car and ran for the school building.*

tumble over (something) to fall over the edge of something. □ *Stay away from the edge. I don't want any of you tumbling over it.* □ *Don't go too close. You'll tumble over.*

tune up [for one or more musicians] to bring their instruments into tune. □ *You could hear them behind the curtain, tuning up.* □ *We have to tune up before the concert.*

turn about See *turn around.*

turn against someone or something to attack, defy, or revolt against someone or something. □ *You wouldn't think that your own family would turn against you!* □ *In the last days, everyone turned against the government.*

turn around AND **turn about** to reverse; to face the opposite direction; to change direction of motion. □ *The bus turned around and went the other way.* □ *Please turn around so I can see who you are.* □ *The bus turned about and returned to the station.*

turn back (from some place) to stop one's journey and return. □ *We turned back from the amusement park so we could go home and get the tickets we had forgotten.* □ *We turned back at the last minute.*

turn in((to) some place) to walk or steer one's vehicle into a place. □ *Turn into the next service station for some gas.* □ *I'll turn in for gas now.* □ *She walked down the street and turned into the drugstore.*

turn off [for something] to go off; to switch off. □ *All the lights turn off automatically.* □ *What time do the streetlights turn off?*

turn on [for something] to switch on and start running. □ *The lights turned on right at dusk.* □ *At what time do the streetlights turn on?*

turn out (for something) [for people, especially an audience] to [leave home to] attend some event. ☐ *A lot of people turned out for our meeting.* ☐ *Almost all the residents turned out for the meeting.*

turn someone down to issue a refusal to someone. ☐ *We had to turn Joan down, even though her proposal was okay.* 🅃 *We turned down Joan, even though her credentials were good.*

turn someone or something back to cause someone or something to stop and go back; to cause someone or something to retreat. ☐ *The border guards turned us back because we had no passports.* 🅃 *They turned back the train because the bridge was down.*

turn someone or something over to someone or something to release or assign someone or something to someone or something; to transfer or deliver someone or something to someone or something. ☐ *The deputy turned the bank robber over to the sheriff.* 🅃 *I turned over the money I found to the police.* ☐ *The police officer turned Max over to the court.*

turn someone or something up **1.** to increase the volume of a device emitting the sound of someone or something. ☐ *I can't hear the lecturer. Turn her up.* 🅃 *Turn up the radio, please.* **2.** to discover or locate someone or something. ☐ *See if you can turn any evidence up for his presence on the night of January 16.* 🅃 *Have you been able to turn up a date for Friday night?*

turn someone out to train or produce someone with certain skills or talents. ☐ *The state law school turns lawyers out by the dozen.* 🅃 *A committee accused the state university of turning out too many veterinarians.*

turn something down **1.** to bend or fold something down. ☐ *He turned his coat collar down when he got inside the house.* 🅃 *Timmy had turned down his cuffs and caught one of them in his bicycle chain.* **2.** to decrease the volume of something. ☐ *Please turn the radio down.* 🅃 *Can't you turn down that stereo?* **3.** to reject something. ☐ *The board turned our proposal down.* 🅃 *They turned down our proposal.*

turn something on to switch on something to make it run. ☐ *I turned the microwave oven on and cooked dinner.* 🅃 *I turned on the lights when the sun went down.*

turn something out **1.** to manufacture or produce something in numbers. □ *The factory turns too few cars out.* 🅃 *The factory turns out about seventy-five cars a day.* **2.** to turn off a light. □ *Please turn the hall light out.* 🅃 *Turn out the light.*

turn something up **1.** to bend or fold something up. □ *Please turn your cuffs up. They are getting muddy.* 🅃 *He turned up his coat collar to keep the rain off his neck.* **2.** to turn playing cards face up. □ *Please turn all the cards up.* 🅃 *Sally turned up the cards one at a time.*

turn to to start working; to start doing one's job. □ *Get going, you guys! Come on! Turn to!* □ *It's time you all turned to and gave us a hand.*

turn up **1.** [for part of something] to point upward. □ *The ends of the elf's funny little shoes turned up.* **2.** to happen. □ *Something always turns up to prevent their meeting.* □ *I am sorry I was late. Something turned up at the last minute.*

turn up (somewhere) [for someone or something] to appear in a place. □ *Her name is always turning up in the gossip columns.* □ *He turned up an hour late.* □ *Guess who turned up today?* □ *Tom turned up in my office today.* □ *Someone I did not expect to see turned up.* □ *My glasses turned up in the dishwasher.*

type something up to type a handwritten document. □ *I will give this to you as soon as I type it up.* 🅃 *Please type up this paper.*

U

unite against someone or something to join against someone or something. □ *We will unite against the opposing forces.* □ *We must unite against the incumbent legislators.*

unite someone against someone or something to cause people to join together against someone or something. (*Someone* includes *oneself.*) □ *The mayor united his people against the federal investigators.* □ *Ted united us against John.* □ *They united themselves against the enemy.*

upgrade someone or something to something to raise someone or something to a higher grade or rank. (*Someone* includes *oneself.*) □ *Please upgrade me to first class.* □ *They upgraded the crisis to code red.* □ *She upgraded herself to a higher rank.*

use something up to consume or use all of something. □ *Use it up. I have more in the cupboard.* [T] *Use up every bit of it. Go ahead.*

usher someone or something in(to some place) to escort or lead someone, a group, or something into a place. □ *The guard ushered the group into the palace.* [T] *They ushered in the visitors.* □ *They ushered the children into the theater.*

usher someone or something out (of some place) to escort or lead someone, a group, or something out of a place. □ *The woman ushered the guest out.* □ *We ushered them out of the room.* □ *They ushered the birthday party out.*

V

vacuum something up (from something) to clean something up from something with a vacuum cleaner. ☐ *Fred vacuumed the dirt up from the carpet.* 🅃 *He vacuumed up the birdseed from the kitchen floor.* 🅃 *He vacuumed up the dirt.*

volunteer for something to submit oneself for some task. ☐ *I volunteered for the job.* ☐ *I didn't volunteer for this.*

vote someone or something down to defeat someone or something in an election. ☐ *The community voted the proposal down.* 🅃 *They voted down the proposal.* ☐ *The citizens voted Roger down.*

W

wade in(to something) **1.** to walk into an area covered by water. ☐ *The horse waded right into the stream.* ☐ *It waded right in.* **2.** to get quickly and directly involved in something. ☐ *Don't just wade into things. Stop and think about what you are doing.* ☐ *Just wade in and get started.*

wait up (for someone or something) **1.** to slow down and pause for someone or something to catch up. ☐ *Wait up for me. You are too fast.* ☐ *Please wait up for the bus.* ☐ *Wait up, you guys!* **2.** to delay going to bed for someone or something or until someone or something does something. ☐ *I won't wait up for you.* ☐ *There is no need to wait up.* ☐ *We chose to wait up for the coming of the new year.*

wait (up)on someone to pay homage to someone. (Stilted.) ☐ *Do you expect me to wait upon you like a member of some medieval court?* ☐ *She waited on her grown children as if they were gods and goddesses.*

wake someone or something up to cause someone or some creature to awaken. ☐ *Please don't wake me up until noon.* 🅃 *Wake up your brother at noon.* ☐ *Don't wake the dog up unless you want to take her for a walk.*

wake up to awaken; to become alert. ☐ *Wake up! We have to get on the road.* ☐ *It's time to wake up!*

walk in on someone or something to interrupt someone or something by entering a place. ☐ *I didn't mean to walk in on you. I didn't know anyone was in here.* ☐ *Alice walked in on the meeting by accident.*

walk off to walk away; to leave on foot abruptly. ☐ *She didn't even say good-bye. She just walked off.* ☐ *He walked off and never looked back.*

walk out (of something) 1. to exit something or some place. ☐ *We walked out of the shop when we had made our purchases.* ☐ *She went to the door and walked out.* 2. to exit the workplace on strike. ☐ *The workers walked out because of a jurisdictional dispute.* ☐ *The workers walked out in sympathy with another union.*

walk out (on someone or something) to leave or abandon someone or something, in anger, disgust, or aversion. ☐ *Sally walked out on Tom because she was fed up with him.* ☐ *Sally finally walked out.*

want in((to) something) to want to come into something or some place. ☐ *It's cold out here! I want into the house.* ☐ *The dog wants in.*

want out (of something) 1. to desire to get out of something or some place. ☐ *I want out of this stuffy room.* ☐ *Where's the door? I want out.* 2. to desire to be relieved of a responsibility. ☐ *I want out of this responsibility. I don't have the time to do it right.* ☐ *This job is no good for me. I want out.*

want someone or something out of something to desire that someone or something leave or be removed from something or some place. ☐ *I want you out of here immediately.* ☐ *I want this box out of here now!*

warm someone or something up to make someone or something warmer; to take the chill off someone or something. (*Someone* includes *oneself.*) ☐ *I put him by the fire to warm him up a little.* 🆃 *We warmed up our feet before the fire.* 🆃 *Could you warm up my coffee, please?* ☐ *Is dinner warmed up yet?* ☐ *I need to get in there and warm myself up.*

warm someone up to help someone get physically prepared to perform in an athletic event. (*Someone* includes *oneself.*) ☐ *The referee told the coach to warm his team up so the game could begin.* 🆃 *You have to warm up the team before a game.* ☐ *Be sure to warm yourself up before playing.*

warm up 1. [for the weather or a person] to become warmer or hotter. □ *I think it is going to warm up next week.* □ *Will it ever warm up?* 2. [for someone] to become more friendly. □ *Todd began to warm up halfway through the conference.* □ *After he had worked there for a while, he began to warm up.*

warm up (for something) to prepare for some kind of performance or competition. □ *The team had to warm up before the game.* □ *They have to warm up.*

warm up to someone or something to become more fervent and earnest toward someone, something, or a group; to become more responsive and receptive to someone, a group, or something. □ *After we talked, he began to warm up to us a little.* □ *I warmed up to the committee as the interview went on.* □ *Jane warmed up to the idea, so she may approve it.*

warn someone against someone or something to advise someone against someone, something, or doing something. □ *We warned them all against going to Turkey at this time.* □ *I warned her against Gerald.*

warn someone away from someone or something to advise someone to avoid someone or something. □ *We warned her away from the danger, but she did not heed our warning.* □ *Why didn't you warn me away from Roger?*

warn someone off to advise a person to stay away. □ *We placed a guard outside the door to warn people off until the gas leak could be fixed.* 🅃 *The guards warned off everyone in the vicinity.*

wash away to be carried away by water or some other liquid. □ *The bridge washed away in the flood.* □ *All the soil washed away and left the rocks exposed.*

wash off ((of) someone or something) to be carried off of or away from something by the action of water or another liquid. (The *of* is colloquial.) □ *The dirt washed off of the floor easily.* □ *The label washed off this can, and now I don't know what's in it.*

wash someone or something away [for a flood of water] to carry someone or something away. □ *The flood washed the boats away.* 🅃 *The high water washed away the shoreline.* □ *The storm washed some people on the shore away.*

wash someone or something off to clean someone or something by washing. (*Someone* includes *oneself.*) □ *She washed the muddy children off with a hose and put their clothes right into the washing machine.* 🅃 *Jane washed off the children.* □ *She washed them off.* □ *She washed herself off and then went down to dinner.*

wash something away to clean something by scrubbing and flushing away the dirt. □ *Fresh water will wash the seawater away.* 🅃 *Let's wash away these muddy footprints.*

wash something off ((of) someone or something) to clean something off someone or something. (The *of* is colloquial.) □ *I have to wash this tomato sauce off my jacket before it stains it.* 🅃 *I will wash off the tomato stains.* □ *Carl washed the stuff off as soon as he got home.*

watch out (for someone or something) to keep looking for someone or something. □ *Watch out for Millie. She's mad at you.* □ *You had better watch out!* □ *I'll wait here out of the rain. You watch out for the bus.*

wear off [for the effects of something] to dissipate or go away. □ *The effects of the morphine began to wear off, and Dave began to feel the pain.* □ *As the drug wore off, she was more alert.*

wear out to become worn from use; to become diminished or useless from use. □ *My car engine is about to wear out.* □ *It takes a lot of driving to wear out an engine.*

wear someone down **1.** to exhaust someone. □ *This hot weather wears me down.* 🅃 *The weather wore down the tourists.* **2.** to reduce someone to submission or agreement by constant badgering. □ *Finally they wore me down, and I told them what they wanted to know.* 🅃 *The agents wore down the suspect.*

wear someone out to exhaust or annoy someone. (*Someone* includes *oneself.*) □ *All this shopping is wearing me out.* 🅃 *The shopping trip wore out the tourists.* □ *They will wear themselves out before the game. They should take it easy.*

wear something down to grind something away; to erode something. □ *The constant rubbing of the door wore the carpet down* 🅃 *The rubbing of the door wore down the carpet.*

wear something out to make something worthless or nonfunctional from use. □ *I wore my shoes out in no time at all.* 🅃 *I wore out my shoes in less than a month.*

wear (up)on someone to diminish someone's energy and resistance; to bore or annoy someone. (*Upon* is formal and less commonly used than *on*.) □ *You could see that the lecture was beginning to wear upon the audience.* □ *This kind of thing really wears on me.*

win someone over (to something) to succeed in making someone favorable to something. □ *I hope I can win them all over to our side.* 🅃 *I won over the mayor to our side.* □ *We can win the voters over!*

wind down to start running or operating slower. □ *Things will begin to wind down at the end of the summer.* □ *As things wind down, life will be a lot easier.* □ *The clock wound down and finally stopped.*

wind something on(to something) to coil or wrap something onto something. □ *Wind this string onto the ball and save it.* 🅃 *If you find the string ball, please wind on this string.* □ *Here, wind some more on.*

wind something up to tighten the spring in something, such as a watch or a clock. □ *Please wind your watch up now—before it runs down.* 🅃 *Wind up your watch before you forget.*

wind up (by) doing something to end by doing something [anyway]. □ *I wound up by going home early.* □ *I wound up eating out.*

wipe someone or something off to clean someone or something of something by wiping. (*Someone* includes *oneself*.) □ *She wiped the baby off and put clean clothes on him.* 🅃 *Please wipe off your shoes.* □ *John fell in the mud, and Sam wiped him off.* □ *She wiped herself off, getting all the mud off her shoes, at least.*

wipe something off ((of) someone or something) to remove something from someone or something by wiping. (The *of* is colloquial.) □ *The mother wiped the ice cream off of her child.* 🅃 *She wiped off the ice cream.* □ *Tony wiped the mud off.*

wipe something up **1.** to clean something up by wiping. □ *Please wipe that spilled milk up.* 🅃 *Jim wiped up the spill.* **2.** to clean something by wiping. ☐ *The floor was sticky so I wiped it up.* 🅃 *Please wipe up the countertop.*

work away (at something) to continue to work industriously at something. ☐ *All the weavers were working away at their looms.* ☐ *They just kept working away.*

work on someone **1.** [for a physician] to treat someone; [for a surgeon] to operate on someone. ☐ *The doctor is still working on your uncle. There is no news yet.* ☐ *They are still working on the accident victims.* **2.** to try to convince someone of something. ☐ *I'll work on her, and I am sure she will agree.* ☐ *They worked on Max for quite a while, but he still didn't speak.* **3.** [for something, such as medication] to have the desired effect on someone. ☐ *This medicine just doesn't work on me.* ☐ *Your good advice doesn't seem to work on Sam.*

work out **1.** [for something] to turn out all right in the end. ☐ *Don't worry. Everything will work out.* ☐ *This will work out. Don't worry.* **2.** [for someone] to do a program of exercise. ☐ *I work out at least twice a week.* ☐ *I need to work out more often.*

work something in(to something) to press, mix, or force a substance into something. ☐ *You should work the butter into the dough carefully.* 🅃 *Work in the butter carefully.* ☐ *Work it in bit by bit.* ☐ *Work the lard into the flour with a fork.*

work something off **1.** to get rid of body fat by doing strenuous work. ☐ *I was able to work a lot of weight off by jogging.* 🅃 *I need to work off some fat.* **2.** to get rid of anger, anxiety, or energy by doing physical activity. ☐ *I was so mad! I went out and played basketball to work my anger off.* 🅃 *I need to work off some anxiety.* **3.** to pay off a debt through work rather than by money. ☐ *I had no money so I had to work the bill off by washing dishes.* 🅃 *I have to work off my debt.*

work something up to prepare something, perhaps on short notice. ☐ *There are some special clients coming in this weekend. We need to make a presentation. Do you think you can work something up by then?* 🅃 *I will work up something for this weekend.*

work up to something **1.** [for something] to build or progress to something. (Usually concerning the weather.) ☐ *The sky is working* *up to some kind of storm.* ☐ *The weather is working up to something severe.* **2.** [for someone] to lead up to something. ☐ *You are working up to telling me something unpleasant, aren't you?* ☐ *I think I am working up to a good cry.*

work (up)on something **1.** to repair or tinker with something. (*Upon* is formal and less commonly used than *on.*) ☐ *He's out in the kitchen, working upon his tax forms.* ☐ *He's working on his car.* **2.** [for something] to have the desired effect on something. (*Upon* is formal and less commonly used than *on.*) ☐ *This medicine should work well upon your cold.* ☐ *I hope it will work on your cold.*

wrap something up to complete work on something; to bring something to an end. ☐ *I will wrap the job up this morning. I'll call you when I finish.* 🆃 *I can wrap up this little project in a week.*

write away to write a lot; to continue writing. ☐ *There he was, writing away, not paying attention to anything else.* ☐ *I spent the entire afternoon writing away, having a fine, productive time.*

write away for something to send for something in writing, from a distant place. ☐ *I wrote away for a book on the rivers of the world.* ☐ *You will have to write away for another copy of the instruction manual.*

write off (to someone) (for something) to send away a request for something. ☐ *I wrote off to my parents for some money, but I think they are ignoring me.* ☐ *I wrote off for money.* ☐ *I need money so I wrote off to my parents.*

write someone in (on something) to write the name of someone in a special place on a ballot, indicating a vote for the person. ☐ *Please write my name in on the ballot.* 🆃 *I wrote in your name on the ballot.* ☐ *I wrote you in.*

write someone or something off (as a something) **1.** to give up on turning someone or something into something. (*Someone* includes *oneself.*) ☐ *I had to write Jill off as a future dancer.* 🆃 *The inventor almost wrote off the automobile as a dependable means of transportation.* ☐ *He would never work out. We wrote him off.* ☐ *Don't write yourself off just yet.* **2.** to give up on someone or something as a dead loss, waste of time, hopeless case, etc.

(*Someone* includes *oneself.*) □ *Don't write me off as a has-been.* 🅃 *We almost wrote off the investment as a dead loss.* □ *We wrote the cash loss off.* □ *They wrote themselves off as a loss.* **3.** to take a charge against one's taxes. □ *Can I write this off as a deduction, or is it a dead loss?* 🅃 *Can I write off this expense as a tax deduction?* □ *Write it off and see what happens.*

write someone or something up to write a narrative or description of someone or something. □ *The reporter wanted to write me up, but I think I am just too dull.* 🅃 *The reporter wrote up the charity ball.* □ *The reporter wrote Sam and June up.*

write something back to someone to write a letter answering someone. □ *I wrote an answer back to her the same day that I received the letter.* □ *Will you please write something back to Julie? She complains that you are ignoring her.* □ *I wrote a letter back to Harry, explaining what had happened.*

write something down to make a note of something; to record something on paper in writing. □ *Please write this down.* 🅃 *Please write down what I tell you.*

write something in(to something) **1.** to write information into something. □ *I wrote her telephone number into my notebook.* 🅃 *I wrote in her number.* □ *I took out my notebook and wrote it in.* **2.** to include a specific statement or provision in a document, such as a contract or agreement. □ *I want you to write a stronger security clause into my contract.* 🅃 *I will write in a stronger clause.* □ *There is no security clause, so I will write one in.*

write something off (on something) to deduct something from one's federal income taxes. □ *Can I write this off on my income taxes?* 🅃 *I'll write off this trip on my taxes.* □ *Oh, yes! Write it off!*

write something out to put thoughts into writing, rather than keeping them in memory. □ *Let me write it out. Then I won't forget it.* 🅃 *Karen wrote out her objections.*

X

x someone or something out to mark out someone or something printed or in writing, with x's. (*Someone* includes *oneself*.) □ *Sally* x'd *the incorrect information out.* 🅃 *Sally* x'd *out the incorrect information.* □ *You should* x *Tom out. He's not coming.* 🅃 *Please* x *out this line of print.* □ *He* x'd *himself out with a pen.*

Y

yell out to cry out; to shout loudly. □ *The pain caused the child to yell out.* □ *I yelled out, but no one heard me.*

yield something to someone **1.** to give the right-of-way to someone. □ *You must yield the right-of-way to pedestrians.* □ *You failed to yield the right-of-way to the oncoming car.* **2.** to give up something to someone. □ *The army yielded the territory to the invading army.* □ *We yielded the territory to the government.*

Z

zero in (on someone or something) to aim directly at someone or something. ☐ *The television camera zeroed in on the little boy scratching his head.* ☐ *It zeroed in on the glass of cola.* ☐ *Zero in when I tell you.* ☐ *Let's zero in on the important points in this discussion.*

zip something up **1.** to close a zipper. ☐ *You should zip that zipper up.* 🅃 *You should zip up that zipper.* **2.** to close a garment by zipping a zipper closed. ☐ *You had better zip your jacket up.* 🅃 *You had better zip up your jacket.* **3.** to close one's mouth. (Usually a command: **Zip it up!**) ☐ *Zip your mouth up, Fred!* 🅃 *Zip up your mouth, Fred.*

zoom in (on someone or something) AND **pan in (on someone or something)** **1.** to move in to a close-up picture of someone or something, using a zoom lens or a similar lens. ☐ *The camera zoomed in on the love scene.* ☐ *The camera operator panned in slowly.* **2.** to focus sharply on a matter related to someone or a problem. ☐ *Let's zoom in on this matter of debt.* ☐ *She zoomed in and dealt quickly with the problem at hand.* ☐ *Sally zoomed in on Tom and demanded an explanation.*

zoom off to leave in a hurry. ☐ *Sorry, I have to zoom off.* ☐ *We will zoom off soon.*

zoom through (something) **1.** to pass through a town or some other location very fast. ☐ *Don't just zoom through these little towns. Stop and explore one or two.* ☐ *We didn't stop. We just zoomed through.* **2.** to work one's way through something very rapidly. ☐ *She zoomed through the reading assignment and went on to something else.* ☐ *Jeff can open a book and zoom through in record time.*

zoom up to pull up some place in a vehicle rapidly. □ *The car zoomed up and came to a stop.* □ *The bus zoomed up and let a few people off.*